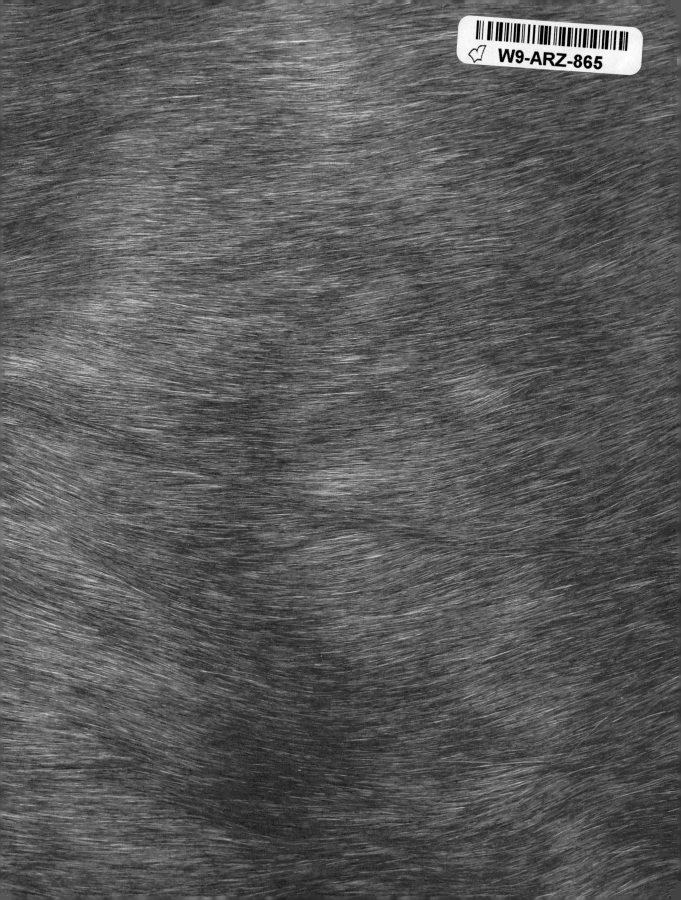

FIELD & STREAM
THE TOTAL DEER HUNTER MANUAL

FIELD & STREAM

THE TOTAL DEER HUNTER MANUAL

SCOTT BESTUL & DAVE HURTEAU

weldon**owen**

CONTENTS

CHAPTER 2

INDEX

ABOUT THE AUTHORS

FROM THE EDITOR-IN-CHIEF

"SO CRAFTY IS THE WHITETAIL, AND SO MUCH JOY TO HUNT, THAT NO ONE WHOSE HUNTING IS CONFINED TO THE WHITETAIL DEER SHOULD FEEL SORRY FOR HIMSELF. HE'S GOT THE BEST."

—Jack O'Connor, *The Big Game Animals of North America*, 1961

When legendary outdoor writer Jack O'Connor penned these words, he was one of North America's most experienced hunters, having pursued everything from grizzly bears to the high-country wild sheep he's best known for. Still, he thought whitetails were the best of the best. Over sixty years have passed, and O'Conner's assessment is more true than ever.

Deer are available nearly everywhere on this continent; whitetails in numbers not seen since colonial days. I many states, seasons are more than three months longer than ever before. Deer provide about a quarter billion— that's *billion*—pounds of tasty, healthy organic meat to hunters and their families every year.

But the truer explanation about why deer hunting is so popular lies somewhere beyond facts and in the realm of emotion. For starters, I think the whitetail is our craftiest, smartest big-game animal, and matching wits with one ignites an atavistic satisfaction, some deeply buried nerve, that modern life seldom fires.

Then there is their striking beauty. All sleek muscle and sinew, they are at once stealthy and fast, delicate and powerful, timid and bold. Bounding across a brushy pasture, melting into the neighborhood woodlot, or cruising through the big timber, whitetails are wildness brought within reach.

Finally, we can't ignore their status as a trophy. Those gleaming antlers, even when ordinary, are for many of us more beautiful than a wildflower. We hang them on the wall as a remembrance of the hunt—and in tribute to the animal that wore them and the country where he lived. Judging from the number of racks that adorn offices and living rooms, barn walls and trophy rooms, there is no doubt that among American hunters, the whitetail is king. And while mule deer numbers have been on the decline in recent years, trophy gray deer still roam the canyons, crags, and badlands, embodying the rugged wildness of the American West.

The two authors of this book take deer obsession to another level. *Field & Stream*'s whitetails editor Scott Bestul and deputy editor Dave Hurteau are two of the most knowledgable and experienced deer-hunting writers in America. All year long they work with the country's top biologists, guides, and experts so they can share that knowledge with sportsmen. This book is a collection of decades of experience and work, and the cutting-edge information it contains will no doubt make you a better hunter. But I think both Bestul and Hurteau would admit that it's just a start. You can hunt deer your entire life and have an incredible amount of knowledge, and a big mature buck can still take you to school. And that is what makes deer, and whitetails especially, our greatest game animals.

–ANTHONY LICATA
Editor-in-Chief, *Field & Stream*

DAVE HURTEAU

Except for the one Adirondack buck I glimpsed briefly before it sailed over the windshield of my Dad's totaled Dodge Omni, I can't remember seeing a deer in the wild before college. The young birch-and-cedar thickets sprouting between the farm fields near my home growing up should have held deer, but didn't to speak of. Then one day while grouse hunting on college break, I crouched to peer into a dark bank of cedars–and saw a whitetail buck staring back at me. That was it.

Converts, as my colleague Phil Bourjaily notes in the *The Total Gun Manual,* make the most committed adherents. The whitetail boom hit my backyard and changed me like it did a whole generation of hunters. I am now obsessed with deer. In the past 19 years of working with *Field & Stream* magazine, I've been lucky to hunt deer in much of the country and work with a host of experts.

Of his classic book *The Still-Hunter,* Theodore Van Dyke said he hoped it was "exhaustive without being exhausting." Styles change, and this book is vastly different, but the goal is the same. We've tried to give you all the information you need and very little you don't, in a format that is easy to access, so you can put the book down and go put its lessons to use right now in the deer woods.

Good hunting.

SCOTT BESTUL

As a boy, whenever the family took a road trip, I would kick off a backseat boundary dispute with my kid sister, Jo, within minutes of departure. Eventually my mother would turn and say in a calm voice, "Scott, look for deer." And I'd stare quietly out the window for the rest of the ride. That should give you some idea of the spell deer had on me then. I'm still under it.

I shot my first buck, a Wisconsin 8-pointer, when I was 12. Not long after, I started building my life around deer. I stalked them with a camera, hunted them in any open season, and read everything I could get my hands on. I picked my college because of the deer hunting, and I quit at least one job for the same reason. When I started writing about deer for *Field & Stream,* I thought back to the boy staring through the car window, because I was now living one of his biggest dreams.

I'm excited about this book, which is full of cutting-edge hunting skills and information on deer biology and behavior. Heck, I didn't know some of this stuff last year. And that is one of the reasons I love deer hunting so deeply. I've been lucky to talk deer with some of the best biologists, hunters, and guides in the country, and they all confess they're still learning about deer. I am, too. If you'd care to join us, perhaps this book will help.

YOU MIGHT BE DEER CRAZY IF

Just 50 years ago, the sight of a deer made the papers in some states. Since 1990, the whitetail population has more than doubled. Today, over 30 million deer roam the U.S. alone, perhaps 35 million in North America—more than have ever inhabited this continent.

In the course of just a few decades, our nation has become a deer paradise, and it has utterly transformed the face of American hunting. All across the land, from Maine to Montana, from Texas to Georgia, we are suddenly, utterly obsessed with deer. Not sure if you're deer crazy? Here are 27 ways to be sure.

☞ **WHILE WATCHING BAMBI WITH THE KIDS, YOU ROUGH SCORE BAMBI'S DAD.** ☞ You became a teacher for the 3 straight weeks of deer hunting over Christmas break. ☞ *When your significant other says "Dear," you reply "Where?"* ☞ YOUR YARD IS PLANTED WITH BIOLOGIC. ☞ YOU PUT MORE EFFORT INTO NAMING BUCKS THAN YOU DID NAMING YOUR KIDS. ☞ You make a gun with your index finger and thumb to take out Santa's reindeer in the neighbor's Christmas decorations. ☞ You balk at deodorant, fearing you won't be scentless—in May. ☞ **"TAXIDERMY BILL" IS A LINE IN YOUR ANNUAL BUDGET**. ☞ You keep your most expensive clothing in a trash bag with leaves and dirt. ☞ Instead of family pictures in your wallet, you have trail camera photos of hit-list bucks. ☞ Your main motivation for starting your own business was more time in the woods. 👍

☞ YOU SCHEDULE YOUR VACATIONS AROUND THE MOON PHASES. ☞ *You follow the price of corn like a Wall Street commodities trader.* ☞ YOU DRIVE A LITTLE FASTER WHEN YOU SEE A DEER CROSSING SIGN. ☞ **You start a fight in church over whether Noah took a typical or nontypical buck aboard the ark.** ☞ THE SMELL OF DOE-IN-ESTRUS TURNS YOU ON. ☞ You put a bigger set of antlers on your 3D buck target because you would have passed him with the ones he came with. ☞ **You consider a shoulder mount fine art.** ☞ YOU PLANNED YOUR WEDDING DATE TO AVOID AN ANNIVERSARY DURING DEER SEASON. ☞ YOU FIRST SAW A DRONE IN THE NEWS AND THOUGHT "MOBILE TRAIL CAM." ☞ Your son's name is Buck and your daughter's is Fawn. ☞ **When a non-hunting friend says "Look at that rack," you scan for deer.** ☞ YOU TOTAL YOUR TRUCK HITTING A DEER AND THINK, "I HOPE THE BACKSTRAPS ARE OKAY." ☞ **Your wife leaves you on November 8th, and you don't notice until the 18th.** ☞ WHEN SHOPPING FOR A NEW FAMILY VEHICLE, YOUR FIRST CONSIDERATION IS "WHERE WILL I PUT THE DEER?" ☞ *You've stood up a date to track a deer you didn't shoot.* ☞ **You broke up with your girlfriend because she refused to bottle her mid-cycle urine like you asked.** 👍

SPOT 10 MODERN DEER HUNTING TRENDS

How, exactly, is today's deer hunting different than in the recent past? Here are ten key ways.

MORE DEER, BIGGER DEER At the turn of the 20th century, there were about half a million deer in the United States. As recently as the 1980s, there were only about 6 million. Today, that number has swelled to a well over 30 million deer. And trophy buck numbers have skyrocketed, too. Since 1970, the number of Boone & Crockett Club record-book whitetail entries have increased by more than 700 percent; Pope & Young entries by more than 4,000 percent.

QUALITY DEER MANAGEMENT For decades, the goal of deer management was to increase the population. But with many herds recovered and some overpopulated by the late 20th century, a new model emerged. In 1988, South Carolina biologist Joe Hamilton started the Quality Deer Management Association with three goals: (1) balancing herd size with habitat; (2) balancing the herd's sex ratio; and (3) balancing the herd's age structure. In many areas, this meant targeting does and passing young bucks—both radical departures from tradition. Today, the QDMA is the US's fastest-growing conservation organization, empowering individual hunters to engage in deer management and habitat improvement on an unprecedented scale. Still, many hunters remain opposed to QDM.

FOOD-PLOTTING Planting forage for deer is the cornerstone of private-land management, so popular that food-plotting is now a commonplace verb among hunters. It started twenty-five years ago when Bass Masters founder Ray Scott started marketing a brand of clover designed specifically for use on deer leases. Today, hunters all over the country have turned into weekend farmers, sowing seeds to feed and attract deer.

ANTLER-POINT RESTRICTIONS The new model of deer management has been codified in many state's official regulations via antlerless tags and quotas—but also antler-point restrictions. A common APR, for example, requires hunters to pass any buck that doesn't have at least four points on one side. Although highly controversial, where APRs have been in place for several years, they typically enjoy overwhelming support from hunters.

ANTLER MANIA Deer hunters have always been fascinated by big headgear, but the recent surge in trophy-size bucks has spawned an unprecedented antler obsession, and hardcore deer hunters can guess a buck's gross B&C score within 10 inches at a glance. Modern antler mania is fun and harmless at best. At its worst, antler snobs scoff at hunters whose bucks don't tally three digits.

SHED MADNESS The spring hunt for shed antlers has become all the rage. At the 9th Annual Whitetail Classic Sports Show and Auction in Dubuque, Iowa—a 3-day event devoted to the sale of shed antlers—a matched set of typical whitetail sheds fetched nearly $19,000. Today's antler geeks want that bone, whitetail or muley, as soon as it hits the ground.

LOSS OF ACCESS Not long ago, you could bang on a door in Wisconsin's famous Buffalo County and be given the keys to a slice of whitetail heaven for nothing. Today, you couldn't lease the same land for less than $40 an acre. All over the country, it's getting tougher and tougher to gain access for a handshake. It's still possible, but you have to knock on many, many more doors.

TRAIL-CAM CRAZE The first commercial trail cameras of the late 1980s were dismissed as either novelties or the latest technological threat to fair chase. Today, most serious whitetail hunters own at least one and usually more, and they use them religiously to inventory, monitor, and pattern deer. It's now perfectly normal for a hunter to have hundreds of pictures of—and a nickname for—a buck before he kills it.

GRAY-DEER DECLINE While whitetails flourish, dominating the deer scene, mule deer numbers have declined significantly from historic highs. Record-book specimens have become increasingly rare, too. Of the B&C's top 50 nontypical muley bucks, only 8 were shot in the last 20 years. Giant muleys are still out there, but they're much harder to find.

DEER-MEDIA FRENZY Historically, outdoor magazines covered the entire sporting experience. In 1982, North American Whitetail, a magazine devoted solely to the whitetail freak, appeared on the scene. Now dozens of media outlets focus specifically on deer. Meanwhile, outdoor TV has grown from a few shows on Saturday morning to a few channels airing mostly deer-hunting shows nonstop, amplifying the influence of celebrity in the deer hunting culture.

001
KNOW THE 5 BASIC TYPES OF DEER HABITAT

If humans outlast deer, the paleozoologists of the future will sift through the fossil record and conclude that *Odocoileus* lived just about everywhere on this continent, from the wildest wilds to the back yard. Biologists have identified more than 30 subspecies of whitetail alone that cover much of North and parts of South America. There's even a growing movement for those avid hunters who want to kill a "whitetail slam," consisting of the 8 major subspecies of America's deer. That's fine, but no matter what species or subspecies you pursue, deer live in one of five major habitat types.

THE BIG WOODS The last stronghold of whitetails when European settlers nearly wiped them out, heavily forested regions of the North continue to host solid populations of deer. But the big woods simply don't offer the abundance of food and edge habitat to support lots of deer. In addition, big-woods whitetails typically face a gauntlet of natural predators—coyote, wolf, bear, and bobcat—and tougher weather that limits their numbers. Big-woods bucks roam widely across large home ranges, so you usually need to cover some ground to tag one.

FARMLAND Whitetails were just about wiped out from America's breadbasket by the early 19th century, but when they bounced back, they did so like a roomful of rubber balls. So much so that when most folks envision deer hunting today, they see a hunter waiting by a woodlot adjacent to a field of corn, alfalfa, or soybeans. Lots of deer, plus lots of predictable food sources, plus broken wooded habitat makes it comparatively easy to pattern the daily movements of deer, which is the key to success on the farm.

PRAIRIE Technically, America has little true prairie habitat left, but we all know what we're talking about here: lots of real estate with durn few trees. In recent decades, CRP acres, grassy swales, cattail sloughs, and cattle pasture have become prime real estate for the ever-adaptable whitetail, as well as some real trophy muleys. Riparian areas concentrate deer, but you're as likely to find a monster buck making a living in an abandoned ranch site. Out here in the great wide open, the hunter's challenge is plain to see: These deer can spot you from a long ways off.

MOUNTAINS When most hunters think "mountain" they dream of sheep, goats, and elk. Drop down-slope just a bit, though, and you're in magazine-cover muley habitat. Descend farther in to the forested glades and foothills and —depending on where you live—you'll be bumping into blacktails and whitetails. How many deer you encounter depends on what lies at the mountain's base. Sprawling ranches with crop fields means deer in abundance. Trees and more trees means big-woods conditions.

THE DESERT You might think rock, sand, and prickly pear is too nasty for deer, but you would be wrong. In the sun-scorched regions of the Southwest lives one of the continent's most sought-after trophies, the Coues deer. This little whitetail ekes out a living in conditions that would cause a farmland buck dry up and blow away. Big muleys also thrive in the desert, so much so that trophy hunters routinely risk bringing guns across the border to chase bucks with 30-inch spreads in old Mexico. Some actually return.

002 START WITH A SCOUTING WALK

There are more deer on the continent now than at any time in recent history, and yet we glimpse them only occasionally. Plain to see, however, is the evidence, or sign, they leave behind as they conduct their daily lives. To get close to deer, most hunters rely on thorough scouting: the finding and interpreting of deer sign.

So let's take a scouting walk.

You can start anywhere deer live, but the best place is at an obvious feeding area: a crop field, an oak ridge littered with acorns, or an old apple orchard. We'll start at an alfalfa field, along the perimeter, where the plants peter out into a strip of dirt and muddy tire tracks against the woods' edge. Here's what to look for.

2. RUBS

Follow the trail into the woods. Right there, just inside the edge, is a rub. Nothing screams "Buck!" like a hashed-up sapling. Folks once believed that bucks rubbed trees to rid their antlers of summer velvet; actually a buck makes most of his rubs after his antlers harden, as a kind of message to other bucks: "Here I am." Keep an eye out for others, mostly on softwood saplings like pine, cedar, aspen, willow, and alder.

1. TRACKS AND TRAILS

The best place to find a deer track is in soft dirt, mud, or snow, and here is one at our field edge. It is basically heart-shaped, with a split down the middle, the narrow end pointing in the direction of travel. Follow it backward to where it joins others to form a narrow trail into the woods where multiple deer enter and/or exit the field. These trails wind through the woods and fields, connecting the places where deer sleep, drink, and eat. Whitetails create trails so they can dash through thick woods quickly to escape danger. Mule deer, typically found in more open terrain, use trails, too, but not as habitually.

3. SCRAPES

Not far from the rub is an oval patch of exposed, moist dirt. This is a scrape. A whitetail buck made it by scraping away the leaf litter with his front hooves, and then peeing in the dirt. Five or six feet above the scrape is a "licking" branch, which the buck worked over with his mouth, eyes, and forehead, leaving a bunch of scent. The whole thing is another, more elaborate, advertisement of his presence. Mule deer do not make scrapes.

5. BEDS

Where the trail eventually leads onto a grassy, brushy knoll is a kidney-bean-shaped depression in the leaves where a deer rested. This is a bed. You'll find others in the places where deer feel the most secure, including ridge ends, thickets, blowdowns, and grassy lowlands. Large, lone beds in rugged terrain usually belong to bucks. Multiple beds of varying sizes tell of a doe and fawn resting together.

4. DROPPINGS

A little farther along, it looks like someone dumped a box of raisins on the trail. Those are deer droppings. Keep an eye out for them whenever you scout. Lots of droppings mean you're in a spot where deer spend a lot of time, usually either a feeding or bedding area. Along with trails, the number of droppings you see on a given property gives you a pretty good sense of the number of deer living there compared with other areas.

003 KNOW THE 5 BASIC METHODS

If you are new to deer hunting, pay close attention. This will be your foundation for understanding the advanced tactics described later. If you are a seasoned deer hunter, to borrow from Monty Python, skip a bit, brother.

STAND HUNTING

There are now so many deer roaming the country that if you stand still long enough, then sooner or later one is going to walk past you. That's an oversimplification, but nonetheless, it goes a long way to explaining why stand hunting has become the method of choice for most of today's deer hunters.

THE BASICS: You scout the woods to find a travel route used by deer and then set up downwind and wait for them to come to you. You can wait in a treestand 20 feet off the ground, in a pop-up blind on terra firma, or on a 5-gallon bucket tucked in some brush.

BEST USED: On the farm and prairie, where small woodlots, tree strips, fencelines, hedgerows, draws, riverbottoms, and other broken cover tends to make deer movements more predictable.

STILL-HUNTING

This is a misnomer, sort of. What makes still-hunting different from stand hunting is that you move. However, your movements should be frequently interrupted by periods of standing, that's right, still.

THE BASICS: You slink through the woods, stopping often to listen and look, hoping to see deer before they detect you. Your pace depends on how promising the area looks. You might cross an open hardwood flat devoid of deer sign in a matter of minutes, hardly stopping. You might spend three hours tiptoeing through a brushy creekbottom, stopping for 15 to 30 minutes at a time.

BEST USED: Wherever there's enough cover to hide you. It's most common in the big woods, though, where deer are comparatively few and covering ground is going to up your odds of seeing one.

DRIVING

Pressured deer have this annoying habit of holing up in some impossible thicket from dawn to dusk, doing more or less nothing but watching out for you and staying out of your way. One solution is to barge into that thicket and kick their butts up.

THE BASICS: A deer drive involves anywhere from 2 to 10 or more hunters split into drivers and posters. The posters first set up along natural escape routes downwind of promising cover. The drivers move into that cover from upwind, trying to push deer toward the posters for a shot. Deer drives need to be highly choreographed to ensure safety.

BEST USED: When deer are not moving on their own during daylight.

SPOT AND STALK

In some areas, deer, especially mule deer and western whitetails, always seem to want to put themselves where they can see you coming from a half mile away at least. To have any chance, you need to see them first from farther than that.

THE BASICS: Use a spotting scope or binoculars to glass distant deer from a high vantage point or from a vehicle. Study the wind, terrain, and cover to figure out how to sneak within gun or bow range without being detected. Then carefully move in for the shot.

BEST USED: In open country—sage flats, prairie hills, grassland breaks, dessert badlands, alpine slopes and meadows, and even farmland crop fields.

TRACKING

Bearded, wool-clad men follow hoof prints miles into the snowy wilderness and come back with a buck. Full of old-timey mystique, tracking is the most romantic way to kill a deer (though the deer may not feel that way).

THE BASICS: After a fresh snow, you drive along logging roads or walk through the woods quickly to find a buck track. You follow it until the trail begins to meander or hook, meaning that the buck has stopped to feed or bed down. You slow to a crawl, combing the cover ahead and to the sides, hoping to spot the buck before he spots you.

BEST USED: In those large tracts of public forest or public-access timberlands where a hunter can follow a track all day without encountering a posted sign or another hunter.

004 MAKE THE CALL

You can rattle (smash a pair of shed or synthetic antlers together to sound like two bucks fighting, which attracts other deer) and call (mimic deer vocalizations, such as grunts and bleats) to great effect in conjunction with the methods in #003. Stand hunters routinely rattle to draw a buck near and then grunt to stop him for a shot, for example. A tracker may track close to a bedded buck and then make a doe bleat to draw him out.

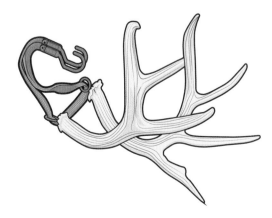

005 BREAK DOWN YOUR DEER SEASON

Deer behavior is dynamic. Because your hunting strategies should be informed by what the animals are doing, it's helpful to break the season down into the following behavioral phases.

EARLY SEASON
LATE AUGUST TO EARLY OCTOBER

BEHAVIOR Deer typically bed for most of the day, and then travel to a major food source (crop field, oak flat, apple orchard) before dark to feed. After feeding again in the early morning, they travel back to their beds.

TOP TACTICS Because early-season deer movement is some of the most predictable of the season, stand hunting rules now. It's simple: Set up overlooking a travel route near a feeding area to ambush deer coming to feed in the late afternoon. Set up closer to the bedding area in the morning.

OCTOBER LULL
EARLY TO MID-OCTOBER

BEHAVIOR As acorns rain down and fruit hangs lower on the branches, deer don't need to expose themselves in open crop fields and food plots to fill up. This decreased visibility is so commonly mistaken for a drop in activity that hunters commonly describe it as the "October lull." But studies show that deer activity actually increases now. You just need to hunt smarter.

TOP TACTICS Stand hunting still works. But if you're not seeing deer, you need to abandon those field-edge spots and set up in the woods, near hard or soft mast.

PRE-RUT
LATE OCTOBER TO EARLY NOVEMBER

BEHAVIOR The breeding ritual begins. Rubs and scrapes are popping up all over. Bucks start actively seeking and chasing does. The woods are suddenly bustling with activity.

TOP TACTICS Stand hunting is hot again. As green foliage dies, spotting deer for both still-hunting and stalking becomes easier, too.

RUT
TIMING: EARLY TO MID-NOVEMBER

BEHAVIOR The spike in activity continues as actual breeding begins, but it soon comes to a abrupt halt as the majority of does come into estrus and bucks are busy tending them. Hunters describe this period as the "lockdown."

TOP TACTICS Stand and still-hunting remain good at first, but during the lockdown, many hunters turn to spot-and-stalk and driving. Tracking can be good if there's snow.

POST RUT
LATE NOVEMBER TO EARLY DECEMBER

BEHAVIOR: Bucks are wiped out from chasing and fighting. Does are tired of being chased. Both are on edge from hunting pressure. Most deer return to a bed-to-feed pattern, but the biggest bucks are still looking for late-cycling does.

TOP TACTICS: Whatever it takes. Stand hunting can be good near a strong food source. But this is prime time for driving and for tracking.

LATE SEASON
MID-DECEMBER TO SEASON'S END

BEHAVIOR: In parts of the South, the rut is just beginning. But elsewhere, it's all about two things: (1) food, because deer need to recover and prepare for the worst of winter, and (2) the second rut, because yearling does and fawns commonly come into estrus a month later than adult does.

TACTICS: When temperatures plummet, deer need to feed heavily; it's hard to beat a stand overlooking a good food source now. That said, the relative lack of cover facilitates still-hunting and driving—and it remains prime time for tracking down a big buck.

006 GEAR UP FOR DEER

You can hunt deer with only a rifle, a cartridge, some clothes (please), and a pair of boots. But you will do better and have an easier time of it if you also have, at a minimum, these accessories.

BINOCULAR To see deer before they see you. Get the best model you can afford. A 10x42 binocular is best for open country. A light, compact 6x32 is perfect for tracking or still-hunting in the big woods. An 8x42 is a great all-purpose choice for deer hunting.

TREESTAND To get you above a deer's line of sight and your stink above its nose. Neither means you won't get busted, but both can help. The more treestands you have, the better. If you own just one, get a climbing stand, which lets you can hunt many different spots.

DEER CALLS To lure deer into shooting range or stop moving deer for a standing shot. At the least, you should have a variable grunt call, a bleat call, and a set of rattling antlers.

THREE COMPASSES As Maine guide and friend Randy Flannery says, "A GPS is powered by batteries. The Earth's magnetic field is powered by God." Why three? If one breaks, which do you trust?

ROPE If you are only going to carry one rope, make it 25 feet of ³/₈-inch braided poly rope. This is the most versatile for deer hunting—not too thick for pulling up a treestand, gun, or bow; not to thin for dragging out a buck.

KNIFE A full-tang drop-point with a fixed 2¹/₂ to 4-inch blade and wood or bone handle is the traditional choice. It's what I carry. That said, a folder with a good saw blade and extra tools sure is handy.

FOLDING SAW AND CLIPPERS To clear shooting lanes, build a natural blind, quarter or bone out a buck in the backwoods, cut a limb for a drag handle, and on and on....

TWO HEADLAMPS Why headlamps? Because you are carrying too much other gear to have a hand free to hold a flashlight. Why two? Because the first one is guaranteed to crap out at the very moment you need it most.

DAY OR FANNY PACK You need something to carry all this stuff in.

007 COMMIT THESE 10 RULES TO MEMORY

Heard them before? Good. They should never escape your mind.

RULE 1 Assume every gun is loaded and treat it accordingly.

RULE 2 Unload your gun when not in use.

RULE 3 Be certain of your target and what lies beyond.

RULE 4 Keep your gun's safety on until you're ready to shoot.

RULE 5 Keep your finger off the trigger until you're ready to shoot.

RULE 6 Wear at least the required amount of hunter-orange clothing.

RULE 7 Know your safe shooting lanes, especially when conducting a deer drive.

RULE 8 Never walk with a nocked arrow.

RULE 9 Never drink and hunt.

RULE 10 Bring a cell phone and make sure someone knows where you are and when you'll be back.

008 BE ULTRASAFE

In hunting, the best policy is to be overly cautious. The first rule in gun safety, for example, is to always treat a gun as if it were loaded even when you know perfectly well that it is not (see above). Why? Because it guards against stupid. Why? Because the average person does something stupid between, like, 8 to 10 times a day. Just go on the Internet. As research for this, I killed a half hour on YouTube watching people fell trees directly onto their cars and houses.

The most dangerous thing in the deer woods is swagger, overconfidence. Never assume that you can't do something dumb. Don't think, "I could never mistake a person for a deer" or "I could never pull the trigger without meaning to." Instead, double- and triple-check your target. Keep your safety on until the moment before you shoot. Always assume you could do something stupid, and guard against it by being overly cautious.

009 STRAP YOURSELF IN

One of the many sea changes in deer hunting during the last 20 years is a huge increase in the use of treestands, which has inherent risks. You should know what they are: Should you fall out of a stand, there's a chance you will walk away a little bruised. There's a better chance you will sprain or break something. And there's a real chance you will be eviscerated by your tree steps on the way down, break a leg when you hit, and be left to die in the woods, alone.

So while we are on the subject of stupid things, I'll point out that one of the very dumbest a deer hunter can do is to hunt from a treestand without using a safety harness, which, when attached to the tree, prevents you from falling. Last year, far fewer hunters were injured by bullets or broadheads than were injured in treestand accidents. Most of those injured were not wearing a harness.

THE DEER HAVEN'T CHANGED MUCH. SO WHY ANOTHER BOOK CHAPTER ON BEHAVIOR AND BIOLOGY? Here's why: In the course of just a couple decades, our understanding of deer and how they behave has taken a giant, soaring, jet-propelled leap forward.

The whitetail's rise to utter dominance in the hunting culture has spurred interest in and funding for research. More than ever, deer hunters want to understand their quarry. Scientists are happy to oblige: A recent examination by David G. Hewitt of Texas A&M University of scientific literature pertaining to whitetail deer found 631 papers published before 1985—and 834 since. This, plus vastly improved research technology, from GPS trackers that can pinpoint a buck on a computer screen to transmitters that can signal researchers the moment a fawn is born, boils down to this: We know a lot more about deer. And the more you know, the better a hunter you'll be.

010 KNOW YOUR DEER

Almost 50 subspecies of whitetail, blacktail, and mule deer range from just below the Arctic Circle to the southern tip of South America, weighing from a mere 80 pounds to more than 400, and eating everything from lichen to cactus. Here is a breakdown in the United States and Canada.

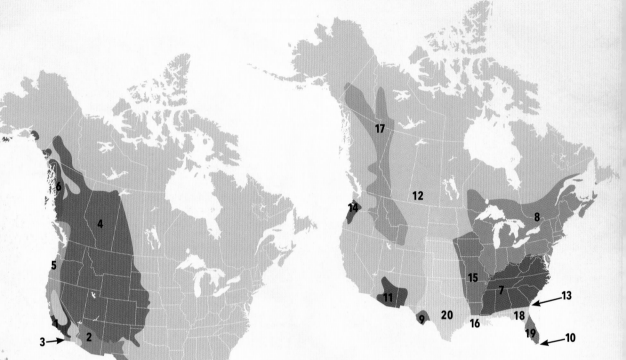

MULE DEER

- 1. California mule deer – *Odocoileus hemionus californicus*
- 2. Desert/burro mule deer – *O. h. eremicus*
- 3. Southern mule deer – *O. h. fuliginatus*
- 4. Rocky Mountain mule deer – *O. h. hemionus*

BLACKTAIL DEER

- 5. Columbian blacktail – *O.h. columbianus*
- 6. Sitka blacktail – *O.h. sitkensis*

WHITETAIL DEER

- 7. Virginia whitetail – *Odocoileus virginianus virginianus*
- 8. Northern whitetail (the largest subspecies) – *O. v. borealis*
- 9. Carmen Mountains Jorge deer – *O. v. carminis*
- 10. Key deer – *O. v. clavium*
- 11. Coues deer – *O. v. couesi*
- 12. Dakota whitetail – *O. v. dacotensis*
- 13. Hilton Head Island whitetail – *O. v. hiltonensis*
- 14. Columbian whitetail – *O. v. leucurus*
- 15. Kansas whitetail – *O. v. macrourus*
- 16. Avery Island whitetail – *O. v. mcilhennyi*
- 17. Northwest whitetail – *O. v. ochrourus*
- 18. Florida coastal whitetail – *O. v. osceola*
- 19. Florida whitetail – *O. v. seminolus*
- 20. Texas whitetail – *O. v. texanus*

011 ANALYZE WHITETAIL ANATOMY

PREORBITAL GLAND Bucks deposit scent from this gland on rubs and over scrapes.

ANTLERS Deer grow a new set every year. Velvet is shed in late summer, turning antlers into weapons for the rut.

TESTICULAR GLANDS This is the source of testosterone–that magical elixir that tells a buck it's go time every fall.

FOREHEAD GLAND Bucks deposit scent from this gland on rubs and on limbs overhanging scrapes.

TARSAL GLANDS The most prominent and funky-smelling glands on a deer. Bucks pee all over them to create a mating-season musk.

NECK Enlarges to nearly three times its normal size during the rut.

METATARSAL GLAND Truth is, no one is sure about this one.

INTERDIGITAL GLAND Located between the toes, it leaves a scent that seems to be unique to each individual deer as it walks or makes scrapes.

012 TAKE HEADS AND TAILS

The easiest way to tell a whitetail from a mule deer from a blacktail is to look at their heads and tails. Here are the tipoffs:

WHITETAIL

HEAD The antlers of a typical mature buck consist of two main beams from which evenly spaced tines grow upward.

TAIL The top side is brown, fringed in white. When alarmed, this deer raises its tail to full vertical and exposes the patch of bright white hair underneath–thus the name, whitetail.

MULE DEER

HEAD The muley's antlers are "bifurcated," which means they fork as they grow. The deer's name comes from its ears, which are are so big that early white settlers compared them to a mule's.

TAIL The mule deer's tail is ropelike and black-tipped. It lies against a large white rump patch, making it easy to spot.

BLACKTAIL

HEAD Bascially, the blacktail deer's head resembles a mule deer's, only with smaller forked tines and a typically less sizeable rack.

TAIL The blacktail has a white rump patch like a muley's but smaller, and its tail is, you guessed it, mostly black, or blackish.

013 NOW HEAR THIS

Remember those hearing tests you took as a kid? Someone would play a sound, and you'd raise your hand when you heard it. Well, researchers figured out how to do that with deer. They put deer of various ages in a soundproof booth and then hooked them to little electrodes measuring brain-wave activity. Computers measured the frequency and volume of sound it took to get a bump in brain waves.

The conclusion? The average deer can hear high-frequency sounds better than we can (human hearing maxes out at 20,000 hertz; deer can hear up to 30,000 hertz), but the volume has to be turned up. Also, they are excellent at pinpointing the source of sound, thanks to their maneuverable ears. Other than that, deer actually don't hear much better than you or I do.

Like us, they hear moderate-frequency sounds best and virtually all the vocalizations they use to communicate with each other are in this range. And they get distracted by background noise in the woods, just like we do. So, you want to know how far off a deer can hear your calls, your rattling, or the sound of your foot cracking a stick? Have a buddy make those noises a set distance away. If you can hear it, so can a buck. If you can't, he probably can't either.

014 GET A GRIP ON DEER SENSES

After my rookie deer season, I was certain that bucks could see through hillsides, hear what I was thinking, and smell what I had for lunch from 100 yards away. We all tend to romanticize the quarry. After all, giving them supernatural powers makes our successes more heroic and our failures more excusable. But let's get real here. If deer were that good, they'd all die of old age, and we couldn't sell you this book. The truth is, deer senses are good, but not great. Only one—smell—is borderline otherworldly. The others . . . meh.

Maybe realizing your role in hunting failure is no fun, but ignoring it can hamper your success. Yes, deer are sharp, they are wary, and you should be careful. But don't let an exaggerated idea of their defenses keep you from making the aggressive moves sometimes needed to fill your tag.

015 KNOW THAT THE NOSE KNOWS

A deer's sense of smell is so spectacular that it's tough to quantify. But here's one yardstick: Researchers estimate that we have about 5 million olfactory receptors (neurons responsible for the detection of odor) in our noses. Bloodhounds—the legendary sniffers of dogdom—are thought to have 200 million. Deer have an estimated 297 million.

In other words, a deer can smell 60 times better than you can. In the right conditions, a downwind deer can smell you from more than 300 yards away. It can smell where you've been long after you leave.

Not only can deer detect minute traces of odor, they can decipher many different scents simultaneously. They can be snuffling acorns, whiffing nearby water, catching the scent of a coyote in the woodlot across the field, and pinpointing the spot where you walked by an hour ago—all at the same time.

A multimillion-dollar industry exists with the sole purpose of defeating a deer's ability to smell a hunter—with little if any tangible success. In the end, a deer cannot see through hillsides or hear your thoughts. But it might be able to smell what you had for lunch. Above all, be careful of a deer's nose.

016 DON'T MOVE . . . OR WEAR BLUE

Deer have excellent peripheral vision and an outstanding ability to detect motion. Their eyes have a high density of rods, a horizontal slit for a pupil, and a reflective tapetum lucidum on the retina, which allow them to see in the dark. They can also spot colors in the ultraviolet spectrum, which means that if your hunting garments contain UV brighteners (as many do) or are blue, to deer you'll actually appear to glow in low light.

That's the good news for deer. The bad: They can't see squat for detail. Researcher Gino D'Angelo actually devised an eye exam chart to measure the visual acuity of a captive doe named Nellie. D'Angelo found that Nellie's eyes were comparable to those of a human with 20/100 vision. Nellie, thank goodness, would flunk the vision portion of a driving test. Deer eyes are also fairly pathetic at depth perception. If you don camo and stand motionless against a broad tree, a deer staring in your direction from just 20 yards won't spot you.

017 KEEP DEER OFF YOUR TRACKS

Knowing that a deer's nose is often compared to a dog's, and hoping to shed some light on a few of the nagging questions about a buck's ability to sniff us out, I enlisted a pair of professionals: Winona County, Minnesota, Sheriff's Deputy Chris Cichosz and Blitz, his 5-year-old German shepherd K-9 partner.

THE COLD TRACK For the first test, I laid down two trails two hours before Chris's scheduled arrival. For the first trail, donning old, smelly leather boots, I walked between a crop reduction program field and food plot, entered a brushy stand of sumac, and dropped a coat. I scuffed the trail repeatedly, touched brush with my bare hands, and walked back on my own tracks.

Next, wearing knee-high rubber boots that I'd thoroughly scrubbed with a paste of baking soda and then air-dried outdoors, I walked a 75-yard-long trail along a wooded valley bottom, taking care to not touch anything before dropping an old shirt by a tree.

The conditions were dry and breezy, and Blitz could not detect either scent trail. This suggests you should get into your stand early. It also suggests that dry, windy days are good ones for speed scouting or hanging a stand without leaving too much residual scent.

THE HOT TRACK For the next test, Chris and Blitz were going to try to nail a track that was minutes old. To try and make things a little bit more difficult for them, I wore untreated boots, zigzagged along a field edge for 100 yards, dropped a dummy at the end of my trail, and then looped wide to avoid a backtrail. For a second trial, I repeated the entire procedure in a new spot, with a few variations. First of all, this time I wore my treated rubber boots. In addition, I walked quickly along a snowmobile trail of very short grass.

Blitz nailed both of these trails with ease. What this says to me is that if you can't get into your stand early, be careful not to walk in the area from which you expect deer to approach, and don't assume rubber boots will help.

THE BODY SEARCH How far downwind can a buck nail your airborne body odor? To get an idea, I walked in from the wooded, upwind side of a small block of timber and hung a stand near the edge of a downwind field. It took Blitz seconds to nail me 275 yards away. I saw the dog jerk to a stop at a distance I wouldn't attempt with a shotgun or muzzleloader rifle. The lesson? Many gun hunters think they can set their stand far enough away so scent won't matter. Stop it—you'll probably kill more deer.

018 MANAGE BODY ODOR (OR NOT)

Every deer hunter frets about B.O., but our attempts to manage it are all over the map. So which approach, if any, gives you the best chance of knocking down your own scent? To answer that question, I enlisted another K-9 cop, Chance, and we played a version of the "Hot Box" game. In this training exercise, six plywood boxes (4 feet x 4 feet x 5 feet) are spaced evenly in two rows across a large field. People are placed in the boxes for 2 to 3 minutes to "heat them up" with human scent. Then, all but one leaves, and the dog has to find him. We tried out three simple tests to see if certain scent-control measures could confuse or perhaps completely fool Chance.

FULL-BLOWN B.O. The hunter had not showered nor attempted any other scent-control measure. He wore street clothes laundered in regular soap and his everyday tennis shoes; it took Chance 20 seconds before he was barking at the hunter's box.

SHOWER AND SPRAY This time, the hunter took a no-scent shower and dressed in camo clothes washed in an unscented detergent. He also wore high rubber boots to keep his walking trail clean and to hide foot odor. It took Chance 18 seconds to find him.

COMPULSIVELY CLEAN Our final test involved every scent-control measure we could think of. In addition to the shower, the hunter wore two layers of activated-carbon clothing. I literally soaked him with a scent-killing spray, and he even chewed a wad of gum designed to eliminate breath odor. It took Chance 13 seconds to find him. No hesitation.

Our test may not reveal how a deer would react under the same circumstances. But it does show that all the scent-reducing measures in the world didn't make a bit of difference to a downwind dog—which suggests, at the very least, that if a deer is downwind and close, he can smell you, no matter what. We are bombarded by claims that a product makes downwind deer oblivious, but our tests would indicate, it probably does not.

019 COVER YOUR SCENT

I'll start with a confession: I expected cover scents to fail miserably. To test them, I booked a K-9, Ike, as my helper and used the "Hot Box" test again. I was prepared for a yawner. What I got was a real eye-opener.

	COVER	RESULT
NO COVER	Our hunter dressed to hunt but with no scent-eliminating clothing and did not use any type of cover scent.	Ike found him in 6 seconds.
PINE & EARTH SCENT	We sprayed the hunter liberally with earth-scent spray.	Ike did not speed directly to the hunter's box. Rather, he ran past each enclosure once, then double-checked one before finding the hunter. Elapsed time: 25 seconds.
ACORN SCENT	We pinned acorn-scent wafers to the hunter's coat and misted him with acorn-based spray. I also soaked a rag with a synthetic acorn scent from an aerosol can.	Once again, Ike ran the entire course, scent-checking each box. Elapsed time before he found the hunter: 45 seconds.
SKUNK SCENT	The hunter used a small canister containing a cotton ball soaked with enough skunk scent to gag an outdoor writer.	It took Ike 45 seconds to find the hunter.

The goal is to delay the inevitable—to fool a buck's nose long enough to make a shot. Scent-reducing products failed utterly. Yet pine-and-earth scents were twice as effective as no cover scent, and acorn and skunk scents confused the dog for a half-minute longer.

020 CALL HIM OUT

The vast majority of deer hunters are call-shy. In 40 years of hunting with and talking to fellow hunters, I'm continually surprised at how few of them call to whitetails even half as much as they should. And almost no one talks to muleys. Meanwhile, deer of both species walk out of their lives that might otherwise have been lured into shooting range.

I know deer don't look or behave like raucous, vocal creatures. They don't howl like wolves, jabber like chimps, or gobble like turkeys. Outside of the occasional warning snort, we just don't hear them "talk" to each other very much. The truth is that deer are actually pretty chatty. Biologists have identified more than 90 different sounds made by whitetails alone. These vocalizations serve a variety of

purposes: contact, reassurance, lust, challenge, alarm, and more. You don't need to mimic all these sounds. Not by a long shot. Learning just the basics will definitely help you get closer to whitetails and muleys as you're on the hunt.

So here's what you do. Start by buying a variable grunt call that comes with an instructional DVD, and begin tinkering with the sounds at home. Then take your call to the woods and practice on deer you don't intend to shoot. Some of those deer will ignore you. Most will give you a look. Hardly any will spook. And some will come, looking for the doe, or fawn, or buck you're imitating. Then, the next time you see a deer you do want to shoot that's walking out of your life, you'll know exactly what to do.

021 DECIPHER DEER SOUNDS

There are eight deer vocalizations every hunter should
know and learn how to mimic. Here's what each sounds
like, how to make it, and what it means.

THE CALL	WHO MAKES IT	THE SOUND	WHAT IT MEANS
CONTACT GRUNT	Every deer in the herd	A half-second burp, made with a variable grunt-tube call	"I'm here. Whassup?"
TENDING GRUNT	Bucks dogging does	Burp, burp, buuurp, made with a variable grunt-tube call	"Who da man? I'm da man! Who da man?"
CLICKING	Bucks really dogging does	Roof-of-mouth tongue clicking—tick, tick, tick, tick—made with a variable grunt-tube call	"Never, never going to give you up . . ."
ROAR	Bucks out of their minds with lust	Grunt on 'roids—BUUURRRP!—made with a "roar" or "growl" grunt call	"I'm one step away from needing a serious cold shower here! How 'bout it?"
SNORT	Alarmed bucks and does	A loud, breathy whoooosh!, often accompanied by a hoof stomp. Can be made by mouth or with snort-wheeze call	Varies from "What the heck is that?" to "Let's get the heck outta here!"
BAWL	Usually fawns, but any deer in danger	A dying rabbit times three—Meaaaa! Meaaa! Meeeaaaa!—made with fawn-distress call	"Get this coyote's teeth out of my butt!"
SNORT-WHEEZE	Aggressive bucks	Couple of quick snorts, and a long, loud exhale—Whish, whish, pheeeewwwwwt!—made by mouth or with snort-wheeze call	"I own this turf, and all the does standing thereon. Dude!"
BLEAT	Does	Similar to a contact grunt, with a hint of sheep—meeaaaah—made with bleat call	"Mommy's right here, honey."
MEW	Fawns	High-pitched, lower-volume bleat—meah, meah, meah—made with bleat call	"Mom? Mom? Mommmyyy?!"

022 READ A TALE FROM THE TAIL

Whoever coined the old English proverb, "The eyes are the window to the soul" wasn't a deer hunter. With deer, it's all about the tail. You can often tell a whole lot about what a buck or doe is thinking or feeling just by watching its flag.

Relaxed and Droopy

"All's well in the world."

Almost Vertical and Flared

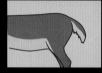

"I'm feeling a little edgy about something."

Vertical and Waving

"I'm outta here, and you other deer should run too."

Straight Out and Ruffled

"I'm dealing with some anger right now."

A Quick Twitch or Two

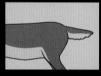

"I checked everything out; it's cool. No danger."

Continual Twitching

"Another week of deer flies, and I'm gonna need therapy."

Tucked Down Tight

"Pay no attention to me; I'm just looking for a rock to crawl under."

023 THINK DIFFERENT FOR BIG BUCKS

If you want to tag mature bucks, the first step is to realize that older deer don't behave the same as younger ones. The second step is to change your hunting strategy accordingly. Here's a breakdown of four key differences.

MATURE BUCKS ARE LAZIER

Telemetry research on south Texas' King Ranch showed that older bucks simply spent more time on their bellies than younger deer. "One old buck was only mobile about 19 percent of the time," says study leader Mickey Hellickson. **HUNT PLAN** Set up closer to the bedding area.

THEY ARE HOMEBODIES

Hellickson's research also revealed that the longer a buck lives, the smaller his home range and core area get. **HUNT PLAN** Find his pattern and be patient; he's around.

THEY ARE SEX MACHINES

Most of us associate the rut with bucks chasing does willy-nilly across the landscape. Not so with older ones, says noted researcher Karl Miller. "Mature bucks have learned the signs that indicate a doe is in heat and wait for those signals before making a move. They don't run around like teenagers, hitting on everything that moves." **HUNT PLAN** Camp on the does during the rut.

THEY MOVE LIKE GHOSTS

An old buck knows how to slip around the woods unnoticed. Instead of barging into a field to look for does, he'll scent-check it from the downwind woods; rather than walking the spine of a ridge, he'll slink along the hidden sidehill. **HUNT PLAN** Back off the main runways and look for faint trails carving covert routes.

024 TAKE A PERSONALITY TEST

Deer are no different from dogs, cats, or horses—all animals to which we readily assign personality traits. Some bucks are brash and combative; others avoid conflict. Most are social, but there's always a shy loner who just doesn't play well with others. Understanding these personality traits can make you a more successful deer hunter. If you know that a buck avoids confrontation, you'd never stake a buck decoy in front of him. Conversely, if you spot a belligerent brawler, you should feel confident challenging him with a loud grunt or snort-wheeze. Here's what to look for.

SIGNS OF AN AGGRESSIVE BUCK

- Stares directly into the faces of other deer
- Lays his ears back and raises the hair on his front shoulders, back, and neck
- Moves toward other bucks that spar or fight
- Kicks or shoves other bucks, even while he's in velvet
- Runs bucks, does, and fawns off his feeding areas
- Has broken antler tines or visible scars
- Comes to the sound of rattling and calling

SIGNS OF A PASSIVE OR SUBMISSIVE BUCK

- Avoids eye contact with other bucks
- Moves to a different feeding area when another buck approaches
- Lower his head and doesn't bristle his hair around other bucks
- Has a clean rack, with no broken tines
- Has a "pretty" face, with no scars or wounds
- Slinks away at the sound of rattling or buck vocalizations
- Tucks his tail

025 KNOW THE BIG 5 DEER FOODS

Just about every hunter knows that deer devour acorns, alfalfa, apples, corn, and soybeans. But to stay a step ahead of just about every hunter, you should also know the following about these five favorites.

ACORNS Deer prefer acorns that fall without their caps, as these nuts tend to have fine, firm flesh. Those still sporting caps often have flesh that is punky or rotten.

ALFALFA Deer love this perennial member of the legume family, but never more so than when it is newly seeded. They'll hammer a spring-planted field all fall and dig through deep snow to get to it in winter.

APPLES Of course deer love the sugary fruit. But remember that they'll keep hitting orchards to browse on the buds and twigs of these and other soft-mast trees long after the sweets are gone.

CORN It's a game changer. When a farmer fires up a combine, it's suddenly a race between deer and host of other critters to clean up the waste grain. That's why deer will temporarily abandon other foods to follow the combine. You should, too.

SOYBEANS In early fall, deer crave this plant's green leaves, but once the foliage turns yellow, the animals move on. They'll be back in winter to eat the beans.

026 SEEK SECONDARY FOODS

Given the choice between an acorn, an apple, and a red maple leaf, a deer will eat all three. You can try to explain to him that he has to choose one. But he won't listen, and it's not in his nature anyway.

Deer are nibblers. Walking to and from primary feeding areas, they nibble on a raspberry stem here, pluck an aspen leaf there, and maybe linger a while under a crab apple tree. Savvy hunters know this and keep track of these secondary food sources because their availability can dictate what path a deer chooses for its daily travels. Plus, when the savviest buck on your ground doesn't show in the crop field or food plot before dark, guess where he is: calmly mowing some secondary food source in the woods, waiting for dark before exposing himself. You might want to meet him there.

027 SCOUT FOR ACORNS

Deer prefer white oak acorns to red. Whites drop earlier. Nuttalls and pin oaks drop even before whites. Reds are the most reliably found from year to year. Those trees with the widest crowns and on south slopes produce the biggest crops. Blue, scrub, and live oak acorns are tops with western deer.

And all of that is perfectly good to know—as long as the deer and the trees play by the rules, which sometimes they don't. Outside the pages of magazines and manuals, deer tend to zero in on the acorns of specific trees in a way that is either somewhat or totally unpredictable. And so as a practical matter, the best way to tell which nuts they're after is to go look.

Walk amid the oaks—be they white, red, or other—and look for freshly fallen nuts without caps, partially chewed acorns, pawed leaves, hoofprints, and fresh droppings that are often pasty and green-hued. Keep an eye out for fresh rubs and scrapes nearby. And remember that the hot tree or trees can change at any time, so keep close tabs.

GREATEST DEER

THE MILO HANSON BUCK

DATE: NOVEMBER 23, 1993
LOCATION: BIGGAR, SASKATCHEWAN
SCORE: 213 5/8" B&C (reigning world-record typical whitetail)

WHY IT MAKES THE LIST:
How does a quiet, unassuming nice guy–who lives in a place almost no one has heard of–get famous virtually overnight? He shoots the world record typical whitetail. No one had heard of Milo Hanson, or Biggar, Saskatchewan, before the fall of 1993. But after the third week of November, suddenly every whitetail nut knew that a friendly farmer from Canada had shot a buck that would dethrone Jim Jordan's B&C world record typical, shot 79 seasons earlier. Taken on a drive, Milo's incredible buck has 14 scoreable points, main beams over 28", 4 tines over 12" and incredible symmetry.

028 FIND FRUITS AND NUTS

Before the moldboard plow made a giant salad bar out of much of the country, deer did just fine thanks in large part to naturally growing hard and soft mast. You know about apples, and acorns from white and red oaks. Here are six other favorite fruits and nuts.

BEECHNUTS A commmon staple where oak trees are absent or few, or when the acorn crop fails, especially in the northeastern United States.

BERRIES Deer actually prefer the leaves, branches, and stems of raspberry and blackberry bushes to the fruit, which is usually gone by hunting season.

HONEY LOCUSTS Deer love the sweet brown pods that drop from these trees in early September and gradually throughout the winter.

ALTERNATE ACORNS White and red oaks get all the ink, but deer devour nuts from more than a dozen other oak trees and shrubs. All told, acorns can compose more than 60 percent of the fall diet for whitetail deer, and more than 50 percent for blacktails. Muleys love them, too. Basically, if it's an acorn, it's deer food.

PERSIMMONS These juicy orange fruits ripen in early fall and drop gradually during wind storms through the late season.

SUMAC Easily identified by its clustered red berries, sumac provides a snack that's available late into the year.

WILD GRAPE The fruits are often available through fall and winter. Deer also eat leaves on vines clinging to trees and shrubs above the snow.

029 BROWSE THE BUFFET

Unlike agricultural crops and mast, the leaves, twigs, and buds of small woody plants, called browse, stimulate the microbes in a deer's rumen, which is critical to digestion. They can't survive without them.

A whitetail needs to consume 7 to 10 pounds of browse every day, which means a good deer habitat needs to include plenty of brush, shrubs, saplings, and vines growing low enough for them to reach. If a potential hunting area has little browse, it will have few deer, even if there are abundant croplands and hardwoods that drop truckloads of nuts. On the other hand, wherever you find plenty of low brush and saplings in otherwise good habitat, you should be in for steady action. Top browse species include the following.

ASH Often growing in low-lying sites preferred by wintering or pressured deer, ash is a widespread browse species.

ASPEN It's a staple in industrial forests and other areas of aggressive logging activity. Deer eat leaves early in the year, buds and twigs late.

BITTERBRUSH A highly digestible favorite of mule deer.

DEWBERRY This vine offers tender shoots that Southern deer favor, and it maintains edible leaves later than neighboring plants.

DOGWOOD Gray dogwood is an important browse species in the eastern half of the country; red osier is key east and west.

GREENBRIER The blue berries of this widespread thorny evergreen vine can last well into November, and the leaves are a favorite all winter long.

HONEYSUCKLE Another favorite vine, particularly in the Southern and mid-Atlantic states where its leaves remain attached through the winter months.

MAPLE High residual sugars give red leaves a special appeal. The twigs and buds of red, sugar, and striped maples are also favorites.

MOUNTAIN LAUREL Without the high-protein leaves of this plant, any number of winter deer would starve in some areas.

030 LOOK FOR EVERGREENS

In autumn's excess, when deer delectables fall from the trees and pop up underfoot (mushrooms are a prime, overlooked food in early fall), most evergreen foliage holds marginal appeal. But when winter hits, conifers become crucial for food and thermal cover.

Northern white cedar, with its waxy, high-energy leaves and buds, is a favorite winter treat for whitetails across the North; the recent whitetail boom has in fact significantly diminished the species. Winter deer in the North also rely on hemlock as a staple; it's one of the few eastern conifers of significant nutritional value.

In the West, fir needles are commonly the best available food where whitetails, muleys, and blacktails take winter shelter.

POPLAR Muleys relish the yellow leaves and the buds of low or fallen branches from this tree.

SAGEBRUSH Not favored, but an important winter species for mule deer because of its availability.

VARIOUS TREETOPS Wind-fallen or cut by loggers, they put mast, leaves, buds, and twigs suddenly at a deer's feeding level.

WILLOW Widespread in western riparian habitats and a key browse species for whitetails, muleys, and blacktails.

031 MAKE A WILD SALAD

You don't have to plant greenery from a seed bag marked "Monster Bucks" for it to attract monster bucks. You don't have to plant it at all. Turns out, the forbs, sedges, and herbs that grow naturally in fallow fields, pastures, burns, prairies, alpine meadows, wetlands, and natural clearings are powerful deer attractants when green and tender, as well as when frosts make certain species less toxic and tastier. Up to 70 percent of a whitetail's summer diet consists of forbs, including pokeweed, aster, ragweed, wild strawberry, and goldenrod, to name a few favorites. In fall, mule deer quickly devour frost-killed false hellebore, cow parsnip, and Russian thistle, as well as a long list of other herbaceous plants.

032 LOOK HIGH AND LOW FOR BUCK BEDS

That deer have been known to lie down on rooftops and in underground bunkers tells you a couple of things about where they bed: (1) no spot is too odd and (2) start by looking high and low.

In hill country, whitetail bucks love to bed up high where it's remote and rugged. Why here? Because most hunters don't like to climb hills, and because it offers a good view of the few who do.

Wilderness bucks will bed high, too, but the old-time trackers swear that the biggest ones hunker in the low, heavy green growth: the cedar swamps, the spruce thickets, the close-growing pines. They may choose a somewhat elevated spot within the lowlands (a dry hummock in a swamp, a knoll within a spruce hollow) but it's relative.

In the mountains, breaks, and badlands, muleys go up to lie down, but they don't need a tangle of cover so much as a good view. A big rock or bushy juniper that casts a patch of shade near the head of a draw or canyon is just right.

On the open flats, muleys, and some whitetails too, hunker down in ditches, swales, and creekbeds--any depression that puts their form below the sage brush or broom grass and their eyes above or peering through the tops.

033 GO TO GRASS

High or low, and especially on flat ground, bedding bucks claim the thickest thickets: the impossible snags of briar and honeysuckle, the impenetrable low conifers, the jumble of blowdowns, vines, and saplings.

But there's another spot.

Hunters are quick to assume that deer bed in the woods. But when you don't find them there, go to grass. All kinds of grass. For a shy, old buck, there's nothing like a dry hummock swallowed up in cattails or loosestrife. Who's going to find him in a sea of switch grass, or goldenrod, or CRP, or standing corn? Remember that some bucks use the woods for travel and tall grass for cover.

034 DON'T WALK PAST THAT PLOW

When late-season bucks get pressured out of their usual haunts, they bed down where few hunters bother to look—right under our noses. Prime examples: Shelterbelts near farmhouses; roadside ditches; abandoned homesteads; near farm equipment parked in hedgerows and pastures; isolated patches of grass, cattails, or brush; backyard borders; right behind the barn; right beside the hay bales.

035 SEX A BED

So you find a deer bed. Buck or doe? Ask yourself these questions, in this order:

QUESTION 1 How remote and rugged is the locale? Compared to bucks, does tend to bed closer to major food sources—often within a few hundred yards—in head-high grassy or brushy cover either on the lower half of a hillside or in flat or rolling terrain. Bucks tend to bed higher, farther from the food, in the real nasty stuff.

QUESTION 2 What's nearby? Does routinely bed in family groups, including yearlings and fawns. So where there's a doe bed, there are often two or three others of varying sizes nearby, as well as a mix of midsize and small droppings and tracks. Bucks (except yearlings and fawns) tend to bed alone and may pepper the area with rubs and large droppings.

QUESTION 3 Where'd I put my tape measure? What? You don't carry a tape measure? Well, grab one before your next scouting run. Because when sexing beds gets tough, such as in the late summer when bachelor groups of bucks lie down together, you can tell the difference between them by measuring them. Buck beds usually go more than 40 inches long; doe and fawn beds less.

036 KNOW THE ANATOMY OF A BUCK BED

This muley buck has bedded near the head of a canyon, but the same general principles apply with a whitetail on a ridge end.

- Cover at his back
- Open view to watch for danger from below
- Wind or thermals tell of danger from behind
- A good escape route
- Approaches from upwind, to smell danger on backtrack

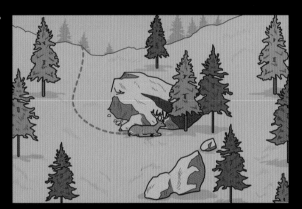

This whitetail is hunkered down in a cattail slough, but he could as easily be a muley in a clump of sagebrush:

- Surrounded by cover
- View out front through screen (or above) cover
- Wind tells of danger from behind
- A good escape route
- Approaches from upwind, to smell danger on backtrack

BEST WHITETAIL BUCK BEDS?

In an age when a growing number of readers can't consume more than 250 words without popping an Adderall, oversimplification rules the day. And so, more than ever, deer hunting articles say simply "find the bedding area" or "set up 150 yards from the bedding area" as if these areas were roped off and all the trees inside were decorated with Christmas lights.

They are not (nor are core areas, but that's another rant). On the contrary, nailing down the exact locations of buck beds is hard work, requiring time and boot leather. And so, to make it easier, we asked the hard-core deer hunters who read our Whitetail365 blog: What are the very best whitetail buck bedding areas?

Here are their top seven spots, in order:

1. CRP or other tall grass

2. Low-growing, dense conifers

3. Bench on a hillside

4. Blowdown

5. Thick fencerow or hedgerow

6. Brushy river or creek bank

7. The end or point of a ridge or spur

037 WATCH THAT SCAT

Locating fresh, large dropping near dense cover means you're close to a buck's bedding site along an oft-used trail or travel corridor. You can set up here for an early-morning hunt designed to catch the buck coming back to bed afer a night's feeding. Or you can back off from the scat in the direction of the nearest major food source, and hang a stand along that route for an afternoon hunt as he leaves the bed and heads for the grub.

Where droppings are in open cover, you're likely close to a feeding area. If you set up here, the deer may not arrive till after dark. So study a topographic map or aerial photo and look for a nearby funnel leading toward bedding cover. Head into the woods a ways and set up to catch the buck coming to the feeding area just after dark.

GREATEST DEER HUNTERS

NAT FOSTER
THE ORIGINAL DEERSLAYER

Boone and Crockett, both legendary hunters, shaped the mythos of the American backwoodsman. But it was the fictional Natty Bumppo of James Fenimore Cooper's Leatherstocking Tales who cemented the American deer hunter, specifically, as a cultural hero—rugged, steady, trustworthy, upright. Historians advance several candidates as Bumppo's real-life counterpart. As likely as not (and according to a 1937 report in *The New York Times*) renowned Adirondack deerslayer Nat Foster (1766–1840) gave Cooper his protagonist. Like Bumppo, Foster was a supremely skilled hunter and crack shot with the long rifle. Unlike Bumppo, he was no cardboard hero and none too friendly with the natives; suspected of killing many, he stood trial and was acquitted by a white jury for the murder of one.

038 GET THE SCOOP ON POOP

Experienced hunters are sometimes dismissive of the whole idea of studying deer pellets, as though paying attention to the sign was something that's valuable only to novices. Don't believe the (lack of) hype.

A close look at the deer scat you come across while scouting and hunting reveals loads of practical, nuanced information about the animals that left it behind. Use the guide below to interpret the droppings you find.

DRY PELLETS
Dry scat is a few days old. If the pellets are hard and lightening in color, they're even older. Move to a different spot.

MOIST PELLETS
Shiny, wet-looking droppings were likely made within the last 6 to 12 hours. This is a smoking-hot sign. Hunt near here now.

SOFT PELLETS
Loosely defined droppings indicate a deer was eating fruit or moist greenery. Look around for an alfalfa field or soft mast.

LARGE PELLETS
A large pile of pellets measuring roughly ¾ inch or more in length indicates a large animal, quite possibly a mature buck. Hunt here before and after the rut.

MIDSIZE PELLETS
Pellets that are only ½ inch or a little more in length were likely left by deer weighing 90 to 125 pounds–typically does but also young bucks. This can be a good rut spot.

SMALL PELLETS
The smallest pellets are a fawn's. Found near midsize pellets, these are a sure sign of a family group. It's a good place to hunt during the rut, as bucks look for company.

FIRM PELLETS
Firm, well-defined pellets suggest a deer was browsing on twigs and bushes. Scout to find a nearby cut, burn, or other area with thick saplings and brush, and hang a stand.

039 KNOW YOUR RUB

Once in a while, a whitetail buck makes a random rub, a light, incidental mark in a place where he's not likely to return. But far more often, rubs are purposeful and telling; they mean something—but what, exactly?

Bucks shred trees from the first hint of fall through the start of winter, in different places, and for different reasons. Understanding what kind of rub you're looking at and how it should factor into your hunting plans can lead to more success in the field.

TYPE	DESCRIPTION	RUB I.D.	HUNTING SIGNIFICANCE
BOUNDARY RUB	Made by mature bucks in the early season as they begin to mark their breeding territory.	Look for large rubs along natural boundary lines, such as creeks, fencelines, and wooded edges.	These make good early-season tree stand sites, often marking a route used about every three days in September.
TRAIL RUB	Made as a buck travels through his core area, typically from feed areas to bed.	Often found in a line, with clusters on either end nearest feed or bed.	Great pre-rut stand location. Determine the buck's direction by the side of the tree rubbed, and set up.
RUT RUB	Made during peak breeding by hormonally charged bucks near a hot doe.	Look for shredded saplings, brush, and 2- to 3-inch-diameter trees near doe bedding or feeding areas. There may be halfhearted scrapes nearby.	If you find a fresh rut rub that wasn't there a few days ago, set up immediately or hang a stand and return in the morning.
COMMUNITY RUB	Worked by several bucks in high-traffic areas.	Found in staging areas or at the intersection of major trails; deeply gouged, typically on 3- to 5-inch-diameter trees.	Can be good spots to simply tag out, but not consistent for older bucks.
FIELD RUB	Marked at the edge of a field by early-season or pre-rut bucks approaching to feed.	Found by walking a field's edge, just inside the woods. They may or may not be part of a rub line.	This reveals at least one place where a buck enters a feeding area—but he may not step into the open until after dark.
GIANT RUB	Made only by the largest bucks to mark their core area, usually during the pre-rut.	Probably a trail rub--but a special one. It's hard to miss blazes made on 6- to 12-inch-diameter trees. They may be found in a line.	These are rare and reveal a 4- to 7-year-old buck's core area. Set up downwind and wait. This could make your season.

040 READ THE RUB

As a buck ages, he becomes increasingly predictable about where he rubs, how he rubs, and what his rubs look like. And you can use that information to set up an ambush. Here are five things to look for when unraveling the rub-making habits of an older buck.

TREE SPECIES Most whitetails pick on trees with sappy, aromatic bark, including aspen, pine, cedar, and sassafras. Once a buck gets older, however, he will often pick one species to the exclusion of all others. I've hunted bucks with a preference for ash, white cedar, or even wooden fence posts.

TREE SIZE Bucks often favor tree trunks of a specific size. One of my buddies tells the story of hunting a huge buck that tortured any red pine with a 3-inch diameter—because they were the biggest trees he could fit between his near-touching antler tips.

TERRAIN AND COVER Bucks can be very particular about where they rub. For example, I've hunted bucks that make rubs only in swamps, even though their favorite tree species also grows on uplands.

UNIQUE ARTISTRY Funky racks make for one-of-a-kind rubs. One buck I tracked all season had a forked brow tine on his right side that left an unmistakable gouge. Really wide bucks often wreak collateral damage on nearby saplings and brush. Some unique artistry is obvious, some not so much. So get in the habit of inspecting rubs closely.

RUB HEIGHT Some bucks only rub down low, topping out at just 2 feet above the ground. Others crane their necks skyward and end up leaving elk-high markings at 5 or 6 feet up. Find a bunch of the latter and you can bet that they were made by the same buck—and that he'd look good on your wall.

MAKER'S MARKS
STUDY EACH RUB FOR HINTS ABOUT A BUCK'S TREE-RAKING HABITS, FOR EXAMPLE:

1. He likes cedars; look for more of that species.

2. He prefers to rub a fairly thick trunk.

6"

4'

3. His wide rack scars adjacent saplings.

4. He rubs fairly high– likely a good-size buck.

041 FIND EARLY RUBS AND SCRAPES

Are you waiting for late October to scout for a buck sign, when it's most abundant and easiest to find? Well, stop it. You need to look earlier. Why? Because according to the latest research, the first rubs and scrapes, which often show up before October, are usually made by the biggest bucks.

On average, a male whitetail makes between 300 and 400 rubs per fall, but young bucks open only about half as many as older bucks. What's more, whereas young bucks don't start making hard-antler rubs until late October, mature whitetails begin savaging saplings and debarking thigh-thick trunks almost immediately after antler shed in late August or early September.

Scraping, too, can begin right after velvet shed, and older bucks make roughly 85 percent of all scrapes. In other words, find early rubs and scrapes, and you've probably found a good-size buck.

GREATEST DEER

THE JAMES JORDAN BUCK

DATE: NOVEMBER 20, 1914
LOCATION: BURNETT COUNTY, WISCONSIN
SCORE: 206-$\frac{1}{8}$" TYPICAL

WHY IT MAKES THE LIST:
Jordan's giant 10-pointer reigned as the Boone and Crockett world-record typical whitetail for 79 years, longer than any other before or since. But the buck proved a bittersweet triumph for the hunter. Shortly after shooting the deer, Jordan gave the antlers to a taxidermist, who moved and took the antlers with him. Fifty years passed before Jordan saw the rack again, after it was found at a garage sale. Even after the buck was declared a world record, B&C didn't verify Jordan as the hunter until after his death, in 1978.

042 SCORE DURING SCRAPE WEEK

Hunting over scrapes can be maddening throughout much of the season. Research has shown that whitetails visit them mostly at night. Also, it's not uncommon for bucks to make one casually and never revisit. And once the peak rut begins, even the hottest scrapes can suddenly go stone cold. For a short time each fall, however, scrape hunting can be fantastic. The key is being in the woods before the peak breeding period.

Your absolute prime opportunity to hunt over this sign lasts about a week and straddles the seeking and chasing phases of the rut, starting about a week and a half before breeding crests. If you locate fresh scrapes then, the odds are very good that a buck will hit them while the sun is up. Even better, you're almost sure to find them: Bucks open more scrapes during this roughly weeklong period than at any other time of the year. Also, with their testosterone levels rising, these boys spend more time on their feet during daylight, opening and checking scrapes and cruising for does—but remain within their home ranges and along their familiar routes. Such predictability increases your chances for a successful ambush.

Don't expect the scrapes to stay hot, though. One of the biggest reasons hunters get skunked over this sign is that they hunt it too late, when bucks have switched their focus from pawing dirt to running down does.

Finally, it's important to understand that even during this seven-day window, some scrapes are better than others. Bucks are more likely to revisit those situated in or near secure cover. Overgrown logging roads surrounded by woods are great spots, as are wooded ridgetops, river bottoms, and evergreen stands. Also, whenever you find one scrape, look for another, and another, along a line that reveals a deer's travel route.

043 GET THE DIRT ON SCRAPES

Check those scrapes carefully, since different factors will dictate different hunting strategies.

	OPEN SCRAPES	HIDDEN SCRAPES	CHASE SCRAPES	RUT SCRAPES	LATE SCRAPES
DESCRIPTIONS	Look for these scrapes in or along the edges of fields, clear-cuts, and other openings. They begin popping up during the pre-rut and are typically worked at night.	As the pre-rut progresses, deer start hitting more and more of these scrapes within the woods. The thicker the cover, the more likely bucks are to work them during shooting light.	Certain scrapes get really hot during the seeking and chasing phases. Fresh dirt will be tossed everywhere, the licking branch will be mangled, and nearby saplings will be newly savaged.	Most scrapes are more or less abandoned once breeding begins in earnest. One key exception, however, is buck sign near doe bedding areas.	When unbred does come into heat, roughly 28 days after the primary rut, bucks may reopen scrapes. These scrapes are comparatively scant but well worth locating.
HUNT PLAN	Back off and seek corresponding buck sign in a nearby staging area with good cover. This is where you can ambush a mature buck before nightfall.	Setting up between the scrape and a known bedding area can be a deadly tactic now. Hang a scent wick soaked with regular buck urine and call with passive contact grunts.	Locating your stand right over the scrape can pay off big as big bucks begin cruising for receptive does. Get aggressive. Put out estrous doe scent and hit the rattling horns.	Hang your stand overlooking scrapes on the downwind edge of a doe bedding area. A combination of doe bleats and estrous scent can bring bucks trotting into shooting range now.	Set up within shooting distance and use tending grunts, doe bleats, and snort-wheezes to attract or challenge bucks competing for the few estrous does left.

044 SEX A TRACK

"Nobody—except possibly Jesus—can reliably tell a buck from a big doe track," writes John Wootters in his classic *Hunting Trophy Deer*. According to the Pew Forum on Religion and Public Life, about 80 percent of the Americans strive to emulate Jesus. If that includes you, here's your chance.

Wooters is of course right that you cannot sex deer tracks at a glance, like we often pretend to do, "Ooh, look at that big buck track right there." But you can, like possibly Jesus, reliably tell the difference. You just need to look closely at a variety of clues in aggregate.

SIZE A track that measures more than 5 ½ inches long with dew claws or 3 inches without, and is at least 3 inches wide, likely belongs to a good buck.

SHAPE The toes of a buck track are often splayed, giving the print a V shape. The tips of those toes are commonly worn round from scraping.

STRIDE The length between tracks, or stride, of the average walking whitetail measures less than 18 inches. That of a good buck may go nearly 2 feet. And it's purposeful; it's going somewhere. A dithering trail of closely set tracks usually tells of a doe.

STAGGER A barrel-chested buck's stagger—the width between the right and left track—is greater, too. The tracks of a doe or young buck run almost in a straight line. A good buck's fall clearly outside the centerline, as much as 6 or 8 inches apart. The old-time trackers say, the wider the stagger, the bigger the buck.

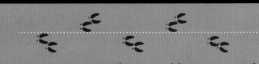

OFFSET TRACKS The rear and front prints on the same side commonly overlap. Because a doe's hips are wider, her rear hoof often lands slightly outside the front track, whereas a buck's frequently lands inside and a little short.

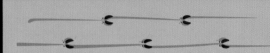

DRAG MARKS Bucks tend to drag their feet when walking, while does pick theirs up daintily. Drag marks are most obvious and reliable on a light blanket of snow, registering as long, skinny troughs cut between the prints. In snow more than a few inches deep, though, does may leave these marks, too.

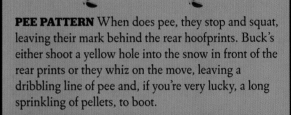

PEE PATTERN When does pee, they stop and squat, leaving their mark behind the rear hoofprints. Buck's either shoot a yellow hole into the snow in front of the rear prints or they whiz on the move, leaving a dribbling line of pee and, if you're very lucky, a long sprinkling of pellets, to boot.

OTHER TRACKS Very small tracks meandering alongside larger ones tell of a fawn shadowing its mother. The exception comes a few weeks after the primary rut, when many fawns come late into estrus and scampering trails of large and small tracks reveal a chase scene in the snow.

RACK REGISTER A rutting buck will bury his nose in any fresh doe track he finds. When he buries it deeply enough to leave an impression of his antlers in the snow, you'll have no trouble sexing his track.

045 TAKE A SURVEY

It's not as easy as counting, say, sheep, but by using a method developed in the late 1960s by the Wisconsin Department of Natural Resources, you can, roughly, count the deer in your hunting area. Here's how.

STEP 1 Head to your hunting area, pick a starting point, and walk 450 yards in a straight line while counting the deer trails you pass (include logging roads and people paths if they show deer tracks).

STEP 2 Stop, move over 200 yards, and head back in the direction you came on a line parallel to the first pass, counting all the way.

STEP 3 Move over another 200 yards and make another pass. Continue doing so until you've completed at least four passes.

STEP 4 When you're done, divide the number of deer trails you counted by the number of passes you made. For example, if you counted 30 trails and you made 10 passes, the number you need to remember is 3.

If the number you come up with is 2, 3, or 4, you have roughly 5 to 7 deer per square mile in your hunting area. If the number is 5, 6, or 7, you can estimate 15 to 20 deer per square mile. If your number is 8 or more, count your blessings.

046 USE THE OLD .30-06 TRICK

A classic trick of the old-time trackers is to lay a .30-06 round across the width of a deer track. If the print is as wide or wider than the cartridge, it belongs to a good-size buck. Happily, .25-06 Rem., .257 Wby. Mag., .264 Win. Mag, .270 Win., .280 Rem., 7mm Rem. Mag, .300 Win. Mag, .35 Whelen, and other cartridges of similar length will do the trick, too.

047 FIND THE FUNNELS

Funnels or pinch points are places where some obstacle or feature—a lakeshore, rocky bluff, road, or open field— forces or encourages deer to pass through a narrow lane. When you find one of the following, hang a stand.

WATER CROSSINGS Where the current is otherwise too strong or deep, deer will cross where it's more gentle and shallow. And they'll beat an obvious path to that spot.

FENCE GAPS Deer prefer an easy crossing, so they'll tend toward a break in the barrier or a low spot, such as where the top strand of barbwire sags.

HEADS AND TAILS When erosion cuts a deep, rugged gash in a hillside, deer will cross above (which is to say, at the head) or below (at the tail) of it.

NATURAL BRIDGES Any time there's a narrow strip of cover bridging two travel barriers (ponds or open fields) deer will walk the strip.

INTERSECTIONS Whenever you find two or more travel corridors that converge to form an intersection, such as a spot where three ridges come together, you can be sure that deer will walk right through the hub.

048 WALK WITH BUCKS

Above all, what separates the really great deer hunter from the mere mortal is a freakishly intuitive understanding of one thing: how bucks travel through the landscape. Just like a great fisherman can "read" the water and tell exactly where trout lie—never wasting a cast—a savvy deer hunter can look at the cover and terrain and know that a buck will enter a field edge or cross a woodlot or cruise a ridge here and not there.

Ultimately you learn this through experience, by noting where you see sign, where you spot deer, where your guesses are right and wrong. But a couple of basic rules do apply: Big bucks are naturally lazy. If they are unpressured, they will take the path of least resistance. Bucks are naturally shy. They will try to use cover and terrain to stay hidden as they travel—especially when pressured, even slightly.

A great way to hone your understanding of how bucks move, is to walk with them. After a thaw, stroll the spring woods (more on this later), following buck sign preserved from last fall and collecting hints about where they travel.

049 IDENTIFY THE CORRIDORS

Travel corridors are areas where bucks prefer to walk when there are other options, usually out of either laziness or for security. Here are five prime examples.

HABITAT EDGES Deer like to walk the line between one cover type and another, especially if one is thicker, such as the edge separating a clear-cut from the adjoining hardwoods.

LINEAR LOW SPOTS Ravines, saddles, ditches, dips, swales, and the like keep deer hidden as they move, even through what looks like otherwise open terrain.

FENCELINES Doesn't matter if it's a stone wall in Vermont or four-strand barbwire in Nebraska—the bucks will consistently parallel this structure. If there are trees, brush, or weeds along the line, even better.

WATER COURSES Dense vegetation typically grows along moving water, making deer feel safe. Stream courses usually provides food, too. And hey, if a buck gets thirsty . . .

RIDGETOPS Deer love to walk along or just off the spines of long ridges, where the terrain isn't too steep and escape is just a bound or two away.

050 CRASH THE BACHELOR PARTY

Several bucks feeding together in a summer alfalfa field isn't coincidence; it's a bachelor group. And if you're smart, when you spot these boys hanging out on your hunting ground, you'll grab your binoculars, set up a safe distance away, and spy on the party. Here's what to look for.

POSTURING One reason bucks band together now is to start working out dominance. These guys will compete for breeding rights in the fall, and answering some basic "Who's the boss?" questions now decreases the chance of a serious fight later between familiar bucks.

The process starts low-key while bucks are still in velvet. Posturing, shoving, hoof-flailing . . . all of this is more attitude than action, but it does give some insight into individual buck personalities.

FIGHTS Bachelor bucks do party on after velvet shed, but as their testosterone levels continue rising, the competition grows more fierce. Typical guys. Suddenly one buck cops an attitude and another ups the challenge. And with no more tender tines to protect, they'll use their antlers as the weapons they are. If the boys just walk toward each other

and lower heads, the sparring will rarely get serious. But if they sidestep, circle, bristle the hair on their backs, and roll their eyes back, sparring can get ugly. Many hunters believe bucks save serious fights for the rut; in fact some of the fiercest battles take place now. Pay attention, and you'll gather critical data about how certain bucks will respond later when you call or rattle to them.

THE BREAKUP Even the best parties must end. As late summer gives way to early fall, the appearance of that bachelor group at evening food sources—once as

predictable as a noon whistle—becomes haphazard. Suddenly there are three bucks instead of five. Or a single buck feeds in one corner of the field while two former buddies stay in another. In any case, the once-cohesive unit goes the way of all boy bands—each member splitting off of the group to go solo.

The good news is that most will stay in the general neighborhood. Continue to watch this field, but also check other top food sources. Set out trail cameras and make midday scouting runs with an eye for new rubs and scrapes. If the habitat is good, odds are you'll find the old boys.

HURTEAU ON:
HUNTING METHODS

If an ethical, legal method of deer hunting isn't your cup of tea, fine. Say so, if you must. But good gravy, don't act like your way makes you a better person. It doesn't, and, if you argue the point for long, you'll find that you're just picking nits. (For example, baiting an animal to kill for food—although not my cup of tea—is unequivocally not unethical and is better by far than how most folks get their meat.)

As Theodore Van Dyke, author of *The Still-Hunter*, wrote, "I have not a particle of interest in the question of [this style of hunting versus that]; for the world is all before me and I shall hunt as I choose . . ."

And as my own sweet mother says, "If you can't think of anything nice to say, shut the hell up."

F&S POLL — WHERE TO AIM

Bowhunters agree: Aim behind the shoulder. Gun hunters, on the other hand, hotly debate the best shot placement on a broadside deer. One camp shoots through the shoulders to drop a buck fast. Most shoot behind the shoulder, which ruins less meat. And some still favor the neck shot. So we showed our online readers this illustration and asked: With a gun, where would you shoot?

Here's how more than 2,000 readers voted:

Other: 3%

Neck: 4%

Behind the shoulder crease: 65%

Shoulder: 28%

3 4 5 6 7 8 8 7

051 FIND A MONSTER BUCK AT HOME

You could have a monster buck living right under your nose. If you haven't seen him, it's probably just because he doesn't get around a whole lot.

For years, researchers and hunters have assumed that as a buck ages, his home range gets bigger. But when Mickey Hellickson, former chief biologist on south Texas's well-known King Ranch, recently took a new look at some old data, he found that just the opposite was true. The longer a buck lives, the more his territory actually shrinks.

Way back in 1992, Hellickson's research team fitted 125 whitetail bucks with telemetry collars and monitored their locations weekly for three years. Technically, the study ended in 1995, but it's still yielding eye-popping information today. After analyzing his original data specifically for buck range

by age class, he published the results in the June–July 2010 issue of *Quality Whitetails* magazine, revealing that "old" bucks (7 ½ or older) have the smallest home ranges, averaging 1,055 acres—less than half that of young bucks (2 ½ and younger) and at least 25 percent smaller than that of middle-aged (3- and 4-year-olds) and mature bucks (5 and 6).

But here's the real kicker: Territory shrinkage holds for core areas, too, with old bucks averaging just 151 acres. And prior to the pre-rut, while deer are still in their summer pattern, home ranges and core areas tend to be significantly smaller than the average. In other words, the oldest buck on your property may also be the biggest homebody. And during the early season, his primary haunt may be no bigger than one corner of your hunting ground.

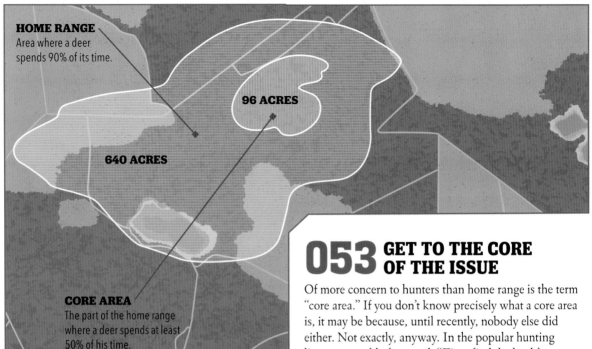

HOME RANGE
Area where a deer
spends 90% of its time.

96 ACRES

640 ACRES

CORE AREA
The part of the home range
where a deer spends at least
50% of his time.

052 HEED HOME RANGES, A LITTLE

An adult deer spends the vast majority of its life on a limited span of acreage called a home range, which provides all of its needs through the seasons. Extreme hunting pressure, other radical disruptions, and the prospect of sex with an unknown partner can push or pull a deer off its turf. Otherwise, it's loathe to leave.

And that, as a practical matter, is about all the average hunter need know about home ranges. Their sizes vary so wildly, depending on a gamut of factors, as to be almost meaningless. I've seen "average home range" estimates from 640 acres (a square mile) to 3,000 acres, and individual home ranges within a single study group from as small as about 300 acres to more than 13,000. What's more, most home ranges overlap several if not numerous properties.

On the other hand, it is somewhat useful to know the meaning of the term "home range," if only for the comfort it provides knowing that you didn't necessarily screw up when the buck you were hunting suddenly vanishes; he may have simply moved temporarily to another part of his home range.

053 GET TO THE CORE OF THE ISSUE

Of more concern to hunters than home range is the term "core area." If you don't know precisely what a core area is, it may be because, until recently, nobody else did either. Not exactly, anyway. In the popular hunting literature you'd often read, "First, find the buck's core area . . ." without the benefit of an explanation.

We understood it to mean—very loosely—"where a buck is currently spending most of his time."

Then in 2008, a real scientist nailed it down for us. In a study that marked the movements of 40 adult GPS-collared bucks every 20 minutes from August through December, Chesapeake Farms researcher Mark Conner defined "core area" as the place within a buck's home range (which averaged about 600 acres in his study) where the deer spent at least 50 percent of his time. "Most core areas represented about 15 percent of the total home range, or about 90 acres," he said.

Now that's a space that the average hunter can get his mind—as well as his feet and eyes and trail cameras—around. It's an area that's worth your attention because it may well exist largely or entirely on your hunting property. And it's worth your patience, because a buck that spends "at least 50 percent of his time here" will be coming back, repeatedly.

It's a safe bet to assume that a deer's core area boasts choice foods within its home range. But don't overlook the importance of thick cover. We hunters are primarily interested in where bucks spend most of their daylight hours, and that would be in and around their daytime beds—in other words, thick cover.

So, from this point on within these pages, when you read the phrase, "First, find the buck's core area . . . ," this is what we mean.

054 FACE IT: THERE'S NO "OCTOBER LULL"

I hate to pour cold water on the "October lull"—that perennial, handy excuse we hunters use to explain why buck movement seems to slow way down during the first part of the month—and to conveniently place all the blame on the deer. You know what I mean—statements like "The bucks just aren't moving now," or "They're laying low, resting up for the rut."

But there's one little hang-up: Bucks actually move more often in October.

Telemetry research conducted at Maryland's Chesapeake Farms by biologist Mark Conner recently proved that deer movement does nothing but increase as the fall progresses. In late summer, his GPS-collared bucks moved an average of 1 ½ miles in a 24-hour period. By October, they'd upped their travels to 2 miles a day. (During the rut, they clocked 2 ½ miles per day.) Conner's data also shows that the timing of these movements didn't change significantly, which means the old "going nocturnal" excuse doesn't wash.

So there is no real "lull" in activity, only a perceived one. Turns out, the problem isn't the deer. The problem is, well, you. But this is good news: Bucks are still on their feet in October; you just need to start looking in the right places.

GREATEST DEER HUNTERS

JOHN JAMES AUDUBON
THE HUNTER-NATURALIST

Though not widely celebrated as a deer hunter, Audubon (1785–1851) was an avid whitetail devotee, and, along with Foster, a strong candidate for Cooper's real-life Natty Bumppo. Audubon's influential 1831 essay "Deer Hunting," widely read in his day and still in print 182 years later, was [1] the first serious how-to manual detailing the popular deer-hunting tactics of the time; [2] a romanticized case for deer hunting as noble recreation; and [3] an early argument for fair-chase hunting. Audubon is America's original hunter-naturalist, who, as deer-hunting historian Robert Wegner writes in his excellent *Legendary Deerslayers*, "studied deer to hunt them and hunted them to study them."

055 FIND THE HIDDEN FOODS

If bucks are more active in October and yet you're not seeing them, then what gives? Most likely, the explanation is a shift in food sources. In late summer and early fall, deer are plain to see as they feed on grains and greens in open crop fields, meadows, pastures, and clear-cuts. But in October, when acorns start raining down and soft-mast favorites like apples and persimmons ripen, deer can suddenly fill up within the security of the woods, where you can't see them as readily. And given that option, they'll usually take it. So, when bucks vanish from the fields and openings you've been watching, speed-scout the woods to find the hidden foods.

056 CONCENTRATE ON COVER

Another factor that makes bucks seem to disappear is the annual leaf drop. Deer seek thick cover. So what happens when the trees lose their leaves in a matter of a week? Right. The buck that felt safely covered up only days ago suddenly feels like he's wearing a hospital gown, or worse. So naturally, he's going to drop any parklike woods from his walking routes and stick to the evergreens, thick brush, and dark shadows.

057 CHECK THE PRESSURE

A lot of hunting seasons start in early fall, and the pressure from small-game and bird hunters can cause deer to shift their patterns. There may be leaf-peeping hikers and bikers, too. And let's not forget you. If you've been hunting the same stands since the start of bow season, the deer you were seeing in September may be wise to you by October. Hang a new stand, walk farther back, or just get away from the roads and trails where a pressured buck won't see so much blaze orange and spandex.

058 GET IN ON THE SECRET RUT

Last fall, my father and I ignored the calendar that told us we were in the "October lull" and headed out to hunt a local farm. That evening—with our stands only about 400 yards apart—I watched a pair of giant bucks working a field of does just out of range, and my dad missed a chip shot at a P&Y 8-pointer. It was October 11, but we enjoyed November-like buck action.

Some time ago, I might have called this a freak occurrence. Although research suggests that some does come into estrus about a month prior to the peak rut, I—like many hunters—assumed this was too scattered to be of much significance. But I started to change my mind

three years ago when a taxidermist buddy called to tell me about a customer's 150-class buck shot on October 10. The next fall, hunters brought three giant whitetails to his shop, all killed within four days of that same date. Those bucks had all been either chasing does or responding to rattling or calling. Along with similar anecdotes from other hunters, this convinced my father and me to hunt in early October last year. And we weren't disappointed.

Of course, early breeding activity won't compare to the rutting peak, but it's definitely worth exploiting, especially since mature bucks seem to be the most active participants. It

makes sense that these deer, which have the most breeding experience, are the ones competing for a small number of early estrous does.

Start with the onset of the peak rut in your area and count backward 28 days. (If you don't know the timing, call your regional game agency and ask a biologist.) For most hunters, this will be sometime around the first or second week of October—right in the middle of the so-called "lull." Plan to hunt during the three- or four-day period surrounding that date. While a lot of other people sit at home assuming the hunting is too slow to bother with, you may get your shot at a monster. Hopefully, you'll shoot a little straighter than my dad did.

059 PINPOINT EARLY RUT ACTIVITY

Knowing that some of the biggest bucks are looking for love a month early is fine and dandy, but to take advantage you need to pinpoint this activity. The key is to find the first estrous does. To distinguish them from the rest of the herd, glass every doe you see and make note of those with the darkest-stained tarsal glands. Also look for the biggest does. As fellow F&S contributor Gerald Almy has written: "Among humans, the dominant male often gets the cutest girl. Among whitetails, he gets the heaviest . . . The largest matriarch attracts the area's dominant buck because she comes into estrus earliest."

Starting from where these does like to feed, follow trails back to their bedding areas—typically grassy or bushy cover that grows eye-high to a bedded deer. Now move downwind of this spot and set up a stand to catch bucks cruising or bedding where they can get a good whiff of the first few hot does. This rutting action is not going to be widespread or easy to spot, so also keep an eye out for any sudden surge of rubbing and scraping near these feeding or bedding areas to tip you off. Also, keep a journal noting when and where you spot early rutting activity to help you pinpoint it in the future. You just might catch a monster thinking more about his love life than his hide weeks before the main event.

HURTEAU ON:
RUB-URINATION

When a buck really wants to smell nice for the ladies, he urinates on his already-stinky tarsal glands, creating a near-lethal cologne that makes Axe body spray smell like roses. Deer biologists call this behavior "rub-urination" or "self-anointing," the latter of which in a survey of normal English speakers was voted the "most ridiculous euphemism in deer hunting." I, like other normal English speakers, call it "peeing all over oneself."

Knowing about rub-urination does have some practical value for the deer hunter; for example, some truly dedicated hunters will actually carry around a deer-urine-doused tarsal gland taken from a killed buck in order to cover their own scent or to lure other deer close during the rut, or both. But, that said, the most important benefit of knowing about rub-urination is that it just makes some of our own rituals seem less weird.

061 SEEK THE FIRST PHASE

We often talk about the rut phases as if a switch is flipped and, click, it's the seeking phase, or, click, the chase is on. But the shifts are far subtler. The transition from the so-called October lull to the seeking phase starts with bucks simply spending a little more time on their feet, venturing into doe areas, sniffing for any hint of go-time, and making more rubs and scrapes. It builds from there.

Technically, seeking and chasing are one phase. Bucks seek does, and when they find one, they're apt to chase. If the doe isn't ready, the buck will break off and seek another. As more does enter estrous, what starts off as mostly seeking gradually becomes mostly chasing. And even then, any buck that isn't chasing a doe is definitely seeking one to chase.

But it's useful to separate them from a practical standpoint—because they hunt differently. The seeking phase is an especially good time for bowhunting because bucks are on the move yet still fairly predictable (which begins to change once they start chasing in ernest). But to take advantage, you need to pay close attention to subtle changes in late October. You need to seek the seeking phase. Do lots of midday scouting and be ready jump on the freshest sign or latest sightings.

062 CUT TO THE CHASE, GRADUALLY

Roughly two days before a doe is ready, she becomes restless, covering more ground (some actually leaving their home range on breeding excursions) and urinating frequently—advertising herself to bucks, which pick up the trail and pursue. However, it may be a day or more before she is ready to accept a mate. This, plus the advances of increasingly frustrated bucks harassing does that aren't ready, can make it seem like every deer you see is either chasing or being chased. Many hunters consider it the very best time to be in the deer woods.

Some researchers believe the whole frantic, conspicuous, noisy process is a way for does to attract as many suitors as possible in order to pick the best mate. What does that mean for you? Well, when you see a doe being chased, don't just take the first decent buck you see. Odds are, the big one will be coming along shortly.

060 WATCH THE LIP CURL

When a pursuing buck catches up to a doe and his lip curls—an act that's technically called flehmening—he's actually sucking the odor of her urine into the roof of his mouth. That's where the vomeronasal organ processes the scent and tells him if she's ready to breed. Several animal species have this gland, and researchers feel that primitive humans might have had it, too. But don't lip curl on your next date. It's considered gauche.

063 TRACK THE RUT

The timing of rut phases isn't perfectly predictable by any means. But it helps to know generally when to start looking for the signs. The chart below is based on typical rut dates for most northern states. To customize it, call your regional wildlife agency; they'll be able to help you pinpoint your area's peak breeding times.

PHASES	DESCRIPTION	APPROXIMATE DATES	THE LOWDOWN	SURE SIGNS
1. SEEKING	About two weeks prior to peak breeding	October 25–November 1	Bucks are on their feet more, seeking females	Explosion of new rubs and scrapes. More buck sightings.
2. CHASING	One week before peak breeding	November 1–8	The first does are coming into estrus, and bucks are more than ready.	You'll see bucks chasing does.
3. PEAK BREEDING	Consult regional wildlife biologist	November 9–16	Most does are in estrus, and bucks are tending them.	Deer movement slows way down. When seen, bucks are with does.
4. IMMEDIATE POST-RUT	One week after the start of peak breeding	November 17–24	Breeding is mostly done, but mature bucks still vie for the last receptive does.	Does reappear at food sources. Bucks freshen rubs and scrapes.
5. POST-RUT	Two weeks after the start of peak breeding	Beginning November 25	Breeding is done for now. Bucks return to core areas and feed.	Bucks hit prime food sources during daylight in cold weather.
6. SECONDARY BREEDING	About one month after peak breeding	December 9–16	Unbred does enter estrus again. Doe fawns and yearlings come in for the first time.	Big bucks chase does and fawns near winter food sources. Fresh scrapes reappear.

F&S POLL

BEST PHASE TO HUNT

We asked *F&S* readers: If you could hunt any phase of the rut all the time, which would it be? Which phase gives you the best shot at taking a good buck?

A: Seeking: 36%
B: Chasing: 49%
C: Peak Breeding: 5%
D: Post-Rut: 10%

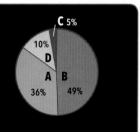

064 DON'T MISS MIDDAY

If you watch a rut funnel during the middle of the day, there's an excellent chance that any buck that you encounter will be a good one. Mature bucks are simply more driven to find estrous does right now, and they have the endurance to travel at times when younger bucks are tired and bedded down for the day. Also, if hunting pressure or predation is a factor in your area, older bucks may have learned that traveling during midday is simply safer.

065 KNOW WHY DEER FIGHT

When ranging far and wide during the rut, unfamiliar bucks sometimes find themselves in the same area, vying for the same does. When they do, look out. Fights can be brief and brutal or long and exhausting. They can settle breeding rights, end in death or, like many battles, achieve nothing much at all.

Serious clashes don't happen often, but when they do, they're a stunning spectacle of power and savagery. Hunters rattle antlers to mimic bucks battling, but I've seen the real thing from 20 yards and can tell you that no rattling session can duplicate the mayhem and brutality.

It's important to understand why bucks fight. It's not about "territory," as many think. Rather, it's about does and dominance, and the major battles are usually between bucks that don't know each other. Among familiar deer, pecking-order issues are mostly settled before the rut. But when dominant strangers bump into each other now, it can get ugly. That said, serious fights are not limited to the rut. Bucks are no different from males of any species in this way; if one cocky troublemaker runs into another, it's on.

066 RECOGNIZE RUT FUNNELS

Willing females make the rut exciting for wide-roaming bucks. But it's the wide-roaming bucks, often on their feet during daylight, that make it exciting for us. According to the latest research, bucks increase their normal travel by a significant percentage during the breeding season. Why? Because with does scattered across the landscape, coming into estrus at various and unpredictable times, finding the one that wants to make it happen right now can take some serious searching. (You may be able to relate.)

With bucks covering so much ground, this is the time to concentrate on travel corridors and funnels. But not just any funnel will do; rutting bucks favor these:

MACRO FUNNELS A buck's world gets a lot bigger during the rut, and you need to see it that way. The stud that's on your property today might be 10 miles away tomorrow. So take a look at your ground on Google

Earth, for example, and zoom way out. Now identify the big, major funnels—saddles, wooded strips, creek bottoms, fencelines, ridges—that connect your property to others. These are key rut funnels.

In the big woods, look for features that either steer roaming bucks on a particular course—lakeshores, river banks, dams between beaver ponds—or just make covering the miles a little easier, such as benches, gentler slopes, and logging roads.

DOE-AREA FUNNELS Knowing where the does in your area feed and bed really pays off now. Rutting bucks are virtually guaranteed to hit these places. They'll cruise the perimeter of feed fields or cutovers and swing downwind of brushy bedding spots to sniff for potential mates. Funnels and pinch points leading to and from these areas now turn electric with buck activity.

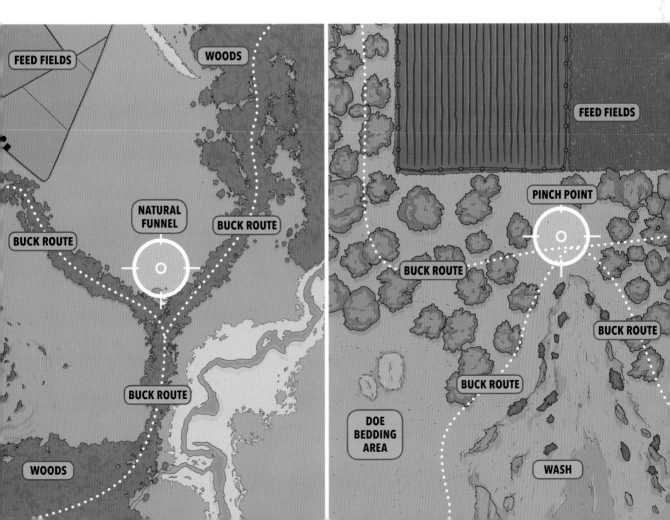

067 KNOW THE RUT PLAYERS

DOE She enters estrus in early to mid-November every fall. When she does, every buck in the neighborhood is after her.

WHAT YOU MAY NOT KNOW: If she's not bred initially, she'll come into heat again, 28 days later, and she comes into estrus earlier than younger does. A mature doe is much more likely to give birth to twins or triplets than her younger peers; in addition, she carries at least half the genetic code that determines whether a buck fawn grows into a whopper or basket rack. She'll most likely continue to birth fawns until she dies; hunters looking for the "old dry doe" are pretty much chasing a myth.

FAWN In healthy herds, some doe fawns are capable of breeding and giving birth.

WHAT YOU MAY NOT KNOW: In some herds, as high as 40 percent of female fawns will enter estrus. Studies show that fawns usually cycle later than mature does, and therefore are often responsible for the bulk of secondary rut activity. They are most likely to throw a single fawn the next spring.

YOUNG BUCK These bucks take part in the seeking and chasing phases of the rut and sometimes even get an opportunity to breed.

WHAT YOU MAY NOT KNOW: Even in highly managed herds, yearling bucks sire up to 35 percent of offspring. These youngsters usually get their chance during peak breeding, when older bucks simply can't get to all the estrous does. While often thought to be genetically inferior, many spike or forkhorn bucks were just born late and haven't had time to grow more bone.

MATURE BUCK This is the King of the Rut. He does the majority of the breeding, fighting off rivals with his superior strength and headgear.

WHAT YOU MAY NOT KNOW: Even the most active "breeder" buck sires surprisingly few fawns each fall. Huge antlers and a large body don't make him dominant; a smaller, more aggressive buck may push him around and do more breeding. He may tolerate the presence of another buck, even when breeding; research proves that twin fawns occasionally have different fathers.

068 WAIT FOR THE PRODIGAL BUCK

If you've nailed down a big buck's core area, the rut can leave you feeling like the prodigal son's father. Sunday-school lessons a little hazy? Like a rutting buck, the prodigal son left home, vamoosed, disappeared to sow his wild oats. But he returned, and so will your buck, most likely.

What's the proof? In a recent study at Cheseapeake Farms, by wildlife manager Mark Conner, bucks began moving more extensively as the rut kicked in, frequently abandoning their core areas and occasionally roaming beyond their home ranges. But here's the kicker: Most returned within 8 to 32 hours. "If a buck was faithful to a core area in the pre-rut," said Conner, "he was coming back." Also, since the activity sensors on the GPS collars indicated that returned bucks were mostly idle, it's safe to assume that those bucks came back to their core areas to rest up. And there's one more thing. Are you sitting down? The data also showed that most bucks made the return trip during daylight hours.

In other words, two of the most widely held assumptions—first, that rutting bucks do not return to their core areas until the rut is over, and second, that hunting core areas is a waste of time during the rut—are dead wrong. So if you're among the many hard-core whitetail hunters who work hard to nail down the core areas of individual bucks, rejoice. The rut is not a time of despair. You just need to keep the faith, brother. Set up in a funnel leading in and out of a core area's best bedding cover, be prepared to sit all day, and wait your buck out. According to this study, there's a great chance you'll kill something far bigger than the fatted calf.

069 GET THE KEYS TO THE LOCKDOWN

When the manic action of the chasing phase comes to an abrupt halt, you have entered the dreaded "lockdown" phase of the rut, when the majority of does come into heat, the majority of bucks get busy servicing them, and the majority of treestand hunters catch up on their reading. The keys to hunting the lockdown are to, first, put down the book and, second, understand how deer behavior during this phase makes some bucks still vulnerable.

IN-BETWEEN KEY Peak-rut bucks do not tend does nonstop. In fact, the latest research suggests that the time spent with any one doe may be shorter than previously thought, perhaps as little as 24 hours. And when a buck isn't with a doe, he is between does—resting back in his core area or seeking a new mate. Set up in the right spot (more on this later) and patience will pay off.

THE LOOK-AT-ME KEY When mates rendezvous, they head off to some odd spot, away from other deer, for their time together. Fairly often, these are places of little cover, such as an isolated patch of brush in an open field, a draw at the edge of a field, or a pasture sparsely dotted with trees and brush. What's more, these are also places where you can glass and spot a breeding pair—and make a successful stalk.

070 DIAGNOSE THE LOCKDOWN

The most obvious sign of the lockdown is not seeing squat for deer in the middle of November. But you can't count on this alone. You may just be in the wrong spot. Or the local yahoos may have driven your property without your knowing it. Or you may just be a really crappy hunter. So look for these other signs to confirm your suspicions: **[1]** The deer you do see are lone fawns, looking lost. They look lost because Mama is off getting some, and, suddenly alone for the first time, they don't know whether to keep walking or stop and lick themselves. **[2]** The deer you do see are yearling bucks, looking clueless. They look clueless because this is their first rut rodeo, and while the older, savvier bucks are having fun, they don't know whether to stand there and self-anoint or run around looking for does. **[3]** Your friends hunting the same general area are seeing—or not seeing—the same thing.

HURTEAU ON: THE PEAK OF THE RUT

Many hunters refer to "the peak of the rut" as if it were a good thing. As in, "I'm going to take a week off work during the peak of the rut." But if the "rut" is the "breeding season," then its peak is the height of breeding activity, which is the lockdown, which is decidedly not good. If by "the peak of the rut," you mean the chasing phase, however, all's well. But if you mean "peak breeding," you'd better take that week off sooner.

If you are allowed to gun hunt during the heart of the chasing phase–when it can seem like every deer in the woods is running willy nilly–take time off about a week before peak rut. If you're a bowhunter, however, two weeks prior is usually better. The deer activity may be less frantic but it's more predictable, and you have a better chance then of calling a buck into easy bow range.

071 PICK YOUR FIGHTS

If you think the peak of the rut is the best time to rattle in a buck, you're right—but maybe not the biggest buck. That's just one of the things that whitetail researcher Mickey Hellickson proved during a two-year study conducted on an 8,000-acre Texas ranch. Hellickson placed observers in elevated blinds, and then had someone rattle a set of antlers at ground level. Teams conducted three 10-minute rattling sessions in a variety of areas and in all kinds of weather. Here are five key lessons they learned that you can put to use for yourself this fall.

1. GET UP EARLY Morning rattling sessions resulted in the most responses from bucks, followed by afternoons. Midday was the worst time to rattle.

2. CHECK THE WEATHER Low winds, cool temps, and 75 percent cloud cover proved to be the ideal conditions for productive rattling.

3. WAIT FOR A GIANT During the pre-rut, yearling bucks were the first-responders, followed by some old bucks. During the peak rut, middle-aged bucks (3 ½ to 4 ½ years old) responded best. The really old boys came in during the post-rut.

4. PLAY IT LOUD, MOSTLY As a rule, loud rattling brought in the most bucks, as you might expect—with one fascinating exception. When truly old bucks came to the antlers in the post-rut, softer rattling (ticking the horns and grinding the bases) was more effective.

5. GET HIGH Ground-level rattlers only laid eyes on 33 percent of the bucks that were seen by the elevated observers, which just goes to show that many bucks may approach the sounds of a fight but not totally commit. This makes rattling from a tree stand a good idea.

072 DON'T DOUBT THE SECOND RUT

The so-called second rut has long been something of a mystery to hunters. Some swear by it. Others doubt it takes place at all. But the latest and most revealing research on the topic leaves little doubt: The second rut is real.

During a four-year study by the Pennsylvania Game Commission (PGC), biologists examined 3,180 road-killed does. By measuring the embryos in these deer, they determined that the vast majority of does age 1 ½ and older are bred during the traditional mid-November rut. Fawn does, however, are bred on average about three to four weeks later. It is these first-time breeders that are responsible for most rutting activity in December.

Researchers also determined that in the overbrowsed, big woods of north-central Pennsylvania, less than 10 percent of the fawn does are bred, compared to about 50 percent of those in the state's more productive agricultural regions.

"It only makes sense that the more productive habitats have more fawn breeding activity," says Dr. Christopher Rosenberry, deer section supervisor for the PGC. "These areas have higher deer birth rates, resulting in more fawns in the population. Those fawns are also going to be larger, healthier, and more likely to breed in their first year."

In short, the key to getting in on good second-rut activity is to focus on the best habitat.

073 GO BIG LATE

Evidence suggests that dominant bucks are particularly active during the second rut because of greater competition for the comparatively few estrous does. "Just about every breeding-age buck takes part in the primary rut," says Penn State University deer researcher Duane Diefenbach. "But I wouldn't be surprised if it's the older bucks that do most of the breeding during the secondary rut. They have higher testosterone levels, and they're more likely to assert their dominance when there are fewer available does."

074 REMEMBER, MULEYS ARE A LITTLE DIFFERENT

The mule deer's mating ritual is very similar to a whitetail's in many ways. Muley bucks dog does for samples of urine; they lip curl to test a doe's readiness; they fend off competing males, sometimes via fierce, head-banging battles; and breeding pairs isolate themselves for the mating act. There are some important differences, though, including the following.

THE SIGNS Leading up to the rut, mule deer bucks make rubs to advertise their presence. But whereas whitetails favor the trunks of individual saplings and trees, muleys are just as likely to savage a large bush. And as a rule, muleys do not make scrapes.

THE SCENE In their open terrain, dominant mule deer bucks can often be seen defending what looks like a harem of does. But this is not a harem. The buck is guarding only one doe—the one in or closest to estrus. Other does voluntarily crowd close, using the dominant buck's presence to keep other pesky suitors at bay.

THE TIME FRAME If there were mood music for the muley mating ritual, it would be Barry White. They take it s-l-o-w. "In mule deer," writes renowned mule deer researcher Valerius Geist in *Mule Deer Country*, "breeding is a much drawn-out affair compared to whitetails, both before and after copulation."

075 DIG THE DOWN LOW

One of the classic survival tricks for a deer is something it learned before it could walk. In the first days of a fawn's life, its only defense is simply not moving. Mostly scentless and barely mobile, a fawn's sole means of avoiding a predator is to lie still, barely breathing, while its mother remains nearby, feeding, loafing, and hopefully distracting dangerous critters. Deer quickly learn to use their legs for the short bursts of speed (or agility in the case of mule deer) that will typically help them escape pursuers. But they never forget the power of immobility, especially when avoiding people. Countless telemetry studies have shown that even when hunting pressure is intense, one of the go-to whitetail escape tricks is to not escape at all but, rather, to simply hold tight and let danger pass. That's why the best still-hunters, trackers, and drivers learn to develop a keen eye for motionless deer.

076 UNDERSTAND PRESSURED DEER

Deer are a prey species. From the time they wear spots, something is trying to kill and eat them. This is critically important for deer hunters to keep in mind, because when deer feel the heat of being hunted, they act differently.

As a species, deer are pretty darn good at survival, thanks to centuries of practice eluding wolves, bears, coyotes, bobcats, and, more recently, us upright hominids. Some individual animals can seem almost supernaturally adept at staying alive, running a gauntlet of peril for so many seasons that they appear to have a sixth sense for danger—something that Hurteau (a skeptic) and I (a believer) regularly debate. But what makes an older buck so savvy is less important than simply acknowledging how tough he is to see, much less kill, after five or more years of living with a bull's-eye on his chest.

You can know all you want about deer behavior on a theoretical level, but once a savvy buck, especially a savvy whitetail, gets an inkling that you're after him, all of his normal needs and habits suddenly play second fiddle to his safety. The bottom line: Pressured deer are different—and tagging one means taking your game up a notch.

077 BONE UP ON BUNNIES

Ever hunted rabbits with a beagle? Then you already understand one of the tried-and-true escape behaviors of a whitetail with a predator on its tail. Jumped by a pursuer (be it a coyote or a four-man drive) a deer will use whatever evasive maneuvers are needed to confuse the chase—bursts of speed, doubling back on its own track, zig-zagging, walking in water— and then, even before it seems safe, the deer will circle back home. Several telemetry studies have proven this, including recent research done in South Carolina by Gino D'Angelo that tracked 13 does as they were pursued by hound packs during actual hunts. Even when intense pressure forced them from their familiar territory, the does would invariably loop right back to their home turf. "The hunts ended each day at 3 p.m.," D'Angelo says. "And by dusk, the does were already heading back to where they'd been jumped." The message for hunters is clear: Just because you bump a buck, it doesn't mean that he's left the country. He won't be easy to hunt, but he's probably still there.

078 MAKE A MULEY GO BOING

When hiding fails and skulking doesn't work, a whitetail leaves trouble behind with a burst of speed that puts distance between it and its pursuer. A mule deer, however, does something very different. It goes a-boinging—boinging up over rock and crag, putting impossible terrain between it and its pursuer. A signature difference between the species, the muley's specialized pogo-sticking gait is called stotting. And when you know a jumped muley buck will go stotting up over a rugged rim, you can make sure someone is waiting there for him.

Also, when you bump a good muley buck, quickly find a good rest, settle in, and get ready to shoot. One way that mule deer keep predators at bay in their classic open terrain is to simply keep an eye on them. And so, after bounding away a ways, mule deer have a strong tendency to look back. But it's an adaptation that hasn't worked out so well for them since the invention of the modern scoped rifle.

079 BELIEVE IN BUFFER ZONES

Back in the 1970s, researchers studying wolves learned a fascinating thing about deer: Whitetail numbers were higher in "buffer zones," neutral areas between wolf packs. When two wolf packs meet, they engage in brutal fights; these buffer zones served as a kind of no-man's-land that packs steered clear of to avoid conflict. Deer learned where they were and used them to avoid wolves.

More recent telemetry research has proven that deer use the same strategy to avoid people. In a Pennsylvania study conducted during rifle season, whitetails retreated to areas protected by some obstacle—a river, swamp, mountain, or simply distance from a road—that discouraged hunter intrusion. Learn to identify these buffer zones, and you'll find more deer during the season.

081 STUDY THE STORM

When chimney smoke leans toward the ground and swirling winds send spent leaves spiraling, take notice. A storm is brewing. Deer, which seem to know when bad weather is approaching, act differently before, during, and after a storm. And you should be ready to react, too.

BEFORE THE STORM Deer don't eat in a downpour or a driving snow, so they fill up before the nasty weather rolls in. If the storm will start in the afternoon, expect deer to feed late into the morning. If it'll come at night, expect them to hit feeding areas early in the afternoon. And if a very powerful storm—especially a snowstorm—is moving in, gear up for an all-day vigil near a prime feeding area.

DURING THE STORM During a driving downpour, slanting sleet, or blowing blizzard, deer head to sheltered areas and stay put. In hilly terrain, deer hole up in gullies, hollows, and lee-side slopes that offer good overhead cover—typically conifer stands. In flatter terrain and farmland, they go to low, thick cover, such as a dry hummock in a cedar swamp or a cattail slough where the bitter wind blows over the top of them.

AFTER THE STORM What deer do after bad weather depends on the type of storm. Heavy rains, for example, rarely keep deer down for long and may bring better hunting with cooler temps. Much the same can be said for a snowstorm that dumps 3 to 10 inches of fresh flakes and ushers in cold, calm conditions. This can make a half-beaten late-season hunter feel brand new. But lingering cold winds can keep deer in their sheltered areas and browsing nearby until conditions stabilize. Even in this situation, however, there is an upside: In the meantime, the deer get very hungry. Once conditions calm down, deer will eagerly hit choice feeding areas.

080 CHECK THE DEER FORECAST

SUNNY AND HOT Expect deer to bed out of the sun—on north-facing slopes or in deep shade where the prevailing wind helps keep the bugs at bay. Swamps and creek bottoms also offer cooler air and access to drinking water. Any activity will take place at the edges of daylight.

LIGHT RAIN AND FALLING TEMPERATURES Deer don't mind a little rain or drizzle; when these cold-front conditions snap a prolonged hot-and-dry spell, they can spur deer movement.

COLD, CALM, CLEAR These are ideal conditions for good daytime deer activity. After a front ushers in cooler temperatures, conditions stabilize, and the barometer starts rising again, it's time to climb into your treestand.

HEAVY PRECIPITATION This will put deer down for a while. Expect them to hole up in protective cover and stay there for as long as rain, snow, or sleet lasts. They'll be hungry when conditions normalize.

SUNNY AND COLD Look for deer to bed on south-facing slopes, where they can soak in what little warmth the winter sun offers. Bitterly cold temps will force them to hit top food sources hard for the energy needed to stay warm.

BREEZY AND COLD A top priority for winter deer is to stay out of the cold wind, which quickly robs them of what little heat their bodies produce. When a bitter breeze stirs, late-season deer stick to hollows, bowls, lee-side slopes, and low, protective cover.

082 DON'T GIVE UP

One of the classic excuses for not seeing a buck is, "He's 'gone nocturnal'." While a smart buck may reduce his daytime activity in response to hunting pressure, very few if any go completely nocturnal. During the rut, even mature bucks will pursue estrous does regardless of sun position. And in very cold winter weather, midday feeding can become a biological imperative.

083 STUDY THE WINTER SHIFT

For northern deer, winter is a brutal season. As food sources diminish, intense cold forces the animals to live off fat reserves to maintain body heat. Meanwhile, deep snow not only ensures difficult travel, it makes deer vulnerable to predators. To endure this harsh season, most deer make some shift in territory. From the subtle to the dramatic, these winter movements give deer an edge in the survival game. Understanding how deer in your area make their winter shift helps you to anticipate their late-season movements. When the hunting is over, the same knowledge will make you a better shed finder and habitat manager, too.

084 BONE UP ON WINTER BEDDING AREAS

Many whitetails, particularly those in farmland environments, don't have to make a dramatic adjustment to make their winter lives easier. Simply bedding and loafing in an area that offers a thermal advantage can make all the difference. One of the textbook places for this is a south-facing slope, which offers more sunlight and protection from prevailing—and bitter—northwest winds. Often these slopes host cedar or pines that offer security cover and additional protection from the wind, but sunbathing winter deer will readily bed in brush or grass if necessary. Whitetails may visit the same food sources that they hit a month before, but the advantages gained by this south-slope bedding shift are huge.

085 NAIL DOWN NORTHERN DEER YARDS

In these days of whitetail abundance, it's hard to imagine the survival of the species hinging on one tree. But in the early 20th century, when the only solid populations of whitetails lived in the vast forests of the northern United States, deer numbers might have crashed further were it not for swamps dominated by northern white cedar.

The browse and thermal protection offered by cedar swamps were so critical to their winter survival that whitetails would migrate great distances—sometimes 30 miles or more—to reach them in the early days of winter. Cedar swamps could hold hundreds of deer at high densities per square mile.

Cedar and hemlock swamps offering thermal protection and winter food continue to be critical habitat for whitetails in northern forest that migrate to traditional yarding areas for the worst of winter. Hunting deer in yards, when deep snow makes them vulnerable, is often frowned upon, but interception of deer moving along traditional migration routes generally isn't.

086 MASTER THE MULEY MIGRATION

The big woods whitetail that walks 30 miles to a winter yarding area may seem like a marathoner, but compared to a mountain mule deer, he's got lead in his britches. Muleys may travel several times that distance (one Wyoming herd covers more than 80 miles from fall to winter range), as intense cold and deep snow force them to lower elevations for the winter months. These mountain migrations are typically started by does and fawns, with young bucks following shortly after and mature bucks bringing up the rear. Many experts say the start date of the migration is highly predictable each fall, but how quickly muleys cover the distance is dictated by the severity of the weather. Knowing the traditional migration routes for mule deer in your area can help you fill your late-season tag.

087 HOME IN ON HOME-RANGE SHIFTS

Even when whitetails do not yard, per se, a home range with meager winter food sources and poor thermal cover may cause deer to abandon entire areas that were attractive in spring, summer, and fall. If you're hunting that area, it can feel as if they bombed off to Bermuda. Rather, they've likely moved to take advantage of a totally different part of their home range—an area with solid winter food sources and south-facing slopes and/or thermal cover that will help them survive winter. Learn these spots, and you set yourself up for some great late-season hunting.

THE PLAN

YOU GO TO SLEEP THINKING ABOUT DEER. YOU WAKE UP THINKING ABOUT DEER. You try, really try, to comprehend the words coming out of peoples' mouths throughout the day, but it's tough, because you're thinking about deer. With you, as my own long-suffering wife says about me, "It's all deer, all the time."

As we've seen, the whitetail boom has spurred major practical changes in America's deer-hunting scene, including more deer, bigger bucks, and longer seasons. But this chapter focuses on the cultural shift—the fact that so many of us are now 24/7/365 obsessed with deer.

Our fathers and grandfathers hunted a Saturday here or there, maybe a week's vacation at deer camp. Today, more and more of us spend every free moment in the deer woods, and there's no real off-season. We hunt hard all fall, scout hard all winter and spring, scour the woods for shed antlers, plant food plots in summer, run trail cams, hang stands, practice shooting, prepare for the next fall, and then do it all over again.

When we are not hunting deer, we are making a plan to hunt deer.

088 FIND THOSE WINTER BEDS

If you aspire to be among the growing number of fanatical deer hunters, then you must realize that the end of deer season is not an end at all but the beginning of the next hunting season. In other words, get ready for about seven or eight months of scouting.

The day after the last day is the first day (you with me?) when it doesn't matter whether or not you spook deer. This is critically important because it means that you are suddenly free to go parading into those recently unapproachable bedding areas to figure out exactly where those elusive deer sleep.

So as soon as the season ends, go for a hike. Scour every potential bedding area, looking for both buck and doe beds (read more on this in Chapter One).

When you're done you'll know precisely where deer were bedding on your property during the late season. If food sources stay mostly the same, it's a good bet those deer will lie down in the same spots during the last few weeks of next year's season. And you'll have them pegged.

089 GET ON THE WHITE TRACK

When there's snow on the ground, every step a deer takes is a matter of public record, and nothing gives you a better big-picture view of how deer use your property than following their hoofprints during the off-season. This is equally true whether you're scouting in the dead of winter or in early spring.

Changing food sources affect the deer's movements to a point, but terrain and cover primarily dictate the ways in which deer navigate the landscape, and these factors stay largely the same all year. So the snow-covered off-season is the perfect time to identify funnels, pinch points, and other travel patterns.

As you follow in their footsteps, pay careful attention to the line of the tracks ahead. When you see the trail swing around the head of a wash, sidehill a particular ridge, or slip through a certain saddle, that's something to make a note of. Deer may not always be moving through that area, but when they are, they'll use the same corridors—and you'll know right where to hang your stand.

090 TAKE AN INVENTORY OF BEDS

Come on, admit it: When you say "bedding area," you are sometimes, if not often, guessing. What you really mean by that is, "over there somewhere, where it's thicker, maybe . . ." With diligence and patience, though, you can be much more precise than that.

First, carry a GPS whenever you are scouting or walking your hunting area. Second, every time you come across a deer bed, make a waypoint whose name indicates whether it's a buck or doe bed, what property you're on, and when you found it.

Finally, transfer your waypoints to Google Earth or a large paper map when you get home. Eventually, you will have an inventory of all the consistent bedding areas on your property. Yes, deer commonly switch bedding areas through the year. But this way, when you find a hot food source in the fall, your map will reveal where deer are most likely bedded in relation to the grub. And that will enable you to formulate a high-odds hunting plan.

BESTUAL ON:
FINDING THE SURVIVORS

One of the coolest uses of a trail camera is to learn which bucks survived the hunting season. The drill is simple: Hang cameras over the best sign on the hottest winter food source immediately after the season closes. If your property is lacking solid winter food–and it's legal to do so–make a spread of shelled corn (about one 5-gallon pile per 40 acres) and get ready to inventory some bucks. In a couple weeks, you should have photos of just about all of your hunting area's survivors.

091 | BECOME A SHED HEAD

Shed hunting is over-the-top huge right now—really, it's become a sport all its own. Massive whitetail sheds command five figures at auctions. There's a shed-antler record book as thick as a metro phone directory, and shed expos have grown big enough to boast the Bud Girls. Want in? Here are four tips that'll make you a better bone collector in no time.

SCOUT FOR THEM You scout hard before and during the deer season to wrap your hands around some heavy horns, right? Well, you have to do the same now. Some bucks live in pretty much the same territory from fall through early spring, but many others migrate to wintering areas with good thermal cover, warm south-facing slopes, or a great food source. That's where those deer are going to drop their horns—and nowhere else. So walk, drive, glass, and speed-scout for tracks and beds . . . whatever it takes to find these spots.

GET THE PICTURE Once you've figured out where some good bucks are spending the winter, don't hesitate to set up scouting cameras near hot feeding areas, well-used trails, or even a mock scrape. If a big buck appears on film with his rack one day and without it the next, you know his sheds can't be far away. Also, this gives you a better idea of when bucks are shedding their antlers in your region, which can save you a lot of tromping around.

GO WITH A GURU He may blindfold you for the ride to his hotspot, demand that he get any horn you find, but an expert (or anyone who's had much better results than you) can show you more in a weekend than you'll learn solo in a decade. Watch him closely. And ask that he call you over before he picks up any horn he finds (which is a great way to train your shed-spotting eye).

BE MOBILE To find sheds, you need to cover lots of ground. You'll walk your winter gut off if you're doing it right. Because bucks commonly drop their antlers in open areas, you can cover a lot of ground quickly by searching via ATV or snow machine (with the landowner's permission). Also keep your eyes peeled while driving down the road; I spotted my best shed ever from my truck two years ago while taking the kids to school.

092 ADOPT A SHED ETHIC

Trespassing to find deer sheds is becoming such a serious and widespread problem that it has a name all its own: "shed poaching." While not literally apt (poaching is usually defined as the illegal killing of a game animal), it seems apt. Internet deer hunting sites include threads devoted solely to foiling or catching shed poachers. A recent post, for example, advised landowners to hang a trail camera 8 to 12 feet high in a tree and place a dummy shed in the frame "so you can get a photo of the scumbag and prosecute him."

We are in desperate need of a shed-hunting ethic. It's a tall order, but it is possible to effect a change with a few simple, slogan-like standards repeated loud and often. Below, my suggestions.

DO NOT TRESPASS

This one shouldn't be necessary, yet many in the shed hunting community figure, it's only a horn. "It's not the same as trespassing to hunt deer." Of course, it is the same. So this phrase should top every shed-hunting website, in bold, and be chanted at shed-hunting events.

GIVE DEER A BREAK

Ultracompetitive shed hunters start pounding turf as soon as the hunting season ends, which can be extremely stressful to deer. That's why several western states have a shed season to protect animals until the worst of winter has passed.

RESPECT YOUR FELLOW HUNTER

Most of us already do this during hunting season. You see someone else legally hunting "your" spot, you move on. Right? I admit that none of this will stop the worst offenders, but the shed-hunting community at large could benefit from a few simple rules to mitigate the mania.

BESTUL ON: SELLING SHEDS

Shed antlers are hugely valuable: They tell you a given buck has survived; they tip you off to buck core areas; and they could pay for your next treestand, deer rifle, or even ATV.

That's right. Antler brokers are paying more than ever for buck bone—some truly heady amounts. How much? Below are some conservative values from Pennsylvania antler-broker Gary Knepp.

TYPICAL	NONTYPICAL
120-inch set: $80	160-inch set: $600
150-inch set: $400	200-inch set: $3,500
180-inch set: $2,500	240-inch set: $10,000

093 TRAIN A SHED-HUNTING MACHINE

We train dogs to hunt and retrieve just about everything else we might find in the great outdoors, so why not include shed antlers on that list? That's what nationally recognized hunting dog trainer Tom Dokken realized a couple years back. Since then, Dokken has not only developed a training program to teach dogs how to find—and bring back—sheds, he runs the annual championships for the North American Shed Hunting Dog Association.

While hunting dogs learn shed hunting more quickly, Dokken says any breed with the hunt-retrieve desire can become a bone finder. Here are his basic steps.

STEP 1 Start in a hallway or in a small room indoors, so you can control the dog. Slide an antler down the hall and let the dog "find" it and bring it to you. Praise your dog and give him a treat.

STEP 2 Once the dog has mastered this basic in-house training, take him outside. Toss an antler 20 to 30 feet and have him fetch it. Use the phrase "find the bone" when you do, so that he associates the command with antler hunting instead of say, finding a duck. Repeat the praising and treats. If your dog wants to run off with the antler, attach a check-cord to his collar so you can reel him in.

STEP 3 Secondary training stays in the yard, or a park with short grass. Scatter several antlers ahead of time, tell the dog to "find the bone," and make a fuss over each antler he retrieves. Increase the difficulty by using larger fields with taller grass. Once that's done, he should be ready for a tryout in the deer woods.

094 SPRING INTO ACTION

If you have just one chance to scout before next deer season, do it in March. There's no other time when so many clues about local deer behavior are laid so bare before you, and spooking bucks is a nonissue so far in advance of fall. For many of us, March is a time when snow is here and gone—and sometimes here again— and in this muddled transition from winter to spring lie the secrets to what deer are doing right now and what they were up to last fall.

WHEN THERE'S SNOW, LOOK FOR

TRACKS In March, as in winter, off-season tracks (1) show you generally how deer move through your hunting area.

BEDS Spring bedding areas (2) may not be used in fall; on the other hand, they may. So be sure to add them to your inventory.

RUBS Rub lines (3) reveal specific routes taken by bucks during the hunting season. As long as the snow isn't deep, last fall's hashed trees will be plain to see. Follow every rub line you can decipher, making note of ambush points. Watch for clusters of rubs, too, that indicate an area that gets a lot of use.

WHEN THE SNOW MELTS, LOOK FOR

SCRAPES Last fall's scrapes (4) are plain to see now too, and it's important to categorize them quickly. Small scrapes and those near food sources were made at night or on a whim. Instead, focus on large scrapes and concentrations of scrapes located in the timber, under a licking branch or branches. Pick out and mark a good stand tree and keep it in mind for next fall.

SECONDARY TRAILS Mature bucks don't leave rubs and scrapes everywhere they go, and they commonly travel off the beaten path (5). Keep an eye out for faint trails that intersect main trails near a food source or that veer just off the obvious runways. I walk every minor trail I can find, and inevitably discover a covert route I've been missing for years, even on familiar ground.

FALL BEDS Yes, beds, again (6), but this is a little complicated. See the next item for details.

095 FIND FALL BEDS IN SPRING

When spring's upstart sun melts the last of the snow and you finally have to face the fact that hunting season is still six months away, don't despair. Instead, remind yourself that this is the perfect time to nail down last fall's buck bedding areas. This simple set of actions will catapult your odds of tagging a brute when the hunt resumes.

Before we go any further, let's get something straight: Unlike at other times of year, the bedding area that you are seeking is not going to be something the size of a yoga mat. If you do find individual beds preserved from last fall, that's great.

For the most part, however, bucks don't bed down in the exact same spot day after day. Given this fact, your goal is to locate a larger area—maybe a quarter acre to a few acres in size—where a buck repeatedly rests in a few, maybe up to a dozen, spots.

The easiest way to find this magic spot is to follow a rub line away from a known fall feeding area. You'll typically see lots of sign in or just off the grub and fewer traces as you progress. When rubs start growing more abundant again, you're close. Once you find clusters of savaged saplings, you're there.

Comb the area around this spot for any supporting signs, but especially beds. You won't always find them. (In pine duff the depressions are barely noticeable.) The first thing a buck does after rising from bed is relieve himself; second, he rubs a tree. That means droppings and rubs are key. Lacking good rub lines to follow, simply walk straight to the most likely bedding cover.

For each buck bedding area you discover, mark a good stand tree along a rub line or funnel leading to the lair. Then go ahead and trim shooting lanes, leave, and stay out. This last step is essential. For trophy bucks to establish predictable bed-to-feed patterns that you can capitalize on later, their sanctuaries must go largely undisturbed.

096 MAKE A FOOD-PLOT PLAN

Food plots can be divided into two types: destination (or nutrition) plots and hunting plots. Generally, hunting plots range from less than ⅛ acre to slightly more than an acre and are meant to draw deer in for a close shot. Destination plots are typically 2 acres or larger, and while they may be hunted over, their main purpose is to provide nutrition, making your property more attractive to deer.

Begin by studing aerial photographs or satellite imagery and mark potential plot sites. Plants need sunlight, so look for clearings, such as fallow fields, pastures, or abandoned homesteads that could become destination plots, as well as smaller openings for hunting plots, such as log landings, small cutovers, or spots where wind has knocked a hole in the canopy. You can clear brush and trees for a plot, but this is the most time- and money-consuming option. Before you rake a leaf or cut a sapling, take your marked-up map, go check out your potential spots firsthand, and take careful notes. How big is the area? How thick is the undergrowth? How much sun does it get? How's the deer sign? Then use that information to make a solid plan for your future plots.

BESTUL ON:
FOOD PLOTS VS. BAIT

Since the beginning of the Food Plot Era, detractors have been chanting: "Food plots are no different than bait." Sorry, but that's mostly hogwash. I'll concede that small hunting plots and bait are roughly the same from an ethical standpoint. But that's where the similarities end. Foods plots are on the landscape longer, benefiting deer long after the season ends. They benefit a host of other wildlife. They have a minimal impact on other hunters—unlike bait, which when used on public land tends to give the baiter a misplaced sense of ownership around the baited area. Finally, plots foster a larger sense of land stewardship. I have no ethical objection to baiting, but I've seen both practices in place, and food plots are simply better—for deer and for deer hunting.

097 GET THE ESSENTIALS

What you need to create your food plot depends on you. What's your type?

	CLEARING	SPRAYING	TILLING	FERTILIZING	PLANTING
THE MINIMALIST Builds small no-till plots on foot and alone.	Handsaw and weed whacker or heavy-duty brush cutter	A 4-gallon pump-operated backpack spot sprayer	Rake or rototiller	Hand-crank broadcast spreader or push-style lawn spreader	Hand spreader
THE ENTHUSIAST Uses an ATV and accessories, making and maintaining several midsize plots.	Chain saw and pull-behind mower	ATV-mounted 12-volt, 15-gallon spot sprayer with boom attachment	Chisel-point field cultivator and chain harrow	A 100-pound pull-behind broadcast spreader	Handheld seed spreader and pull-behind cultipacker (roller)
THE LAND MANAGER Has a large piece of property, lots of big plots, and a tractor.	Chain saw and PTO-driven rotary cutter	A 100-gallon, 12-volt or PTO-driven sprayer with folding boom or multiple nozzles	Moldboard plow and tandem disc harrow	PTO-driven cyclone spreader (fertilizer) and pull-behind drop spreader (lime)	Tow-behind seeder-packer and grain drill

098 PLOT OUT THE TOP PLANTS

Most plots are sown in spring or early fall (although if cold temps come early in your area, you may want to move fall plantings to early summer). Below are six favorite food-plot plants, when to sow them, and what they're best for.

SPRING PLANTS

CLOVER (PERENNIAL)

VALUE TO DEER
This high-protein legume is relished most of the year.

ASSETS
A clover plot lasts 3 to 5 years with proper maintenance.

DRAWBACKS
Requires good soil prep and maintenance; should be clipped 2 to 3 times per season. Attraction ebbs somewhat after hard frosts.

BEST FOR
Hunting or nutrition plots.

SOYBEANS (ANNUAL)

VALUE TO DEER
Foliage is a late-summer/early-fall favorite; bean pods make prime late-fall/winter forage.

ASSETS
Easy and inexpensive to plant; Roundup-ready varieties make weed control easy

DRAWBACKS
Not attractive to deer for several weeks after green foliage turns yellow.

BEST FOR
Nutrition plots.

CORN (ANNUAL)

VALUE TO DEER
A favorite high-carb food source, especially during late fall and winter. Some cover value.

ASSETS
Readily available and inexpensive; Roundup-ready varieties make weed control easy.

DRAWBACK
Requires a seed drill to plant in volume. Minimal attraction for deer in early season.

BEST FOR
Nutrition plots.

FALL PLANTS

RYE (AND RYE-BASED MIXES; ANNUAL)

VALUE TO DEER
Young shoots are easily digestible and highly attractive.

ASSETS
It's the easiest food plot to establish; requires minimal soil prep and little moisture.

DRAWBACKS
Poor late-season attraction in colder climates.

BEST FOR
Hunting plots; can sow between rows of corn or soybeans to increase attraction.

OATS (ANNUAL)

VALUE TO DEER
A favorite when young and tender early, and again in winter when available.

ASSETS
Readily available, usually inexpensive, easy to plant and maintain.

DRAWBACKS
Loses its attraction if not kept cropped by good numbers of deer.

BEST FOR
Hunting plots.

BRASSICAS (ANNUAL)

VALUE TO DEER
Good fall forage that only gets more attractive as cold weather increases its sugar content. A late-season favorite.

ASSETS
Easy to plant; no maintenance required.

DRAWBACKS
Tiny seeds are expensive.

BEST FOR
Hunting plots.

099 MAKE ONE-MAN MINI HUNT PLOTS

No tractor? No ATV? Just you? Well, it won't be easy, but you can still get in on the food-plot craze by making mini plots (a quarter acre or less, often much less) to improve your hunting spots.

Don't expect your small plots to pull bucks off the neighbor's cornfield. The goal here is simply to make an area that deer already frequent even more attractive—and to steer them to a specific ambush point. So go get yourself some no-till seed mix (usually a combination of at least rye and brassicas; the best I've used is Whitetail Institute Secret Spot) and plant it along existing travel corridors, in staging areas, near water sources, or just off bedding areas. Here are two ways.

BLOW AND GROW By far the easiest places to make mini plots are where you need to only remove sticks and leaf litter to expose bare soil: log landings, woods roads,

around dead trees, anywhere sunlight hits the forest floor. You can even fell some low-value trees and plant around them, leaving the crowns for cover.

With your spot chosen, backpack in a leaf blower or rake, one bag each of pelletized lime and fertilizer, and the seed mix. Blow or rake away leaves and sticks, rough up the soil a little, put down the lime and fertilizer, work it in, sow the seed, and hope for rain.

KILL AND TILL More difficult but manageable are existing openings grown up with herbaceous plants. (If the area is dominated by thick grass and/or woody brush and vines, don't bother—it's too much work.) Hack the greenery down with a hand scythe or weed whacker and kill what's left with Roundup. Come back a week later with a steel rake or small rototiller to loosen the soil. Then it's lime, fertilizer, seeds, rain, and, pretty soon, bucks.

HURTEAU ON: "EASY" NO-TILL FOOD PLOTS

If you read today's popular deer-hunting literature, you've been told that you, too, can lure big bucks with easy-peasy mini plots whipped up in an hour with nothing more than a rake and a bag of no-till seed.

Baloney. It takes a half hour just to get in and out of your big-box garden center to buy the lime and fertilizer. By all means, you can make small, effective hunting plots. But if you *are* going to do it by yourself with hand tools, you should know this: Most will take much more than an hour and, from a bust-your-ass standpoint, will range from not-too-tough, through not-at-all-easy, to downright god-awful.

100 4-WHEEL A FOOD PLOT

The first ATV accessories designed for making food plots were iffy at best. But recent models have revolutionized small-scale land management. Although not cheap, they cost a small fraction of full-size implements—and they actually work.

With today's equipment, you can clear areas of even thick growth to create killer hunting plots and midsize destination plots of high-protein perennial forbs that provide deer with quality, year-round forage. Here is a four-step plan for planting a 2-acre plot of clover.

STEP 1 Pick a site that gets at least six hours of sunlight. Test the soil. Use a pull-behind mower to hack vegetation.

STEP 2 Wait a week and then kill any and all persistent grasses and weeds by spraying with an herbicide. Give the chemicals a week to work.

STEP 3 Break up the soil with a harrow. Then spread the required lime and fertilizer, lightly harrow it in, and roll the site with a cultipacker or lawn roller to create a firm, smooth seedbed.

STEP 4 Spread the seed and roll once more. Once the plot is established, mow periodically to promote new growth and deter grasses and weeds.

101 SOW THE BEST SEED FOR BAD CONDITIONS

We'd all like rich, sun-drenched, bottomland topsoil with no rocks, no weeds, a high pH, and perfect moisture in which to sow our food plots. Naturally, it rarely works out that way. So, here's what to plant in tough conditions and still get the best food plots possible.

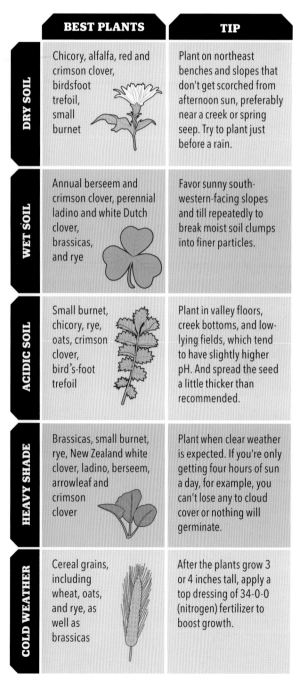

	BEST PLANTS	TIP
DRY SOIL	Chicory, alfalfa, red and crimson clover, birdsfoot trefoil, small burnet	Plant on northeast benches and slopes that don't get scorched from afternoon sun, preferably near a creek or spring seep. Try to plant just before a rain.
WET SOIL	Annual berseem and crimson clover, perennial ladino and white Dutch clover, brassicas, and rye	Favor sunny south-western-facing slopes and till repeatedly to break moist soil clumps into finer particles.
ACIDIC SOIL	Small burnet, chicory, rye, oats, crimson clover, bird's-foot trefoil	Plant in valley floors, creek bottoms, and low-lying fields, which tend to have slightly higher pH. And spread the seed a little thicker than recommended.
HEAVY SHADE	Brassicas, small burnet, rye, New Zealand white clover, ladino, berseem, arrowleaf and crimson clover	Plant when clear weather is expected. If you're only getting four hours of sun a day, for example, you can't lose any to cloud cover or nothing will germinate.
COLD WEATHER	Cereal grains, including wheat, oats, and rye, as well as brassicas	After the plants grow 3 or 4 inches tall, apply a top dressing of 34-0-0 (nitrogen) fertilizer to boost growth.

102 PERFECT YOUR PLOT

Forget picture-book plots. Those rolling green carpets, where a single plant species grows uniformly lush from one edge to another—they don't cut it for mature deer. The ultimate big-buck food plot looks ragged, uneven, disheveled. The traits that make this plot ugly are the very things that will make savvy older bucks visit during shooting light.

1. SIZE
Look for a plot site that is ½ acre to 2 acres. If it's any smaller, deer will destroy the crops before they grow. If it's any larger, mature bucks will be wary of using it during daylight or may show up too far away for a clean shot.

2. WIND DIRECTION
You need to be able to approach and hunt from stands with the wind in your face or blowing perpendicular to the direction of typical deer traffic.

3. SUN ANGLE
Choose flat sites whenever possible. Otherwise, pick a slope facing east or northeast, which will get morning sun when the soil is cool and avoid full late-afternoon sun that can wither crops in dry, hot weather. If you can, position the plot so that deer look into the sun as they approach.

4. SHAPE
Follow the natural contours of the land. Long, skinny plots are preferable to square ones because they provide more edge, where a big buck can feel safe using the plot, only steps from cover.

5. BEDDING AREAS
Put your plot strategically close—from 100 to 200 yards—to prime doe bedding cover (e.g., grassy fields or areas with scattered cedars, pines, and honeysuckle), and twice that distance from thicker, more rugged, and remote buck beds. A funnel with good cover leading from beds to feed seals the deal.

6. THE VIEW
Plant a row of white pines, if necessary, to shield any view of the plot, or the big bucks using it, from a road or public hunting area.

7. STAND LOCATIONS
Make sure that your site offers good stand trees for both bow and gun hunting. Look for potential staging areas to catch a buck waiting for dark to enter.

8. SUMMER ANNUALS
To draw bucks in summer and early fall, plant lablab, cowpeas, sorghum, buckwheat, sunflowers, or a mixture such as Power Plant in May or June. Add a few rows of corn and forage soybeans. Together, these yield tremendous food production, and some grow tall enough to provide extra cover.

9. FALL AND WINTER ANNUALS
As summer annuals die off, deer favor brassicas and cereal grains as frosts raise their sugar content. From June through August, plant a mixture of rape, kale, and turnips, plus a separate patch of sugar beets or pure turnips. Between August and October, put in wheat and/or oats mixed with crimson clover.

10. PERENNIALS
Planted in spring or fall, these are plants that last three to seven years and provide food for deer year-round in the South and for nine or ten months in the North. Large white clovers

(ladino), intermediates like Durana, and blends such as the Whitetail Institute Imperial Whitetail are best. Mixtures that include chicory are good for summer droughts. Alfalfa-and-clover mixes do well in drier uplands and sandy soils. Small burnet is great for poor-quality soils.

11. TALL GRASSES
Plant a few strips of native warm-season grasses around your plot. These might include switchgrass, Indian, and bluestem. These grow 5 to 7 feet tall and make bucks feel secure using the plot during daylight.

12. JUNK
Pull deadfall or large treetops into the plot with a tractor for added cover. Or cut some cedars and pile them by hand.

13. ROUGH EDGES
Mature deer don't like a stark switch from older, mature woods to a low, open plot. Create transition cover along the edge by felling or hinge-cutting some low-value trees. If there's a possible buck approach route that would swing downwind of a good stand location, block it with some of these cuttings.

14. SHRUBS
Red osier dogwood, Tatarian honeysuckle, Chickasaw plum, chinquapin, indigobush, Lespedeza, and blackberry provide security and an extra food source where deer enter.

15. FRUIT TREES
For the ultra-wary buck that refuses to come out in the open, plant a few apple, pear, or persimmon trees at the plot's edge and hang your stand upwind. His sweet tooth will bring him right to you.

103 CREATE A KILLER LICK SITE

The early weeks of spring present a nutritional challenge to deer. Lactating does need a lot of nutrients, and bucks are pouring the coals into antler growth, depleting the rest of their bodies. In addition, spring and early summer foods are high in potassium and rich in water, which leaves deer craving salt. Where legal, help whitetails overcome these hurdles by starting a mineral lick, which provides the calcium, phosphorus, and trace minerals they need—as well as the sodium they crave. Mineral licks also make fantastic spots to hang trail cameras for a summer census of your deer. The standard recommendation is that you put in one lick per 50 acres of habitat.

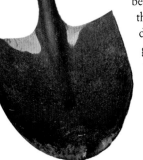

STEP 1 Buy a bag of loose whitetail minerals, or save some cash by getting trace mineral salt from a feed store. It works just as well.

STEP 2 Pour half of the mix into a plastic pail.

STEP 3 Take the pail and a shovel to an area with good deer traffic and remove any sod and leaf litter from a 3-foot-square area. Pour two-thirds of the bucket contents on this spot, then use the shovel to spade the mineral into the dirt. Pour the remainder on top of the soil.

STEP 4 Use what's left in the bag to repeat the procedure in another likely spot nearby. Deer may ignore minerals at one site but demolish a lick at a seemingly identical location only 100 yards away.

STEP 5 Check back in one week and replenish only the sweet spot. It will be easy to identify by the large amount of deer tracks; the ground will be torn up by deer digging for more minerals. Revisit licks every two to four weeks to recharge them if necessary.

104 MANAGE DEER ON $200

If you don't have the mountain of cash it takes to buy tractors, ATVs, plows, discs, seed drills, and on and on, don't worry. You're not out of the game—not by a long shot. All you really need to vastly improve the habitat and hunting on your property is a chain saw, which shouldn't cost more than a couple of C notes. Here are five great ways to put your saw to work.

MAKE COVER Good bedding and security cover comprise the single most important factor affecting the quality of your habitat and hunting. Deer will walk a mile each day for food. But to call a place home, they need cover. And you can give it to them, cheap. Find an open, wooded area near the middle of your property that's already difficult to hunt, such as a deep bowl, ravine, or ridge end. Cut down all low-value trees in a 1/4- to 2-acre circle, creating a tangle of felled trees that will thicken as new growth emerges in their place.

SET THE STAGE Bucks are far more apt to approach open feeding areas during daylight if they have a staging area that offers some food and good cover. So find a spot along the edge that has mast or browse. Then hinge-cut several trees. This, along with new growth, will create a dense edge where bucks will feel safe loitering—plus one heck of a spot for a treestand.

STEER DEER If your property lacks natural funnels, make some. Just fell trees in a line. The trunks, tops, and new growth form a wall of cover that deer feel safe traveling near but won't want to cross—a perfect travel corridor. Make these long or short. Use them to steer bucks closer to a prime stand site or to prevent bucks from circling downwind.

RAISE THE MAST Most hard- and soft-mast trees do better with less competition. "Release" them by felling lower-value trees nearby. Also use your saw to prune fruit trees, which will pump out more grub after you remove suckers and dead or dying limbs.

CLEAR THE PLOT Head into the woods and, near thick cover, drop a cluster of low-value trees to create an opening where the sun comes through. Return in late summer with a steel rake, some pelletized lime, a bag of wheat or clover seed, and a stand. Then return again in fall, get in the stand, and kill a giant.

105 HINGE-CUT A TREE

Hinge-cutting is the secret to creating bedding and staging areas, barriers and travel corridors. Here's how.

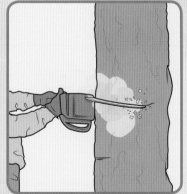

Cut trees 3 to 4 feet off the ground, sawing just far enough into the trunk that the tree will tip over with bark attached.

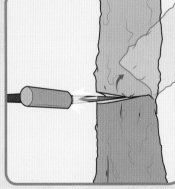

Smaller trees can be pushed over in the direction you choose. Use a plastic wedge to tip and steer larger trees.

To create a higher screen and more structure, fell two or more trees on top of each other in a crosshatch pattern.

106 ADD WATER

To steer bucks to your setup, offer them a drink. With a few hand tools and a little sweat, you can create a small pond that will attract deer right to your stand. Here's how to do it right.

PICK A SPOT Put your pond in or near security cover, such as a brushy transition area, an overgrown logging road, or a forested ridge. Big bucks are more likely to visit these hidden spots, and the shade will protect the water from evaporation.

CHOOSE A TREE Select a place to hang your stand that will take advantage of the prevailing wind, keep the sun out of your face, and offer good concealment. Once you've got a likely location, probe the soil nearby with a spade. If there are too many large rocks, you may want to look for another suitable tree.

HAUL IN THE TUB A 100-gallon plastic landscaping tub is reasonably light and fairly easy to get into the woods. The simplest way is to drag yours—carefully—behind a four-wheeler. But you and a buddy can accomplish the task by hand with a little bit of effort.

START DIGGING Use a quality steel spade for loose soil and a pickax to loosen rocky spots or sever tree roots. Dig a hole large enough to fit the tub, and then backfill with dirt along the sides so that runoff drains into your pond. Now lean a wrist-size stick against one side to allow rodents that fall in to escape.

WAIT If there's rain in the forecast, nature may fill the pond. But if time is short and the weather is dry, it's possible to haul in water as long as you can drive close to the site. Either way, check the water hole for tracks a few days after it's filled. By then, your manufactured hotspot may already be drawing bucks.

107 GIVE SANCTUARY

One of the single most effective steps you can take to keep deer on your property is also one of the simplest. Just keep out. That is, designate a portion of your ground with good security cover as off limits immediately before and during the season. Keep your feet and your stands and your scent and your dog and your cousins and your buddies out of the sanctuary proper, and instead carefully hunt the periphery to catch bucks coming to and from the safe haven.

Ideally, the sanctuary should be situated near the middle of your property, so you can thoroughly hunt the entire periphery. And, if possible, it's wise to choose a spot that's already difficult to hunt effectively (as noted in item 104). Over time, you can improve your sanctuary by planting pines, bushes, or switchgrass, or by felling low-value trees to create a tangle of logs, treetops, and regenerating saplings, vines, and brush.

It won't take long for the deer in your area to take advantage of the sense of security—however false—your sanctuary offers. And when the bullets fly, a bruiser or two from the neighboring farms may come seeking refuge, too.

108 MAKE HIS BED

While you're improving a sanctuary or cutting timber to enhance bedding cover, take a few extra steps to encourage bucks to lie down right where you want them. We know what bedding bucks prefer: the wind at their backs or sides, an obstacle behind, and a view out front. So give it to them. Drop or hinge-cut a couple of low-value trees on a wooded knoll, for example, where a buck can easily see and smell danger. Then take one more step to seal the deal—one that Iowa's Bar-Y Ranch Outfitting owner John Tharp recently explained to us: "Deer like to lie on bare dirt. So clearing a nice smooth circle of ground will cause a deer to plop right down."

When it works, making a specific bedding site puts you in control of precisely where deer bed, which is a huge advantage when formulating a hunting strategy. What's more, when you find a natural bed whose location facilitates a high-odds ambush, don't hesitate to enhance the spot to make it not just a buck's bed, but a buck's favorite bed.

109 STEER YOUR DEER

Intercepting deer on natural movement via scouting and careful observation is cool and all. But radical landscape manipulation is where it's really at these days. As you know, with some farming equipment and a chain saw, you can influence where deer sleep, eat, and drink. But remember that just because you've installed bedding areas, food plots, and water hazards, there's no reason—such as moderation—to stop there. With some strategic environmental modifications, you can actually steer deer to a stand location that put all the factors—wind, cover, shooting lanes—in your favor.

BLOCK A TRAIL When you want deer to use the trail that leads to your stand and not the one that swings downwind or out of range, simply place a sizeable obstruction—such as a log, some cut brush, or a toll booth—that will block the deer from walking onto the wrong trail.

REROUTE A TRAIL If there's only one trail and it doesn't lead to the best stand location, you can block it and reroute it. Simply create an obstruction as above—whether it's a limb, bush, or shopping cart—and then carve a new trail to your stand, kicking the leaves away down to bare ground and removing any major obstructions. It won't take long for deer to start using it.

CUT A CORRIDOR Deer will take the path of least resistance through thick cover, and you can cut just such a lane—with clippers through brush or a weed whacker through tall grass—so it leads right to your stand. Just don't cut the path so wide that a wary buck might feel exposed.

PLANT A CORRIDOR A lane lined with edible bushes, fruit trees, and cedars or pines that leads to a stand overlooking a food plot, for example, provides cover and food that deer will quickly take advantage of. If you plant it, they will come.

110 BOOST YOUR FRUIT

Any wild-growing fruit trees on your hunting property will already draw deer. With a few simple tools and a weekend or two, you can sweeten the deal, resulting in bigger, healthier, heavier-horned bucks.

First, walk your property to identify what you have to work with. Look for wild apple, crab apple, pear, plum, persimmon, and pawpaw. Also pinpoint fruit-bearing shrubs and vines, such as grapes, greenbrier, honeysuckle, and wild berries.

Use pruning shears and a chain saw to trim back overhanging branches and cut down low-value trees that are competing with the food plants. Wherever grape or honeysuckle vines climb these trees, saw the trunks partway through and lean them over so the food grows where deer can easily reach it.

Fruit trees bear more and higher quality mast when pruned. Start by removing any dead or dying branches. Then get rid of any small "shooters" or "suckers" that grow straight up from main branches, cutting close to but not into the latter.

Now, test your soil. If the pH is below 6, sprinkle a few pounds of lime onto shrubs, 5 to 8 pounds around a prime fruit tree. Also, scatter a couple of pounds of 10-10-10 fertilizer on the shrubs or 5 pounds along the drip line of trees. Alternatively, you can insert several time-release fertilizer spikes. Either method will lead to more-favored food to tempt bucks.

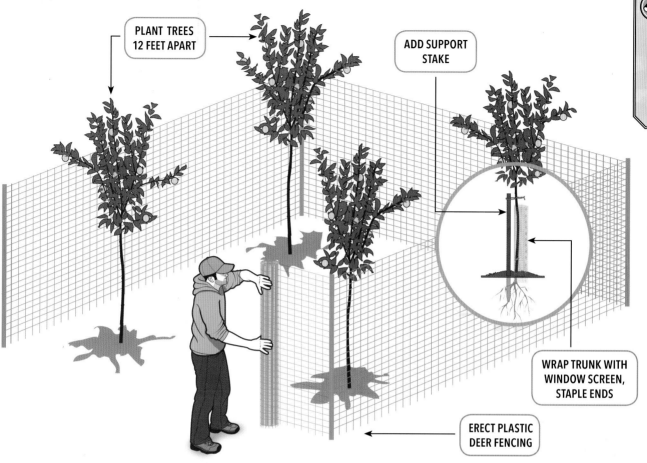

PLANT TREES
12 FEET APART

ADD SUPPORT
STAKE

WRAP TRUNK WITH
WINDOW SCREEN,
STAPLE ENDS

ERECT PLASTIC
DEER FENCING

111 PLANT AN ORCHARD

You don't need a tractor, ATV, or even a Rototiller to plant an apple orchard. Choose an area with full sun and well-drained soils, and (as long as you're patient) your trees will bear fruit and attract deer for decades with very little maintenance compared to most food plots. Here's how to sweeten your ground in four simple steps.

STEP 1 Buy container-grown trees or bare-root saplings. Choose disease-resistant, semidwarf varieties (at least two for cross-pollination) that begin producing quickly and hold their fruit late into fall. Soak the roots. Larger trees can be planted in the spring or fall; bare-root saplings should be planted in spring only.

STEP 2 Place each tree in a hole that you dig to be about twice the width of the root ball. Once it's planted, backfill

the hole with soil, tamping it down firmly and making sure the root graft is 1 to 2 inches above the surface. Water well and add mulch to suppress weeds. Brace the tree with a stake.

STEP 3 You'll need to protect your tree plots from browsing deer for the first five or six years. To do this, surround plots with plastic deer fencing. The advantage of this fencing is that it can easily be lowered in fall. Wrap trunks with wire window screen to guard against gnawing rodents and boring insect larvae. As the tree grows, it will push apart the stapled ends of the screen.

STEP 4 After the first growing season, fertilize and prune trees annually in late winter to produce well-spaced horizontal branching and vigorous new growth.

112 CREATE A STALKING TRAIL

When I bought 100 acres 20 years ago, I cut trails through it so my family could explore the land. By fall I found they also served a different purpose. They made great stalking trails.

With a carefully laid out, precut trail, you can walk more quietly, with less movement. Your trail should typically be oval in shape but let it zigzag as needed to approach prime spots, including thickets, ponds, food plots, fruit trees, and oak ridges.

You'll need a mower or weed whacker to cut through soft vegetation, and a chain saw or machete to trim trees and saplings. Don't overdo it. Make your trail only wide enough for you to move along without making a racket. Keep in mind the prevailing wind, so it blows toward you or crossways as you work prime areas. And be prepared to find your buck standing in the trail as you still-hunt it. Turns out deer like these easy walking routes, too.

113 MAKE BUCKS SCRAPE CLOSE

Want a buck to paw the ground under your stand? Limit his options. Bucks are not going to open primary scrapes where there are no licking branches. So grab your saw and take a little stroll, removing the potential licking branches in the immediate area. This trick can work along field edges, logging roads, in clear-cuts, and even in mature woods. But, of course, it works best where the number of potential natural licking branches is limited and can be easily manipulated.

If there are no suitable licking branches near your stand, just make some. Take a few of the branches you cut and lash them with stout rope—or attach them with wood screws, or both—to a nearby tree so their ends hang 5 or 6 feet off the ground. Make a mock scrape underneath, and wait for the bucks to show.

114 GROW SOME COVER

Growing tall strips of cover in and around your food plots can increase daylight deer traffic, hide you as you walk to your stand, and steer deer right into your shooting lanes.

THE CORRECT COVER In the South, a fallow field may grow 8 feet tall by September; so creating a strip of cover around your plot may be as easy as not mowing the edges. In cooler places, plant native grasses like bluestem and switchgrass or an annual grass. Strips of 16 to 20 feet wide will be about right.

STRATEGIC PLANTING For an open plot, plant cover strips on all sides, leaving a few gaps near the best stand or ground-blind sites for deer to access. Or put strips on any open edge to hide roads, houses, the approach to your stand, or any view of human activity that might keep deer from using it during daylight. The bottom line is that it takes only a few narrow lines of cover to turn an open plot into a sweet spot where monster bucks—and you—can hide out.

115 MOCK UP SCRAPES NOW

Whenever you happen to be reading this, it's a fine time to make a mock scrape. You may think of scrapes as pre-rut buck sign—and that is indeed when most pop up—but bucks open and visit them year-round. And so, mock scrapes can be effective anytime, for a variety of purposes, including:

TRAIL-CAM SETUPS The best way to get pictures of a buck is to lure him in front of the camera and get him to pose there for a bit. A mock scrape does a great job of this, especially where bait and minerals are not legal.

BUCK TRAINING Making mock scrapes near a good stand site long before the season can get bucks in the habit of visiting your fakes on a routine basis—setting a trap for opening day.

STEERING DEER Making a quick mock scrape or two near a new stand also creates a visual cue that can help lure bucks closer for an easy shot.

116 MAKE A FAKE SCRAPE FOR $1.79

You do not need a $10 bottle of deer urine or a $20 mock scrape kit. Just an overhanging branch, exposed dirt, and your own (free) pee. (In fact, you don't even need the last item; a scrape is a visual cue as much as anything and will draw bucks even without pee. I add it for good measure. And for the $1.79 investment in a 20-ounce drink, why not?) Down your soda, grab a pair of pruners, and hit the woods to fire up mock scrapes. Here's what to do.

STEP 1 Go to an area with good deer traffic and find a limb that's 4 to 7 feet off the ground.

STEP 2 Use the pruner to knock down weeds, brush, and branches as needed.

STEP 3 Kick away leaves and debris directly under the branch, exposing bare dirt in an oval shape the size of a truck tire. If you need to, you can loosen the dirt a bit with the tip of the pruner.

STEP 4 Pee in the scrape.

The above recipe works great for all my off-season scrapes and trail-cam setups, and I have hundreds of buck photos to prove it. That said, when I'm hunting over a mock scrape, I'll often run a trail of buck or doe-in-estrous urine to the exposed dirt, and I may add a bright, fresh mock rub nearby, both of which can really get the attention of a cruising buck.

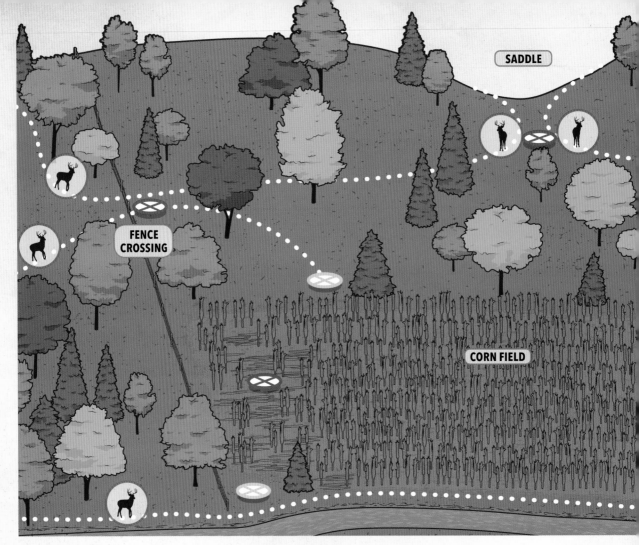

SADDLE

FENCE CROSSING

CORN FIELD

117 PICK YOUR SITE

Wildlife biologists use trail cams to measure herd densities, buck-to-doe ratios, and the like. Your goals should be simpler: learning about the deer on your property, figuring out where to hunt them, and having fun in the process. You can pinpoint ideal spots before you buy a camera, and the locations you choose can determine what model is best for you. Here are four types of sites for four different periods.

⊗ TIME: LATE SUMMER

SITE Mineral lick

GOAL To start an inventory of buck numbers and quality on your property.

SETUP Find a spot with moderate to heavy deer traffic and spade up dirt in a 2-foot circle. Pour in half of an ice-cream pail of stock salt or commercial deer mineral and spade it into the loosened soil. Pour the rest on top of the soil.

TIPS
- Establish one or two licks per 80 acres. Allow deer up to a week to find them.
- Situate each lick 10 to 30 feet from a tree for mounting a camera.
- Jam a stick behind the camera's top edge to point it down toward the lick.

⊗ TIME: EARLY SEASON

SITE Mock scrape

GOAL To find bucks after velvet shed, when they often relocate. Mocks can draw up to 90 percent of the bucks you'll hunt.

SETUP Rake grass and forest debris 5 feet away from a tree that has a green, overhanging licking branch 5 to 7 feet above the ground. Activate with your own "product" (drink plenty of liquids) or use bottled deer urine.

TIPS
- If you are not getting clear shots of a buck, aim the camera at the licking branch instead of the scrap. Most bucks will work the branch with their antlers.
- Establish multiple scrapes in each area and hang cameras only on the most active ones.

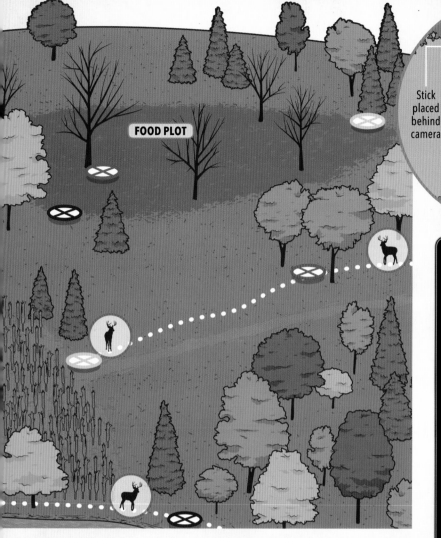

FOOD PLOT

Stick placed behind camera

5' TO 7'

118 LEARN THE LINGO

BLACK FLASH Typical infrared sensors emit a dull red or orange glow that can be detected by game; a black flash supposedly doesn't.

BURST MODE Shoots multiple images in quick succession when the shutter is triggered.

DETECTION ZONE Cone-shaped area formed by the maximum distances at which the camera's sensors can detect an animal and shoot a photo.

MP Stands for megapixel. High-MP cams can produce higher-quality photos, but other factors also affect picture quality.

PIR Passive infrared, or PIR, sensors detect the heat and/or movement of an animal and activate the camera.

RECOVERY RATE How long it takes a camera to rearm before taking the next photo.

TRIGGER SPEED Time elapsed from when a camera's sensor detects an animal to when a picture is taken. Speeds vary greatly, and faster is almost always better.

⊗ TIME: RUT

SITE Funnel

GOAL To determine where resident bucks are traveling and whether traveling bucks are in the area.

SETUP Find terrain features that channel buck movement and hang a camera near fresh tracks and rubbing activity. Check the camera every three to five days; the rut moves quickly.

TIPS
- Mount the camera at a 45-degree angle to the trail. Bucks move through funnels quickly; a camera set perpendicular to the trail might miss the shot.
- Scuff dirt in front of the camera with a boot. Such a mini mock will often make a moving buck pause and get "shot."

⊗ TIME: LATE SEASON

SITE Food source

GOAL To find out where to fill a last-minute tag and to know which bucks have survived the bulk of the hunting season.

SETUP Scout widely to find the hot food sources in your area, such as waste grainfields and clear-cuts. Place the camera within 30 feet of the most heavily trafficked area. Load it with fresh batteries if you hunt in an extremely cold area.

TIPS
- Set up and check cameras at midday to avoid spooking feeding deer.
- If no trees are located near the food source, mount the camera on a tripod and camouflage it with grass or brush.

119 MAKE A TRAIL CAM KIT

Besides the obvious—the cameras—you need a few more pieces of essential gear for setting up and checking your trail cams.

[1] EXTRA MEMORY CARDS It's easier (and less obtrusive) to swap out cards instead of removing the camera. **[2] DEER URINE** For freshening mock scrapes. **[3] CAMERA TRIPOD** For mounting a camera in treeless and fenceless landscapes. **[4] SURGICAL GLOVES** Keep human scent to a minimum as you handle cameras. **[5] SPADE OR TROWEL** Great for starting a mineral lick or roughing up ground for a mock scrape. **[6] COMPASS** Direct sunlight can trigger a camera when sensors detect extra heat, so avoid facing the camera directly south, east, or west. Straight north (or some variation) is the best angle. **[7] FRESH BATTERIES** Nothing is worse than leaving a camera out for a week, only to find the batteries died after just two days. **[8] PRUNING SHEARS AND HANDSAW** For removing grass, brush, or tree limbs that can obstruct a good photo or trigger your camera if blown by the wind.

HO COVERT

120 OPTIMIZE YOUR SETUP

Here's how to get the most out of your new cam.

HANG THEM HIGH Place cameras 5 to 7 feet high for best results. Leave some slack in the mounting strap, then place a stick crossways between the camera and the tree, tipping the lens so it aims down. You'll get a better view of the buck's rack, and the flash is less likely to spook him.

MAKE BUCKS POSE The best pictures are always of deer standing still at a specific spot; accomplish this by setting up a bait pile, mineral lick, mock scrape, food scent, or other attractant (depending on what is legal in your area) in front of the camera.

COME IN CAREFULLY Approach cameras in sensitive areas (such as those near a natural scrape or close to bedding cover) as you would a treestand: Keep the wind in your face, walk quietly, and avoid touching vegetation. On field-edge or feeder setups, drive your vehicle or ATV as close to the camera as possible, and always check it at the same time of day to habituate deer to your presence.

GO HIGH POWER Use high-quality lithium batteries. They cost more than alkalines but last much longer in trail cams. For even longer-lasting juice, go to auxiliary power; some newer cameras come with an external battery port for use with a 6-volt battery, and you can jury-rig (at your own risk) older models to do the same.

GET ORGANIZED Make a system of folders and file names for storing photos on your computer. I use separate folders for each property I hunt. Then I rename pics using a short nickname of the buck(s) shown, an abbreviation of the site, and the date. Use the tips above, and you'll soon have so many photos of bucks that you'll have no choice but to get organized—a good problem to have.

121 TEST YOUR CAMERA

Here are simple tests to determine your camera's detection and flash ranges, ideal focal point, and trigger speed.

Program your camera for its simplest function. Mount it 4 to 5 feet high on a tree, telephone pole, or tripod in an open area. Stand next to it and pace off 10 feet directly in front of the lens. Place a white stake or easily visible object at this spot. Pace off another 10 feet and repeat, until you have a straight line of stakes every 10 feet out to 60 feet. Turn your camera on and give it time to power up.

Now it's time for the "walk test." Walk a wide loop off to one side, and then walk by at the 10-foot mark. Give the camera time to rearm and repeat the walk-through at each stake. Repeat after dark. The images will reveal your maximum detection range in distance (the farthest stake at which the camera detected you) and width (how far into the field of view you had to walk). The clearest photo will tell you the ideal focal distance.

I then like to have my son Bailey and our retriever Lucky stand off-camera together. Bailey throws a ball past the 10-foot stake and tells Lucky to fetch. As soon as Lucky gets going, Bailey runs after him. We repeat at each stake. Cameras with slow trigger speeds get Bailey just before he leaves the detection zone. Faster cameras get him early. The fastest get the dog.

 GREATEST DEER HUNTERS

MESHACH BROWNING
THE BUCK BRAWLER

Browning (1781-1859) was not the first to chronicle hunting life on the early frontier, but his *Forty-Four Years of the Life of a Hunter* focuses more squarely on deer. Browning was, first and foremost, a deer hunter—and one of legendary drive and toughness. His knife fight with a wounded 10-pointer in October of 1819 became the famous subject of a popular Currier and Ives lithograph that was made in 1861.

Browning chronicled the hunt with charm and authenticity, in what remains one of the most important records of pioneer hunting.

122 PLAN LIKE A CAM EXPERT

Most of us are happy if our trail cameras do nothing more than snap a buck's picture. Most of us are not Marc Anthony. A Goodfield, Illinois, whitetail expert who has arrowed four net Boone and Crockett bucks, Anthony forsakes traditional trail-cam locations, such as food-plot edges, mineral licks, and mock scrapes. Instead, he moves his camera along the travel corridor of a trophy buck until he nails down the deer's exact route and finds the perfect place to stage an ambush. Here's how.

STEP 1 Start your scouting at home, by looking at satellite images online to determine generally where you should place your cameras. Any area where a big buck doesn't have to travel more than 200 yards for prime food, bedding, and water is a great starting spot. Mark the most likely spots on a map or GPS and then move in for a closer look.

STEP 2 Next, get out in the field. Anthony scouts each site carefully to figure out precisely where to place his trail cameras. He usually starts close to the best feeding area, looking for buck sign or faint trails that connect the food to water sources and potential bedding and security cover.

STEP 3 Once he sets his cameras where he thinks a buck will come through, Anthony lets them sit for two weeks before checking them to keep disturbance to a minimum. "I carry a card reader in the field and look for two things: if a good buck was in the area, and if so, his direction of travel. I set my cameras to snap multiple exposures of each event, which usually gives me a pretty good idea." In the evening, for example, the direction from which a buck approaches usually points to his bedding area.

STEP 4 The final step is to move in closer. When Anthony marks a good buck, he moves the camera 30 to 40 yards along the trail toward the buck's bedding area. "Then I wait another two weeks," he says. "If I've got more pics, I keep moving the camera, until I'm as close as I dare get to the buck's lair. As I study the pictures, I'm also nailing down the best places, times, and conditions to ambush a buck. When it's time to hunt, I feel almost certain that he'll show up in my bow sights."

GREATEST DEER

THE ED BRODER BUCK

DATE: NOVEMBER, 1926
LOCATION: CHIP LAKE, ALBERTA
SCORE: 355 ²/₈" (world record nontypical mule deer)

WHY IT MAKES THE LIST :

To reign as a B&C world record for eight decades is tough enough; to do so without serious threat is nearly unheard of. But that's what this massive, chocolate-horned buck has done. And with truly huge mulies getting tougher to find, who knows how long this mark will stand? Unfortunately, this monstrous buck also serves as a cautionary tale; Broder died without leaving a will, one of his sons sold the rack to a collector, and the family has feuded over this tremendous buck ever since.

123 MOUNT A CAM ANYWHERE

Many new trail cameras have a ¼-20 threaded socket in the bottom of the housing, similar to what's used to attach a regular camera to a tripod. This means you can use handy aftermarket mounts that screw into trees or attach to metal posts. But for a fraction of the cost, you can make a simple lightweight mounting pole that will let you set up a camera just about anywhere.

MATERIALS LIST

One ¾-inch-diameter wooden dowel, about 2 feet long
One 1 ¼-inch long (or longer) ¼-20 bolt or machine screw
A good wood-to-metal adhesive
One 3/16-inch-diameter steel rod, about 10 inches long
Camo tape or matte spray paint

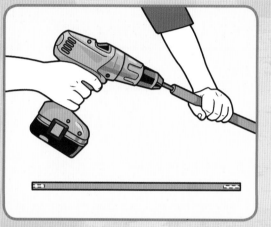

STEP 1 Use a ¼-inch drill bit to make a 1-inch-deep hole in the center of one end of the dowel. Then use a 3/16-inch bit to drill a 2-inch-deep hole in the other end.

STEP 2 Cut off the head of the bolt or screw with a hacksaw. Coat the cut end with Gorilla Glue and insert it into the 1-inch-deep hole. You want about ¼ inch of the threaded end protruding. Then coat one end of the steel rod with glue and insert it in the other hole.

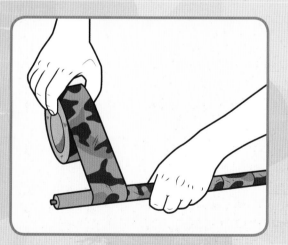

STEP 3 Let everything dry. Wrap the dowel with camo tape or spray-paint it an earth-toned color.

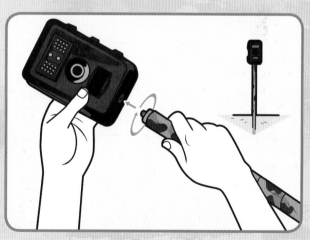

STEP 4 In the field, attach your camera to the pole using the ¼-20 threaded socket, and push the steel rod into the ground. The rod is strong enough to support compact trail cams, yet flexible enough that you can push the pole forward or backward to obtain an ideal camera angle for taking great pictures of your next buck.

BUCK BEDS

TREE STAND

RUB LINE

DOE BEDS

TRAIL CAM

124 FIND BUCKS BY SATELLITE

Google Earth can help you locate the perfect hunting ground, mark buck sign, pick treestand locations, make the coolest custom hunting map you've ever seen, and more. It's easy—just download the latest version of Google Earth (GE).

Type the name of a town into GE's Fly To search bar, hit Enter, and you're off. GE's most basic feature—the ability to seamlessly view satellite images of Earth in detail from above—is a revelation to so many of us accustomed to fumbling with topo maps. The app's navigation controls let you jet from your local farms to the nearest national forest to far-flung trophy-buck destinations in seconds. With the zoom slider, you can focus in so close as to practically see which tree to put your stand in, or zoom out enough to examine how a mile-long ridge funnels deer.

Now click and hold the top arrow on the Look tool, watch the world tilt, and "fly" right into the map. GE's default perspective is from directly overhead, like a paper map. But GE does what no paper map can begin to do—it takes you into the landscape. By tilting the perspective, you can dive low into the land's folds and wrinkles as if you were tree-topping in a helicopter. Slopes, benches, saddles, and ravines lie before you in a format far more intuitive than contour lines.

KNOW YOUR ICONS

Google Earth has a wealth of useful functions that, for example, allow you to mark your favorite spots, overlay photos you've taken, and share your information with your buddies.

ADD PLACEMARK
Mark any spot, such as a treestand location.

ADD POLYGON
Highlight bedding, feeding, or other areas.

ADD PATH
Mark linear features, such as deer trails or rub lines.

ADD IMAGE OVERLAY
Place a map or photo over the satellite imagery.

RECORD A TOUR
Create a tour to show off your custom map.

HISTORICAL IMAGERY
See what your hunting area looked like 15 years ago.

SHOW SUNLIGHT
See how sunlight hits the land throughout the day.

EARTH AND SKY
Switch view from Earth to sky or other planets.

SHOW RULER
Measure actual distances at ground level.

E-MAIL
Share your custom map with a friend.

PRINT
Print a paper copy of your custom map.

VIEW IN GOOGLE MAPS
Send the link to a friend for directions to your ground.

125 GET THE MOST FROM YOUR GPS

GPS has been a revolutionary technology for scouting deer for well over a decade. But when you learn to use it in conjunction with Google Earth or mapping software, well, the sky is the limit.

MARK HOTSPOTS AT HOME Before you head out, use Google Earth to locate promising areas such as funnels, pinch points, and potential bedding and feeding areas. Mark these spots on your computer, and then transfer them to your GPS as waypoints. Now you'll hit the ground running.

PINPOINT DEER SIGN Once afield, use your GPS to mark the location of all the deer sign and potential ambush points you find while scouting. Cover as much ground as you can and create waypoints for rub lines, scrapes, bedding areas, food sources, pinch points, fence crossings, trail intersections, and more.

RECORD A BUCK ROUTE As long as you keep the "track" or "path" mode turned on, your GPS will be mapping wherever you go. You can use this function for a number of useful things, notably to record deer trails, rub lines, logging roads, access paths, and other linear features. Simply walk a trail and save that portion of the track.

NAIL DOWN STAND LOCATIONS Once you're back home, you'll want to transfer those waypoints and tracks that you've recorded back to Google Earth, or mapping software on your computer (see item 124). This gives you a big-picture perspective of the on-the-ground info, and it lets you identify the best sites to ambush a buck. By marking these locations and transferring them to your GPS as waypoints, you can slip back in and hang a stand in the perfect spot—even in the dark.

126 MARK UP YOUR MAP

Virtually anything you can mark on your GPS can be transferred to Google Earth, and then properly named and organized. You'll have a customized, dynamic hunting map like you have never seen. Use GE's Add Path tool to mark access trails, deer trails, rub lines, or any linear feature. Use the Add Polygon tool to highlight areas of virtually any shape or size, such as bedding and feeding areas. And use the Add Placemark tool to mark a specific spot, such as the location of a rub, scrape, pinch point, trail camera, treestand, and on and on.

In each case, you can name and color-code the feature (and use various icons for placemarks), as well as add a description or other important information in a pop-up window. For a treestand location, let's say, you can indicate which way the deer typically approach and what wind directions you can and cannot hunt.

Everything you mark can be saved in the My Places folder of the map's sidebar. There, you can instantly view any one of your places by double-clicking on its name. You can also turn places on or off; if you want to see only this fall's rubs and scrapes, uncheck the boxes next to the older ones. If you want to view buck sign through the years, to understand general trends, turn them all on.

127 GO PUBLIC

Hunters are always complaining that public lands don't have good deer. Not true: Many contain bucks any hunter would be proud to tag, but to be successful, you'll have to prepare better, scout smarter, and hunt differently from anyone else. And the key to all of this is to start early. Get a topo map of the area or view it in Google Earth. Zero in on the tract you plan to hunt, plus one or two backups in case your spot doesn't produce or is discovered by others. As you study your maps, consider the following.

THE UNBEATEN PATH Deer quickly learn normal hunter traffic patterns leading from roads and parking lots; slipping in from an unusual angle can make all the difference. At one site, a river might be a perfect canoe route to a bedding area. A friend of mine uses a state bike trail. He straps his gear to his bicycle and pedals to within 100 yards of his stand. Trace possible covert entry routes on your map with a blue marker.

TOUGH SPOTS Most hunters try to avoid terrain that makes travel difficult. Scan for rugged hillsides, broad swamps, and thick areas that can intimidate other guys. You can count on less competition on the back side of these areas. Circle them with a red marker.

DISCREET FEED Public-land deer have figured out that feeding at open-cover sites in daylight is a good way to get shot at. Find secluded food sources like hidden oak flats, aspen clear-cuts, beech ridges, and apple and persimmon stands. If you can't identify these on your map, call the local wildlife manager or forester and ask about native food sources on this tract. Circle these spots in green.

HIDEY-HOLES Most public-land big bucks find sanctuary where hunters don't think to look. Search for nonclassic cover: a broad Conservation Reserve Program field, a secluded willow thicket, or an abandoned farmstead. Mark these with a yellow marker.

THE BACK DOOR Accessing public land through private land is an excellent way to reach the back side of an area. On your scouting trip, visit some farmers whose land borders the ground you're targeting. Tell them where you plan to hunt on the public area and explain that you're looking for a more efficient route to that spot. If the landowner agrees, ask him to show you a specific route to take and a place to park. Give him a card with your name, phone number, and vehicle description on it. Since you're asking him months before the season, this will help him remember you in the fall.

GREATEST DEER

THE TIMOTHY BECK BUCK

DATE KILLED: NOVEMBER 17, 2012
LOCATION: HUNTINGTON COUNTY, INDIANA
SCORE: 305 $^7/_8$" NONTYPICAL

WHY IT MAKES THE LIST:

The Hoosier State has been coming on like gangbusters in recent years; this buck will not only cement that reputation, it will go down as the second largest hunter-killed nontypical whitetail in history. Tim Beck shot this incredible buck during Indiana's firearms season and word of the giant buck spread like wildfire, and it's little wonder; with 37 scorable points, a 23-$^4/_8$" inside spread, and 6-$^3/_8$" bases, the massive non-typ missed topping the Tony Lovstuen buck by less than two inches.

128 SHOOT (IN SPITE OF) THE BREEZE

It's simple, really: Either you know how wind behaves on your hunting property, or you rely on luck to fill your tag. My friend, whitetail expert, and consultant Neil Dougherty is so ardent about understanding wind behavior that he creates a wind map for each property that he hunts. Below is an illustrated hypothetical example of just such a map. Get started on one now, and you'll learn the perfect places to hang a stand or put a blind this fall.

OPEN WOODS

Every area has winds that come mainly from one direction. The prevailing west wind depicted here sails right through the stand of open hardwoods above. Wind seeks the path of least resistance, and the wide gaps between these trees let it pass unchanged.

BUILDINGS

Man-made structures, such as this barn and outlying farm buildings, deflect wind and cause it to shear off on either side of the obstacle. This is important because whitetails are often unfazed by the presence of buildings, and there may be good stand locations nearby.

WATER AND FIELDS

A stream like this offers a straight shot for this west wind. The field to the north is another example of a place where the breeze should be unaffected and where you'll find the true course of the prevailing wind.

UPSLOPES

Significant terrain changes have the greatest influence on wind. On this steep slope, for example, the wind rides directly up the hill and continues straight over the top for about the same distance as the hill's elevation while gradually falling.

DOWNSLOPES

On the lee side of the hill, the wind currents drop and swirl back toward the opposite side of the slope. Such "vacuums" of swirling air make hunting here difficult–unless thermal winds are strong enough to carry them up or downhill.

STANDS

Creating a wind map can help reveal excellent stand locations. The east edge of the conifer stand or the north side of the swamp are particularly good sites, as both are on the upwind side of convergence points where bucks feel comfortable yet can't smell a hunter in a well-placed stand.

CONVERGENCES

Bucks quickly learn to take advantage of convergence points, where two or more wind currents will meet in one area, so they can check a large area for danger–or does–from one spot. Bucks will usually pause for long periods at these points before continuing on to a food source.

THICK WOODS

A point of dense timber like the conifer stand (above left) or the finger of thick timber jutting into the field (below) can cause wind currents to diverge, or separate–much like water does when it encounters an island.

LOW SPOTS

Ravines and gullies are one of the major wind changers on a property. The wind drops into the ditch, swirls on itself, and bounces around before emerging . . . somewhere. Ravines often contain good buck sign, but the deer have all the advantages here.

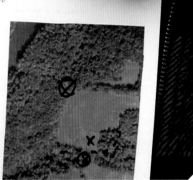

Date: 11·3·12
Time: 3 – 5 pm
Location: Hanson Farm / Corner Sta...
Weather: Clear, high-pressure 42°
Sign: ____
Companions: ____
Deer Sightings: 120" & 140" bucks crossed
by the funnel stand

Hunt Summary and Comments:

A doe entered
the SE corner about
an hour before dark.
Half hour later, just
inside the woods,
these two good bucks
crossed under the
funnel stand. I think

129 GET THE MOST FROM A JOURNAL

Most sports shops sell at least one type of hunting diary; if you're just beginning to do this kind of record-keeping, choose the simplest style with the fewest blanks to fill in. The key thing is to record simple, pertinent facts. If keeping a log becomes exhausting or boring, it's easy to give up. You might want to make your own personalized templates, print them out, and keep them in a binder. Here are some useful categories to include.

WHERE AND WHEN Start your journal with a simple record of the day, date, and time you went hunting.

LOCATION Record not only the hunting area you visited but also the stand you sat or the ridge you still-hunted.

WEATHER Make spaces for temperature, wind direction and intensity, cloud cover, and precipitation. I also record moon phase and whether the barometer is rising, falling, or steady.

SIGN Record the location of any new trails, rubs, beds, or scrapes that you come across. Some guides I know like to pencil this information in on an aerial photo or map.

COMPANIONS I note if I hunted with someone and what they saw. I might want to check back with them.

DEER SIGHTINGS Note the number and sex of deer observed, their location, and when you saw them. Behavior notes (feeding, chasing, bedding) are helpful, too.

SUMMARY AND COMMENTS The other categories can be filled in with a word or two, but this part allows you to make observations about the hunt. I leave at least a half page for this area. When I don't feel like writing or haven't seen deer, I just make sketchy notes, but I definitely jot down something—you can learn a lot from getting skunked! On memorable days, I try to spend more time recording events and impressions.

131 KEEP A BUCK LOG

I once asked Kentucky outfitter and friend Patrick Willis how a hunter can create his own luck. "Forget luck," Willis told me. "There are reasons why a big buck hits certain areas at certain times." And while you may not be able to figure out why, you can figure out when—by keeping a log.

In a journal, Willis writes down the date, wind direction, weather, high and low temperature, and moon cycle. Next to that he reports all deer activity for all of his stand sites. And over time, patterns emerge.

"It's definitely worth your while," Willis says. "We have several stands that the average guy would never hunt judging by the visible sign and cover. Yet if the log says it'll get hot from say Halloween to November 7th, we hunt it. Sure enough, the big bucks show."

133 HANG IT AND HUNT IT

About ten years ago, Scott Bestul introduced me to the nutty, nutty method called hang-and-hunt, which seems to be so popular with the bowhunting kids these days. When he told me that he routinely goes into an area, hangs a lock-on stand, hunts, and then breaks it all down immediately afterward, I said, "You're a freaking nut."

For hit-and-run deer hunts, I have always been more of a climbing-stand guy—plus it used to take me a half hour, on a good day, to hang a lock-on. But if you can learn, as I have, to hang a stand in just a few minutes, the upside of using a lock-on for one-stop hunts becomes clear: Not limited as you are with a climber to straight, branchless trees, you can hunt from whatever perch puts you in the absolute best spot to fill your tag..

134 HANG A TREESTAND IN 7 MINUTES

How long does it take you to hang a lock-on stand? Twenty minutes? A half hour? More? Well, you can do it much faster. All you need is the right equipment and a method that keeps you from going up and down the tree 15 times. Last year, I posted a short video series on our Whitetail 365 blog (which you can see by Googling the headline above), in which I safely hang a stand and am ready to hunt in about 7 minutes.

It's not a race, of course (no matter how much it may appear to be so in the video), but it is handy to be able to shave minutes from your setup time.

Bring a lightweight lock-on stand with a cinch strap (as opposed to a ratchet strap). It's just easier to pull up and set. You're also going to need three or four climbing sticks. They're faster and safer than using tree steps.

Make sure everything you may need—extra sticks, clippers, a saw, safety line—is readily at hand in a fanny pack or pockets. Now you're ready to hang that stand.

Tie one end of a pull-up rope to your stand and the other to your safety harness. Do the same with your gun or bow if you plan to hunt now.

Attach one climbing stick to the base of the tree with your feet on the ground. Grab the second's strap in one hand. Clip the third to your safety harness.

Climb halfway up the first stick. Attach the second stick. Unclip the third from your harness and attach it. Add a couple tree steps if needed. Pull up the stand and hang it. Get in. Pull up your gun or bow. Sit down. Hunt.

132 PICK THE PERFECT STAND TREE

Whenever possible, pick a tree that is perpendicularly downwind and well off the animals' direction of travel to avoid their line of sight and to keep passing deer from winding you. For bowhunting, it should be located 12 to 20 yards off the best sign. Farther makes for a long shot; shorter makes for a steep angle. For gun hunting, the tree should be as far from the hottest sign as you can get and still have a high-odds shot, ideally with a long view of the terrain. Make sure it offers entry and egress that doesn't spook deer. Your choice needs to be wide enough to hide your silhouette but narrow enough that you can get your arms around it for easier climbing and stand hanging. Finally, ensure that it has several branches, forks, or trunks to give cover and for hanging equipment.

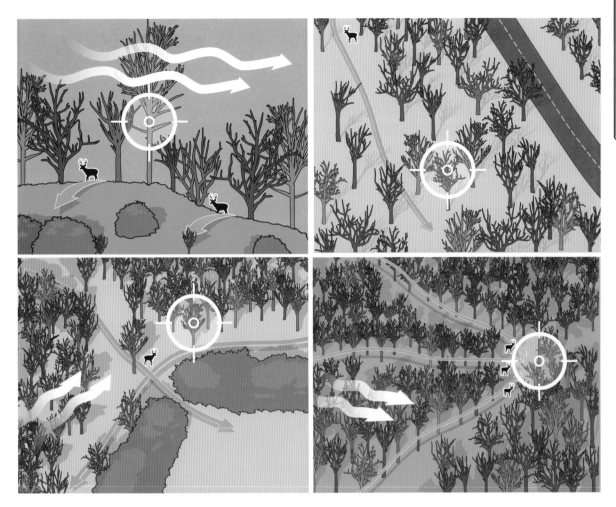

135 CHOOSE A KILLER STAND LOCATION

You can find a buck's hot sign, but what you really need to pinpoint is the spot where you can kill him. Somewhere along his route is a place where cover or terrain (or both) puts the odds most heavily in your favor. That's the definition of a good treestand location.

THE TOP EDGE The backbone of a ridge, lip of a ravine, or shoulder of a plateau is a natural funnel. You can shoot the top side and the downslope. Your rattling reverberates. And as long as the wind is pushing steadily past the drop, you're not getting busted, as your scent will drift over just about any downhill deer.

THE LONG EDGE Just within woods that are found running alongside a road, open field, lakeshore, or parking lot, a natural travel corridor parallels the edge—and you can slip easily to and fro without dropping scent on a buck's path. What's more, the road (as shown) discourages bucks from circling downwind of you.

THE CORNER Feeding bucks will routinely come into fields at an inside corner; cruising bucks love to swing around them. Your job is to find where the feeding and the swinging trails intersect and then hang your stand just downwind. The best of these spots also bottleneck a short way off the field, pinching bucks through the corner.

THE HUB If you know a buck's basic bed-to-feed pattern, the next step is to eyeball an aerial map or satellite image. Is there a place along his general route where two or more ridges, spurs, ditches, wood strips, or fencelines meet? Yes? Set up there. You just doubled—maybe tripled—your odds of seeing him.

136 GET THE RIGHT STAND FOR YOU

No specific number of stands is just right—or ever enough. That said, these five types are great to have. Don't skimp on the climbing stands; you really get what you pay for here. You can, however, find mid-priced ladder stands and even dirt-cheap hang-ons that work great. Just shop carefully

LADDER It's a pain to put up, but nothing is easier or safer to hunt from. Perfect for the reliable hotspot that you can drive right up to.

STEALTH CLIMBER For exploring new, remote spots, nothing gets you in more quietly and up more quickly than an ultralight compact climber.

COMFY CLIMBER Suppose you find a public-land hotspot that's begging for an all-day sit. That's when a little more padding is worth the extra weight.

STEALTH HANG-ON You need a featherweight model that goes up fast for short-term sets where you can't use a climber.

COMFY HANG-ON Use this type for long sits in consistent hotspots where it's not practical to carry in a ladder.

137 FOLLOW A TREE-STAND TIMELINE

Where you hang your stands should change with the season. Smart hunters typically sit in the least obtrusive places (feeding areas) early in the season, get increasingly aggressive (travel corridors and bedding areas) as the rut nears and peaks, and then back off again for the late season. Follow the timeline below, and both you and your stands should be in the heat of the action from the opener until the season's end.

TIME	TIPS
EARLY SEASON	It's all about evening hunts over late-summer/early-fall food sources now. Hang stands on the edge of crop fields or near food plots or soft mast in the big woods.
OCTOBER LULL	Remember, the deer are active; they're just not as visible. So hang your stand over a hidden fall food source, such as acorns, fruit, or the edge of a young clear-cut.
PRE-RUT	Bucks are starting to put some turf under their toes, so set up along rub lines and active scrapes. Buck bedding areas are killer in the last days of this phase.
RUT	Bucks are really moving now, looking for does; the two best spots are pinch points along travel corridors and doe bedding areas.
POST-RUT	It's back to food now. Find the very best grub—a clear-cut, white cedar swamp, standing corn, or a food plot—and camp out.
SPRING	No, you can't hunt, but you can get a huge jump on next fall's action by hanging—or at least prepping—stands over perennially active terrain funnels, which you find by scouting for last fall's rub lines.

138 CLIMB INTO DEER

I do at least half of my deer hunting from a climbing stand. And why not? As long as there are straight-trunked trees free of large lower branches handy, a climber has huge advantages. You're up and hunting in minutes; no steps, no sticks. When you leave, there's no trace left to expose your hotspot. You can easily tweak your stand locations to keep bucks guessing. And nothing is better for exploring and trying new spots. That said, it does help to know a few tricks.

GO LIGHT Ditch the daypack. It's a lot easier to carry a climber in on your back if there isn't something else there, too. Pare down. Use a fanny pack. Strap extra clothes to the stand.

SEEK COVER Straight, branchless trees lack cover. So look for a trunk growing in a cluster, near a leafy sapling, or surrounded by conifers.

FIND A FORK If cover is light, choose a tree that forks at 18 or 20 feet. This will give you a little more back cover.

GET HIGHER Another trick for low-cover situations is to go higher. I arrowed two deer from skinny, utterly naked trees this past fall. Just get a little closer to the sky and keep your movements to a minimum.

DON'T HANG OUT If your climbing stand kicks out from under your feet, your harness will catch you. But then what? There are no steps or sticks to get back onto. Make sure you have a controlled-descent device.

139 GET A LIFELINE

A life line is a thick rope that runs from above your tree-stand down to the base of the tree. Attach a Prusik loop that slides up and down this main line. Clip your harness tether to this loop at ground level and slide it up as you ascend. Then slide it down when you descend. There. You were safely hooked in from when your feet left the ground until they touched down again. You can buy a premade life line or construct one at your own risk.

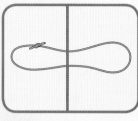

STEP 1 Tie a loop in a 4-foot length of rope slightly thinner in diameter than the main line.

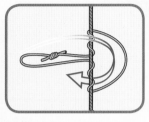

STEP 2 Hold it against the main line; run one end of the loop three or four times around the main line.

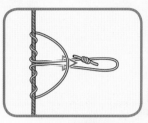

STEP 3 On the final pass, run this end through the other; snug everything up against the main line.

STEP 4 Be sure your rope is securely tightened but can slide up and down.

140 MAKE A STAND-HANGING KIT

Before you head out into the backwoods, follow this checklist to make sure you have everything you might need to get your lock-on stand in place.

DAY PACK A tough, roomy model with plenty of pockets, plus shoulder straps for greater comfort.

STEPS I wrap enough steps for one setup (about 12 steps for me) in strips of cloth to keep them from clinking and clanking.

ROPE I always have several 25- to 30-foot sections of rope handy for pulling up a stand, a backpack, a bow, or a gun.

SAFETY HARNESS I have one in my hunting pack and another in my stand-hanging kit so I am never without protection.

LIFE LINE A stout rope that runs from the ground up to your hung stand, with a sliding Prusik knot, to which you attach your harness tether.

PRUNING SHEARS I like a bypass style that can easily lop off a finger-thick limb.

FOLDING SAW Zipping through larger branches is easy with a quality model made for this purpose.

COMPASS Nothing fancy needed here; just a simple, sturdy unit for determining proper wind direction(s) for sitting the stand.

WIND CHECK To double-check thermal flows or unique wind currents from a hung stand.

TRAIL MARKERS Trail-marking tacks that glow in a flashlight beam are perfect for marking entry trails to morning tree-stand setups.

FOUR CLIMBING STICKS If I need to hang a stand fast, I'll use climbing sticks instead of steps.

POLE SAW Essential for any long-term set that needs to be thoroughly brushed out.

141 BRANCH OUT

You've found the almost-perfect stand tree—except that it's got no cover. Or it has cover now but won't as soon as the leaves drop. Either way, here are two simple, inexpensive ways to solve the problem.

INSTALL LIMBS

You can add limbs to your tree using flag brackets. First, find an evergreen tree or a deciduous species that holds its leaves late, like oak or beech, and use a folding saw to cut a few limbs to a diameter that will fit into the brackets. Hang your stand. Then use a cordless drill and a handful of screws (be sure you have permission to use them on a live tree) to install the brackets to the sides and behind your perch. Pull the branches up with a rope and push them tightly into the bracket to install. Done.

ADD LEAVES

If your tree already has limbs at stand height but they've lost their leaves, use the existing branches as a framework to add foliage with a handful of zip ties. Again, cut several pine, cedar, oak, or beech branches, this time any diameter you want. Haul them up into your stand, and simply cinch down some zip ties tightly around limbs to hold them in place.

142 SHAVE YOUR HANG TIME

Here are seven tips that will get you in your stand faster each year.

SHARPEN DULL TREE STEPS with a file or grinding wheel (at your own risk).

USE A CORDLESS DRILL on the hardest trees to make pilot holes for steps. Carry it in a drill holster.

USE A SHARP STEP as an auger for any dull ones.

TIE A LOOP in your pull-up rope, near the stand. At hunting height, hang it on a tree step so you don't have to hold the weight of the stand as you attach it.

USE A THICKER PULL-UP rope for heavy stands.

USE A RANGEFINDER to quickly choose the perfect tree for bowhunting.

ENLIST A FRIEND to help you get set up faster and safer.

143 FOLLOW THE GROUND RULES

Brooks Johnson, cofounder of Primos Double Bull Blinds, has hunted from pop-up blinds exclusively since 1995. Here are the tricks he's discovered for fooling whitetails on their level.

USE THE 50-YARD RULE If a deer won't have a visual line to your blind until he's 50 yards away, you need to completely camouflage the hide into the natural cover. At that short a distance, a buck won't tolerate being surprised by any hint of a foreign object.

USE THE 100-YARD RULE On the other hand, if a buck has a visual line to the blind from 100 yards or more—such as in a field setup—set the blind in the wide open so he can see it from every side. Put the blind out a day or two ahead of time so the deer get used to it.

HIDE THE ROOF The hard edge of the roofline is one of the first things a buck spots. When hiding a blind, cut some limbs and put them on the top of it.

CLOSE THE WINDOWS You want it as dark as possible inside. If there's too much light, deer will see you when you move, even a little.

WEAR BLACK The goal of camo is to match the background. When you're in a ground blind, your surroundings are dark.

HIT THE NET Use shoot-through netting on the windows. It camouflages the dark holes of blind openings and conceals your movement.

STAKE A FAKE Whenever possible, use a buck decoy to attract nearby deer and thus pull their attention away from your blind.

144 CUT IT OUT!

Want to start a hot deer camp debate? Ask your buddies how aggressively they trim shooting lanes. Half will insist that sparing the saw spoils the shot. The rest will argue that too much hacking spooks deer and ruins the spot.

Who's correct? Both are—but only about half the time. An either-or approach doesn't allow for the fact that proper trimming is highly situational; it should depend on the specifics of each setup.

About half of the stands I hang are located near a terrain funnel or pinch point that isn't apt to change, like the head of a wash, a bench or saddle in hill country, or a brushy fenceline or creek bottom connecting crop fields. These spots will dictate deer movement year after year, so I brush them thoroughly. With the landowner's permission, I use a small chain saw to remove scrub trees and major limbs that might block a shot. The obvious alterations or residual scent might temporarily spook deer, but I know they'll be back; I'll have plenty of chances to hunt them.

Ideally, I do such brushing in the off-season. But even after the opener, I've found I can hunt these sets within a couple of days, because they're usually situated some distance from buck bedding or core areas. If I'm worried about leaving too much scent, I'll trim just prior to a rain.

145 HIT THE HOTSPOT, LIGHTLY

When a certain area is suddenly hot with buck activity, I strive for minimal trimming. I have no idea how long the action will last, and I can't afford to alert them. I search for a fairly open spot to hang my stand, and the limbs that need cutting can be tackled from the stand with pruning shears or a small folding saw.

For thicker cover, I enlist the help of a partner. One of us gets in the stand, and directs the other, who uses a telescoping pole saw to remove the minimum of twigs and limbs. Two people can do a perfect job quickly, wearing rubber boots and gloves to keep human scent to a minimum.

146 GET GOOD GLASS CHEAP

This is the Golden Age of Cheap Glass, in which the quality of low- to mid-priced ($200 to $400) scopes and binoculars has shot straight up through the rafters. The trend became unmistakable for me in 2009 when I picked up the then-new Bushnell Legend Ultra HD 10x42 binocular and said, "Holy s**t! These can't possibly cost $240!" But they do.

Today, Bushnell, Nikon, Leupold, Vortex, and others make shockingly good glass in this price range. It may not paint the world in a magic light that gives even your thoughts more clarity, like the really high-end stuff (Swarovski, Zeiss, Leica) can, and which is great to have if you can afford it. But if not, these will perform admirably.

147 ASSEMBLE A $1,000 DEER COMBO

What's remarkable is that today's deer hunter can get a very capable combo—rifle, scope, and binocular—for under $1,000. Even the long-range deer hunter, who typically has to spend more to spot and drop faraway critters in the great wide open of the West, can come in close to a cool grand.

On a recent eastern Oregon mule deer hunt, for example, I carried a Weatherby Vanguard Series 2 Synthetic in .257 Weatherby Mag (about $490 street price and guaranteed to shoot a minute of angle) topped with a 4.5-14x44 mm Bushnell Legend Ultra HD Scope (about $280 street price) and a Bushnell Legend Ultra HD 10x42 binocular (about $240 street price). That comes to $1,010. I've used guns and glass costing much more, and I don't believe any of them would have served me substantially better as a practical matter.

148 ACHIEVE AFFORDABLE ACCURACY

By happy coincidence, this is also the Hyper-Accuracy for Peanuts era of bolt-action rifles. I declare this because after spotting an emerging trend at the 2012 Shot Show, David E. Petzal and I tested five new or newish bolt-action rifles that retail for around $500 or less. At the range, two of the five guns averaged three-shot groups of nearly a minute of angle. The other three shot well under—under, I say—a minute of angle. And they just so happened to be the three least expensive guns.

They were, in ascending order by accuracy:

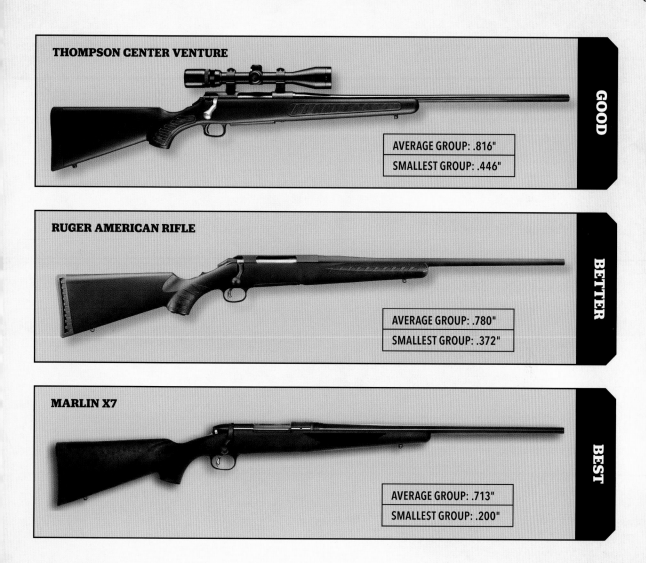

THOMPSON CENTER VENTURE

AVERAGE GROUP: .816"

SMALLEST GROUP: .446"

GOOD

RUGER AMERICAN RIFLE

AVERAGE GROUP: .780"

SMALLEST GROUP: .372"

BETTER

MARLIN X7

AVERAGE GROUP: .713"

SMALLEST GROUP: .200"

BEST

Each of these rifles has a real-world price tag of under $400, and the most accurate, the Marlin, sells at most shops for a paltry $330 or so. Not long ago, sub-minute-of-angle performance cost big bucks, and so the dawning of the HAFP era may bring pain to those who've already spent thousands for gilt-edged accuracy. However, especially in the wake of the Great Recession, it should bring unbridled jubilation to any practical-minded hunter looking to buy a tack-driving deer rifle today.

149 SHOOT THE BEST DEER RIFLE

Only a fool would argue with the great David E. Petzal about the best rifles and cartridges for deer hunting. And so I am very tempted. Nonetheless, here are Petzal's picks, from *Field & Stream's Total Gun Manual*.

BRUSH GUNS

Marlin Model 1895G Guide Gun, .45/70 Very short, unstoppable, and a proven deer killer.

Remington Model 7600, .35 Whelen Quick-shooting, very reliable, and in .35 Whelen, capable of a lot more than deer hunting.

Ruger Gunsite Scout, .308 Not designed for peaceful purposes, but it excels in the deer woods nonetheless.

Blaser R8 Professional, 7x57 A unique rifle that is, among many other things, very compact and gets off aimed shots with blinding speed.

BEANFIELD RIFLES

Savage Model 11/111 Long Range Hunter, 6.5/284 So accurate that it will leave you talking to yourself.

Kimber Sonora, .25/06 Just as wonderful as all the other Kimber rifles and, like them, a bargain, considering what you get.

Weatherby Mark V Accumark, .257 Weatherby A truly hellish combination that makes it difficult to be a deer.

McMillan Long Range Hunting Rifle, .300 Win Mag Simply, a superb firearm. Nothing better anywhere.

ALL-PURPOSE GUNS

Weatherby Vanguard Series 2, .270 One of the great rifle bargains around and a damned near flawless firearm.

Winchester Model 70, .270 This is a far better "rifleman's rifle" than your daddy ever dreamed of.

Ruger American Rifle, .243 Ruger's break with the past and a terrific gun.

Thompson/Center Dimension The first affordable interchangeable-barrel rifle ever, so you have a choice of 12 deer cartridges.

BEST SIGHTS For very short, very quick deer shots, use iron sights. The best rear sight is a large peep, with a front sight consisting of a sizable gold or white bead. With cover open enough for longer shots, use a compact low-power scope that's bright with a large field of view; 1X–4X is ideal. No more than 2X by 7X.

BEST CARTRIDGES The .30/30 Winchester is the classic deer cartridge. The .35 Remington is a dandy big-woods round, light-kicking but with plenty of thump. The .308 Winchester is a great choice, too. The .45/70 Government is more than you need, but highly effective at close range in thick cover.

BRUSH GUNS

BEST SIGHTS These rifles are too heavy to carry far, so you will do no harm to yourself by adding a big scope. Thirty-millimeter tubes and 50 mm objective lenses are favored for gathering light, and a magnification of up to 20X is in vogue—all of which help you make the long shots these guns are made for.

BEST CARTRIDGES The .257 Weatherby Magnum: Roy Weatherby's favorite cartridge, for good reason. The .270 WSM: Faster than the .270 Winchester, with just a bit more kick. The 7mm Remington Magnum: Simply hard to beat. The .300 Winchester Magnum: more than you need, but incredibly accurate.

BEANFIELD RIFLES

BEST SIGHTS An all-purpose deer rifle needs to be light enough to carry all day. Don't undermine this by adding a monstrosity of a scope. A 2X–7X model is dandy for a lightweight bolt; 3X–9X is all you need; 12X should be the limit. Keep the objective lens under 40mm.

BEST CARTRIDGES The .25/06 Remington: A great deer cartridge that could be more popular. The 7mm/08 Remington: Low in recoil but accurate and powerful. The .270 Winchester: Perennial finalist for "best all-purpose deer cartridge." The .30/06 Springfield: A bit much for hunting deer but very popular and effective.

ALL-PURPOSE GUNS

150 PICK A WINNER

Basketball? What basketball? All I know is that March means the Sweet Sixteen of Deer Guns (and Loads) on our fieldandstream.com blog, Whitetail 365. In 2011, our online readers named the ever-popular Marlin 336 lever-action Whitetail Brush Rifle Champ. Last year, they gave Whitetail All-Around Rifle Champ honors to America's favorite bolt-action, the Remington Model 700.

Here's how the Final Four broke down for each contest.

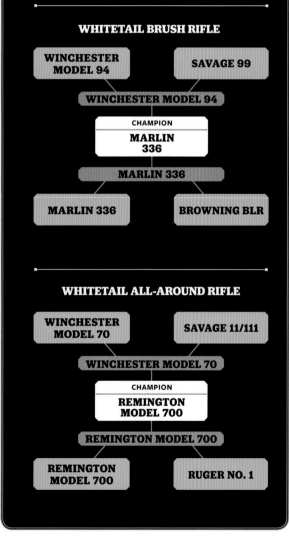

WHITETAIL BRUSH RIFLE

WINCHESTER MODEL 94 — SAVAGE 99

WINCHESTER MODEL 94

CHAMPION
MARLIN 336

MARLIN 336

MARLIN 336 — BROWNING BLR

WHITETAIL ALL-AROUND RIFLE

WINCHESTER MODEL 70 — SAVAGE 11/111

WINCHESTER MODEL 70

CHAMPION
REMINGTON MODEL 700

REMINGTON MODEL 700

REMINGTON MODEL 700 — RUGER NO. 1

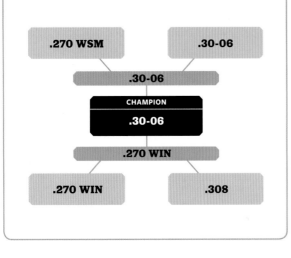

151 HUNT DEER WITH AN AR

The first hunting AR-15s to hit the market were works in progress at best. But with feedback from a growing number of AR-toting deer hunters, manufacturers are starting to get it right. The latest stocks are adjustable; triggers are infinitely crisper; and hand guards are free of Picatinny rails except where needed. What's more, as the best new hunting ARs have slimmed down to a nimble 7 pounds or less, the number of available calibers has beefed up to include a handful of deer-perfect rounds, such as the 6.5 Grendel, 6.8 mm SPC, .30 RAR, and .300 Blackout. None of these three excellent examples is cheap, but you only need to buy a new upper to make it your plinker or varmint rifle, too.

AMBUSH FIREARMS 6.8 This camo carbine weighs just 6 pounds and is chambered for 6.8 mm SPC, which has become a huge hit with hunters wanting a low-recoil, moderate-range whitetail cartridge. The Magpul MOE stock is adjustable, and the Geissele SSA trigger is just this side of perfect. The hammer-forged barrel is guaranteed to produce MOA accuracy.

ALEXANDER ARMS LIGHTWEIGHT 18-INCH 6.5 GRENDEL Pushing 120- to 130-grain bullets, the 6.5 mm Grendel has mild recoil but enough horsepower for any whitetail, even at long ranges. This 7.5-pound rifle has a lightweight, carbon-fiber fore-end and adjustable stock, a great trigger, and a quality barrel cut to just the right length to make it a great all-around deer rifle.

PRIMARY WEAPON SYSTEMS MK116 MOD 1 RIFLE .300 BLK At just 6 pounds, 7 ounces, the MK116 Mod 1 is lightweight, quick-handling, and available in one of the newest AR cartridges, the .300 Blackout, which shines as a mid-range, light-recoil round for whitetails and uses standard .223/5.56 mm magazines to boot. The Geissele trigger is outstanding; the Magpul MOE stock and grip make for comfortable shooting; and the free-floating fore-end enhances accuracy.

BEST DEER CARTRIDGES

When we are not debating the best deer rifles on the Whitetail 365 blog, we are debating the best deer cartridges. In 2010 we launched our first March bracket with the Sweet Sixteen of Deer Cartridges, as in general-purpose cartridges. We put 16 popular rounds head-to-head, and readers voted for the winners. Here's how the Final Four went down.

.270 WSM	.30-06

.30-06

CHAMPION
.30-06

.270 WIN

.270 WIN	.308

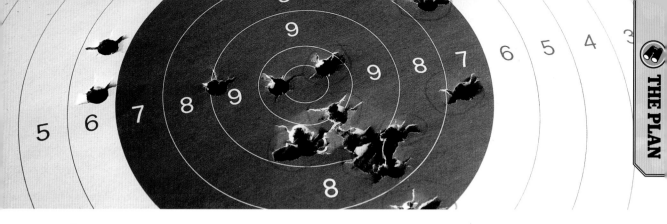

152 CHOOSE THE RIGHT BULLET

In a perfect world, every deer bullet would expand quickly, penetrate just enough to pass through, and then, having expended all its energy in the deer, fall straight to the ground next to a big, bright blood trail. Alas, perfect bullet performance is tricky, because it relies on a host of variables, including bullet construction, velocity, shot placement, and more. The best you can do is get the right bullet for the type of deer hunting you'll be doing. Here's a rundown.

JACKETED LEAD-CORE	This is your basic, inexpensive deer bullet, made with a soft lead core and a thin brass or copper jacket that gets thicker toward the bottom. It's designed for rapid expansion and moderate penetration.	**BEST FOR** Slow- to moderate-velocity rounds at moderate ranges—a good basic bullet for most deer hunting.	**DRAWBACK** At very high velocities, it's apt to fly apart and penetrate little.
BONDED LEAD-CORE	Same as above, except that the lead core is chemically bonded to the jacket, resulting in better weight retention and thus more penetration.	**BEST FOR** Higher-velocity rounds at moderate to long ranges.	**DRAWBACK** They cost a bit more.
CONVENTIONAL CONTROLLED-EXPANSION	Produce reliable moderate expansion with a wide range of velocities, while retaining 70 to 90 percent or more of the original weight for deep penetration. They typically have high ballistic coefficients and can be exceedingly accurate.	**BEST FOR** High-velocity rounds in open country, where you don't know if your buck will show at 40 yards or 400 yards.	**DRAWBACK** They cost a lot more and simply aren't necessary for many deer-hunting scenarios.
ALL-COPPER CONTROLLED-EXPANSION	Also built for reliable moderate expansion, these bullets provide maximum penetration through the toughest hide and bone. These, too, tend to be highly efficient and accurate.	**BEST FOR** Same as above, or if you have to shoot through a Volkswagen in order to hit your deer. Or if you choose to or must hunt lead-free.	**DRAWBACK** Generally the most expensive bullet you can buy—and often not necessary for deer.

153 GET THE RIGHT SLUG GUN

Your smoothbore turkey gun will kill deer dead. If you don't shoot beyond 50 yards, it's all you need. But if you'd like a shotgun that acts more like a centerfire rifle in the deer woods, get a dedicated slug gun with a fixed, rifled barrel. Today's best models come ready for scope mounting and feature vastly improved triggers. Also consider that a 20-gauge gives up very little in performance to a 12, and you'll probably shoot the former better because it kicks less. These three dedicated deer guns are deadly out to 150 yards or more.

SAVAGE 220 SLUG GUN

This is a slug gun that feels and shoots like a centerfire bolt action rifle. Equipped with the company's excellent, adjustable AccuTrigger, the 220 is capable of MOA groups at 100 yards.

ITHACA DEERSLAYER III

A classic remade for the modern hunter, the Deerslayer's rifled barrel is fixed to the receiver and free-floated. The trigger breaks crisply at 4½ pounds. The company claims 4-inch groups at 200.

REMINGTON MODEL 870 SPS SURESHOT SUPER SLUG

The heavy, fluted, rifled barrel is pinned to the receiver for optimum accuracy. Spend a little more to have your gunsmith tune the trigger.

154 IDENTIFY SLUGS

FOSTER SLUG
For smoothbores. The "vanes" don't make it spin; they help it swage down through a choke.

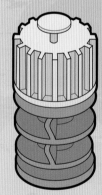

ATTACHED WAD SLUG
For smoothbores and rifled barrels. The attached wad keeps the slug flying straight, like the feathers on a badminton shuttlecock.

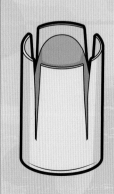

SABOT SLUG
The flaps of the sabot separate and fly off after the round leaves the muzzle. Expensive and worth it in rifled barrels where they are accurate enough to take deer to 150 yards. Very inaccurate in smoothbores.

155 SHOOT A CLASSIC

Many classic deer rifles aren't nearly as accurate as today's models. So what? They often don't need to be, and many of today's models aren't nearly as cool as the old guns. Here are five classics I own and four I want.

WINCHESTER MODEL 94 (PRE-64) *The* American deer rifle for a good part of a century. Wonderfully light, slim, and graceful. Nothing carries better or handles faster. Mine is in .30/30.

REMINGTON MODEL 14 The company's original centerfire pump and precursor to the 760/7600 ubiquitous in today's North Country deer camps. Mine, in .35 Rem of course, shoots pretty close to a minute of angle.

WINCHESTER MODEL 70 (PRE-64) Widely regarded as the best American factory bolt ever made. If you're going to get Jack O'Connor's favorite rifle, you might as well get in .270. If you can't find an old Model 70 to your liking, look for a Model 54.

SAVAGE MODEL 99 Perennial contender for best all-around deer rifle ever made—almost certainly the best lever. Chambered for high-intensity rounds from its debut in 1899, it was vastly ahead of its time then and is still a fantastic deer rifle. Mine's in .300 Savage.

WINCHESTER MODEL 100 CARBINE Though not an especially accurate gun, I have seen some shoot quite well. This unique, full-stock auto is, however, the best-looking short, light, slick-handling self-loader you can get your hands on. Mine, in .308, is perfect for the big woods and easier on the shoulder than the similar Model 88 lever (also a classic).

WINCHESTER MODEL 1886 EXTRA LIGHT Teddy Roosevelt's one complaint about the original 1886: Too heavy, at 9 pounds. In 1890, Winchester rolled out this 7½-pound version. Rare and expensive, it's still one hell of a big-woods thumper in .45/70.

REMINGTON MODEL 8 Remington's first autoloading rifle, designed by John Browning, this is just one crazy-cool gun. It's the rifle that killed Bonnie and Clyde—and quite a few deer—during the first part of the last century. Mine is chambered in .35 Rem.

MARLIN MODEL 1893 The Winchester 94 gets all the love, but Marlin's lever-gun design, with solid-top, side-ejecting receiver, has won the test of time and lives on today in the 336, which I also own. Good ones are fairly rare and coveted. I recently offered $900 cash for a nice old one in .30-30. I should have offered more.

MANNLICHER-SCHOENAUER MODEL 1903 I like American deer guns. But the Austrian-made Mannlicher is probably the best and unequivocally the best-looking factory gun ever made. In 6.5x54, at 5½ pounds, with a roughly 18-inch barrel, it's like it was made for the American whitetail woods.

156 CHOOSE THE RIGHT COMPOUND BOW

A compound bow is a simple pulley-and-lever system. The energy you get out is proportional to what you put in. (Today's bows are better in part because they are more efficient, meaning they give back a higher proportion.) As such, a faster bow is generally harder to draw. And some of the very things that make it fast can also make it harder to shoot well. Getting the bow that's right for you means giving and taking wisely and understanding the tradeoffs.

ACCURACY Archers never tire of debating the lethality of various broadheads and the relative speed, smoothness, and quietness of different compound bows. None of it matters a hoot if you can't hit what you're aiming at. By the same token, with perfect accuracy you could kill deer with a sharpened oil dipstick shot from a washtub bass. As a rule, less-skilled shooters need a bow that's more forgiving of operator error, which often means something on the longer and heavier side (more stable and easier to hold on target) and on the slower side (easier to hold at full draw without creeping forward and apt to have a longer brace height). Good shooters, who don't need a much forgiveness, can reasonably opt for something shorter, lighter, and faster. The trick is to find a bow that you can potentially shoot accurately and then shoot it until you do.

SPEED If you can shoot it accurately—a big *if*—a faster bow has major advantages. It shoots a flatter arrow, making exact range estimation less critical. And if it spits the average hunting arrow of around 400 grains out at an honest 280 fps or better, then it should let you shoot out to 30 yards with one pin without having to hold outside the vitals, simplifying things enormously in the field. The biggest advantage to a blazing bow is that it lets you shoot a heavier arrow sporting a heavier head without giving up too much in trajectory. This means more momentum and better penetration. Neither makes any difference if you make a perfect shot, but if you screw up, they can turn an otherwise nonlethal shot into a filled tag.

157 DON'T TRADE ACCURACY FOR SPEED

You can set up a bow to maximize one or the other—speed or accuracy. Unless you are such a good shot that you can give up a little accuracy and still be hell on wheels in the deer woods, favor accuracy. Here are two examples of how this works in real life.

CRANK IT DOWN Cranking up your bow's draw weight increases arrow speed. But if you shoot better with it turned down—then turn it down.

DRAW SHORT Some hunters shoot a draw length that is too long but don't want to give up any speed by shortening it. Just give it up. Too long a draw puts too much of your face against the string, can make it difficult to maintain a consistent anchor point, and can cause you to lock your bow arm out straight, as well as creep forward with your string arm. It's not worth it. Not sure if your draw is too long? See a good bow-shop pro.

HURTEAU ON: TRENDS

The current hype is that an ultralight, supershort bow is easier to carry and maneuver. That's fine, I suppose, but I don't understand why a 6-pound rifle is a wand and a 4-1/2 pound bow is an anchor. And I don't know any archer who has ever said "I would have killed that deer if my bow were 2 inches shorter." The fact is, longer, heavier bows are easier to shoot accurately, especially at long distance. Short, light bows are indeed handy and some shoot fine. Just remember that radically short and light models can wreak havoc on accuracy.

158 UNDERSTAND THE TRADEOFFS

FORGIVING

MODERATE (280–320 FPS)

FAST (325–360+ FPS)

OLD SCHOOL Longer, smoother-drawing bows with generous brace heights are perfect for finger shooters.

THE CADILLACS The top bows from the top companies are fast, quiet, and forgiving. And you pay for it.

SOLO CAM Most single cams combine moderate speeds with ease of shooting.

FAST ENOUGH International Bowhunting Organization claims usually exceed real-world speeds, but are a useful apples-to-apples comparison. Fast, forgiving bows will run in the 325–345 IBO range.

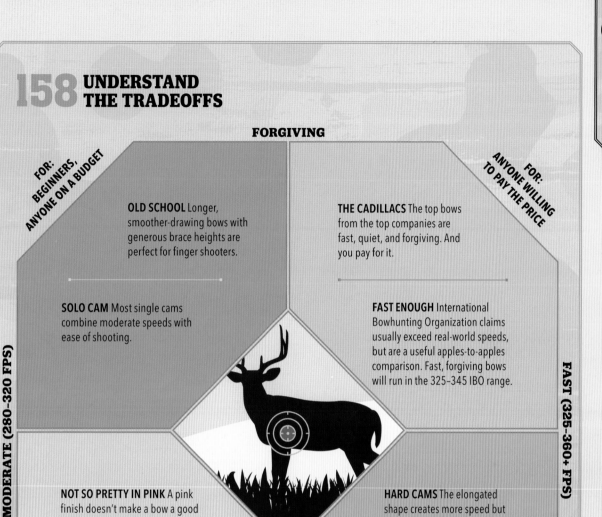

NOT SO PRETTY IN PINK A pink finish doesn't make a bow a good shooter. Women, think more Katniss Everdeen, less Molly Ringwald.

HARD CAMS The elongated shape creates more speed but commonly means a rougher draw cycle and a shallow valley.

SHORT AND LIGHT Though not fast, these bows are tough to shoot, often because they are radically short and light.

SHORT BRACE HEIGHT The arrow stays on the string longer and thus goes faster. And is more affected by shooting errors, too.

DEMANDING

159 SHOOT A STICK AND STRING

Every now and then, I hear a hunter say that traditional archery—hunting with a longbow or recurve—is "making a comeback." The truth is, stick-bow shooting has never gone away. Many custom bowyers are so swamped with orders that it can take more than a year to get your hands on one of their bows. Graceful and full of character, longbows and recurves are fun to shoot and certainly deadly on deer.

But behind the romance, there's this hard truth: It's not easy to shoot a stick bow well. The key is to learn the proper form and then practice—a lot. So let's get started.

STANCE Forget that straight-up compound posture. Assuming you shoot right-handed, point your left foot at a slight angle toward the target and bend just slightly at the knees.

GRIP This is the only similarity with shooting a compound; you want the grip against your lower palm, meeting bone. Keep your fingers relaxed.

ANCHOR You'll need to find a consistent anchor point, but it's rarely the same one you'd use to shoot a compound. I like my middle finger to hit the corner of my mouth at full draw. I also put the tip of my nose on the string.

DRAW Cant the top limb slightly to the right (again, for righties), which will keep the arrow on the rest and give you a better sight picture. Pull back smoothly using your back and shoulder muscles as your eyes focus on the target.

RELEASE When you hit your anchor, your eyes should be burning a hole into the target. Keep that focus as you relax your fingers and let the arrow go. Follow through by holding your form and looking the arrow into the target.

160 KNOW YOUR LIMITS

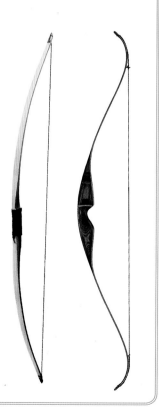

Unless you're truly exceptional, you'll learn in a hurry that you can't do the same things with a stick bow that you can with a compound. Your effective range will likely be 25 yards or less. Your arrows will travel half the speed of a garden-variety compound. You won't draw as heavy a bow. Some hunters, acknowledging these truths, save their traditional bow for the range—or for the curio wall of their man cave, which is perfectly fine. Others embrace the challenge and limitations of traditional archery and recognize these bows for the incredible hunting tools they are. I shot one of my largest whitetails at 15 yards with a recurve a year ago; it's probably the buck I'm most proud of in 40 years of whitetail hunting.

161 GET USED TO CROSSBOWS

A medieval weapon, the crossbow is suddenly the hot new thing. A few decades ago, only three states (Ohio, Arkansas, and Wyoming) allowed crossbows during the general archery season. Since 2003, at least 17 states and five Canadian provinces have boarded the crossbow-during-archery-season train. More are sure to follow, but not without some controversy.

What's the beef against the crossbow? With buttstock, forearm, and scope, it looks more like a rifle than a bow. Once cocked, all you have to do is aim and pull the trigger. It sounds unfair until you consider that crossbow bolts lose energy quickly, making it a close-range weapon. Also, crossbows are heavy, difficult to maneuver, and typically hard to reload if you miss in a hunting situation. I've shot quite a few, and I'd pick my vertical bow for hunting any day.

But there's also this: Some folks don't have that choice. Many would-be hunters—including the very young, old, and some women—simply can't pull the legal weight necessary to hunt with a vertical bow. At a time when we're losing hunters, and game managers are struggling to control deer numbers, the crossbow deserves a place around the bowhunter's campfire. They have already proven that they're here to stay, so you might as well get in on the trend. Here's what to look for.

STOCK It should fit comfortably, just like a deer rifle. The lighter the better if you'll still-hunt, stalk, or have to walk far to a stand. An adjustable stock is a plus.

STIRRUP This is where you plant your foot to cock the crossbow. It should be plenty roomy for a late-season boot.

TRIGGER Just like on your rifle, it should break crisply; a few of the most recent models have excellent triggers that will break between 2 and 3 pounds.

SAFETY A quality crossbow has at least one safety mechanism that engages when the bow is cocked. The stock design or extra safety should keep your fingers away from the rail.

RAIL This is the platform for the bolt, usually made of aluminum, though weight-shaving (and more expensive) carbon models are gaining ground.

SIGHTS Many crossbows come as kits that include a scope with a range-compensating reticle.

LIMBS Recurve limbs are more durable, lighter weight, and less expensive, but they typically result in more noise and vibration, and less speed. Compound designs are more expensive, faster, and often quieter as well.

AXLE-TO-AXLE LENGTH This distance affects the maneuverability of the bow, which can be important if you hunt from a ground blind or shooting house.

QUIVER Typically holds three to four bolts and mounts on the stock. Should be out of the way and detachable.

162 BE A PIONEER

Other than the added fun of not being entirely sure if your gun will go bang, the main reason to hunt deer with a traditional muzzleloader is to connect to our hunting forefathers. The question you need to ask yourself is, do you want to be a pioneer or a mountain man; Daniel Boone or Jedediah Smith?

Around 1725, German gunsmiths in Pennsylvania built the first distinctly American rifle, alternately known as the Pennsylvania or Kentucky long rifle. Typically .50 caliber with a 42- to 46-inch rifled barrel, this flintlock was the most accurate thing anywhere for decades—the sniper rifle of the Revolutionary War and the long-range game-getter of early frontiersmen.

Flintlocks still kill deer out to 100 yards or so. However, they have two major downsides. First, the lock time is slow. When you pull the trigger, it takes a little while for the hammer to drop, the flint to strike steel, the shower of sparks to light the priming powder, to light the main charge, to finally make the gun go bang. Second, the priming powder is exposed to the elements and may not ignite in damp or wet weather.

But there's a major upside: It's the most traditional of deer guns, probably the loveliest, most graceful-looking rifle we've ever produced . . . and wouldn't it be something, really something, to get a deer with one?

163 BE A MOUNTAIN MAN

Soon after the introduction of the percussion cap in the early 1800s, flintlock rifles were widely replaced or converted to caplocks. The new mechanism improved load time, lock time, and especially reliability in bad weather. Here, a closed copper cap laced with explosive mercury fulminate is placed over a hollow tube called a nipple. The hammer hits the cap, which shoots fire through the nipple, straight to the main charge, and the gun goes boom!

Starting in the 1820s, the Hawken Rifle—a shorter, beefier, half-stock caplock typically in .50 or .54 caliber—became the rifle of the plains and Rocky Mountains, where a handier, more-powerful rifle could drop bison and elk, or stop a bear if needed. Today's caplocks have all the same advantages over flintlocks. And they still kill deer, too, out to about 100 yards.

164 GET IN-LINE

If it's more important to you to kill a deer than to feel nostalgic about it, or if you just want to take advantage of the extra season to fill a tag, then get yourself an inline muzzleloader. Yes, these rifles do load from the front and use black powder (or a substitute), but otherwise, they are thoroughly modern guns, capable of MOA accuracy and plenty deadly for deer up to 200 yards.

The modern inline muzzleloader debuted in the late 1970s, and after 40 years of tinkering and refining, manufacturers have largely settled on a few closed-breech designs that use 209 shotgun primers for almost-guaranteed ignition in any weather.

The most popular of the muzzleloaders currently being marketed to hunters is the simple break-action. These are typically lightweight and quick-handling, and you'll find that the best models are going to feature tool-less, virtually instant breech-plug removal, making them the easiest to clean and maintain.

Bolt-action and pivoting-breech models, which have solid, unhinged barrels, are considered more accurate but typically require a wrench to remove the breech plug for cleaning. A few open-breech designs are still sold, as they are required in several northwestern states. (Check your local regulations closely.)

165 KNOW YOUR BLACKPOWDER AMMO

Here's a rundown of the most popular types of bullets used with both traditional and modern muzzleloaders. For deer, go with .54, .52, .50 (the most popular by far), or .45 caliber.

PATCHED ROUND BALL A patched round ball typically shoots best from traditional-style rifles with a slow rate of rifling twist, about one turn in 60 inches.

CONICAL BULLETS These hit harder, shoot flatter, and load more easily than patched round balls. Conicals shoot best from a fast-twist barrel.

SABOTED BULLETS The plastic sabot lets you shoot a slightly smaller-diameter bullet optimized for higher velocity, and better expansion. Best in fast-twist barrels.

POWERBELTS A full-bore projectile with a plastic base that seals the bore and pops off in flight. Powerbelts are easier-loading than sabots and can be shot in slow- or fast-twist barrels.

PATCHED ROUND BALL

CONICAL BULLETS

SABOTED BULLETS

POWERBELTS

166 PRACTICE FOR THE BIG WOODS

In the big woods, most of the bucks you see are jumping out of their beds, running for cover, or circling to get your scent. To put these whitetails on the wall, Maine Guide Randy Flannery shoots an open-sighted rifle like it's a shotgun, keeping both eyes open and concentrating on the front sight. Below is his practice regimen. Follow it, and you will learn to mount the gun properly, get the front sight on target, and shoot quickly and accurately. With a little practice, when a deer jumps up in front of you, your reaction will be automatic.

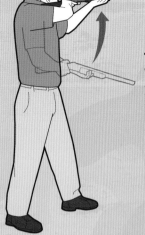

THE STANDING SHOT

With an 8-inch target at 40 or 50 yards, stand with your feet perpendicular to the target, mount, point, and shoot in one fast, fluid motion. Don't slap the trigger. The movement should be smooth–but not slow–like tightening your fist. Bring the rifle back to port arms and repeat. Take 25 shots.

THE STALKING SHOT

Put six milk jugs spaced 20 to 30 yards apart in a row, at the same distance as before. Walking parallel to the jugs, stop, pull up, and shoot. Fire at all six targets going in one direction, and then turn around and repeat going back the other way. Shoot until you're hitting most of the jugs on a round-trip.

THE QUICK AIM

The day of your hunt, grab your unloaded rifle and pick six or eight targets around you in the form of stumps or knots in trees before heading into the woods. Now quickly pull up and put the front sight on each target. These are like practice swings a batter takes before stepping up to the plate. Do 25 repetitions.

167 KEEP SHOOTING SIMPLE

Perhaps you've noticed the new legion of long-range riflemen on TV spinning turret-mounted knobs before taking the shot, or you've peered into the latest range compensating scope and figured, *that must be the secret.*

But hold on a minute. I know some spectacular riflemen who can turn target turrets as fast as I can recall a drop chart. But they are very, very few. And I have used range-compensating scope reticles that function wonderfully . . . as long as you remember to crank them up to full power. Theoretically, either can save you the inherent imprecision of holding off your target.

On the other hand: [1] In the real world, big bucks are not in the habit of milling around stupidly while you spin knobs and count hashes. [2] Without a lot of practice, doing either can go very wrong while your brain is swimming in adrenalin. [3] Most of you needn't ever worry about holding off.

A great many deer hunters simply don't have the time to shoot a bunch. If that's you, it's probably best that you keep your shots at deer within 300 yards—and just about any reasonably flat-shooting round sighted a little high at 100 will keep you well in the hair at that range. For the small remainder who can reasonably shoot to 400, there is no shortage of very flat-shooting rounds, even some non-magnum rounds, that can do the same. This covers about 99 percent of you, and the 1 percent who can hit reliably beyond 400 don't need my advice.

Take your typical 115-grain .25-06 bullet. Sighted 3 inches high at 100, it is damn near dead on at 300 and drops only about 10 inches at 400. A 130-grain .270 WSM sighted 2.5 inches high drops about the same. Meanwhile, the chest of a good muley or whitetail buck, measured from back to brisket, spans about 20 inches. In other words, no need to aim out of the hair.

The best system is the simplest: Shoot your rifle with your chosen hunting round to learn the point of impact at various ranges. (Don't rely on ballistics charts.) Then write it down and either memorize it or tape it to the rifle's butt stock. In the field, range your target, or estimate the range if you must, and then simply remember or glance down to see that you need to hold 4 inches high at 350, or 10 at 400, or whatever. Compensate and shoot. That's it.

168 GET OFF THE BENCH

This is the drill that will make you into a true marksman. Go to the range and burn some ammo, shooting at National Rifle Association 50-yard slow-fire bull's-eye targets, which have an 8-inch bull's-eye.

Assuming you've sighted in your rifle, get off the bench. Why? Because shooting from a perfect rest is not the same as shooting under most field conditions.

Working at 50 yards, firing offhand, take 10 shots, never giving yourself more than three seconds to get the rifle up, aim, and shoot. Next, fire five shots kneeling, taking no more than five seconds per shot. Finally, if you'll hunt from a treestand, take another five while sitting in a chair. For these, you take your time. This is precision shooting.

Take these 20 shots twice a week. When you can get all of your shots from kneeling and sitting, and nine out of 10 from offhand, in the black, it's time to move back to 100 yards and repeat.

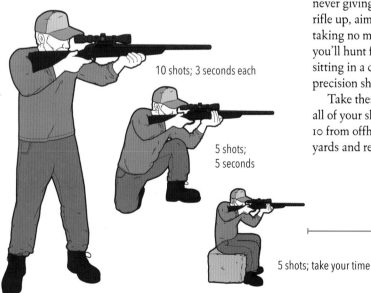

10 shots; 3 seconds each

5 shots; 5 seconds

5 shots; take your time

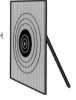

50 YARDS

GREATEST DEER HUNTERS

JUDGE JOHN DEAN CATON
THE ORIGINAL DEER DOCTOR

It is not unusual these days for prominent deer biologists to mingle hard science with popular hunting craft–but this isn't new. Judge John Dean Caton (1812-1895), Chief Justice of the Supreme Court of Illinois, preceded today's Ph.D. hunters by more than a century. Though not a formally trained scientist, Caton studied deer with a rigorous, systematic approach. In 1858, he created the country's second deer park–a 200-acre enclosure for observing deer. That said, the wilds were also his laboratory, and hunting a favorite scientific method. In 1877, he published *The Antelope and Deer of America*, the first scientific treatise on deer and deer hunting. *Forest and Stream* (now *Field & Stream*) called it "the most important publication ever printed on the subject…."

169 GET A GOOD REST

Well, I suppose I should tell you about how I embarrassed myself on a recent mule deer hunt.

I know academically that hitting stuff out in the great wide open mostly boils down to getting a really good rest. But when a muley buck springs up and goes boinging across the cheat grass, it's easy to forget all that, which is what I did.

And so with nothing preventing a sitting or even prone shot, I knelt up high, without so much as a butt cheek on a heel, gun waving on the sticks, and whiffed two otherwise makeable shots. Then I took the long walk of shame—back to the trucks, where a gaggle of fellow writers and guides watched the whole scene through binoculars and spotting scopes.

But it turns out that temporarily feeling like an idiot can be a useful thing. The next morning, when we glassed a decent buck feeding at the base of some far-off rim rock, I made sure to get prone, rest my gun on my pack, and make a killing shot. The other buck was bigger, but this one came with a lesson.

If you don't do a lot of long-range shooting, you may believe that there is some deep mystery behind making a bullet go exactly where you want it to beyond 200 yards, some magic you are not privy to. Just remember: Whatever it is, you don't need it if you have a really good rest. So don't forget this basic rule: *Before you do anything else, get a good rest. If you can't get a good enough rest, don't shoot.*

170 DON'T GET TOO FAR AWAY

Extreme long-range shooting, which we can define here as "anywhere between 300 yards and halfway to the dwarf planet Ceres," seems to be all the rage these days, particularly for hunters seeking mule deer and western whitetails. A very small handful of folks can do this kind of shooting ethically. For anyone else who might be thinking, *That doesn't look so hard*, it's important to at least try to cure yourself of that notion. Indeed, every deer hunter should learn to access his or her real-world accuracy at a variety of ranges.

So first, let's agree that before pulling the trigger on any poor deer that stands to give it all up for you, there should be a high probability of making a shot that will end things quickly. Agreed? Okay, now do this:

STEP 1 Starting at 150 yards, shoot five shots from a kneeling position (with or without sticks, as is your normal practice in the field) at a target with an 8-inch bull. If you put four out of five in the black, move back 25 yards and do it again. When you reach the point when you can't put four out of five in the black, that's it; you're done. Your previous distance is the maximum at which you should shoot kneeling at a deer.

STEP 2 Now do it sitting (with or without sticks), starting at 200 yards and moving back 25 yards at a time.

STEP 3 Finally, prone (with or without bipod or pack, as is your normal practice), starting at 250 yards and moving back 50 yards at a time. There, that should cure you.

171 GET GOOD FORM

Good form is the reason why Sam Snead has more than 300 top-10 finishes and why Mariano Rivera could probably pitch until he's 50. It's also what will get you to shoot your bow better. So practice the following routine until you can do it in your sleep.

Stand with your feet shoulder-width apart and perpendicular to the target. A lot of guys like to turn their lead toe open a bit for better stability and balance.

Maintain a consistent anchor point. Find where your release hand meets your face comfortably at full draw and put it in the same spot every time. And because two anchor points are better than one, drop your nose down on the string or use a kisser button.

Don't grip the bow handle like it's a hammer, which introduces torque. Instead, turn your palm up and rest the bow's grip against the bony part of your palm's heel, between the fleshy pads. Lower your fingers safely under the shelf and well away from the arrow, but leave your hand relaxed and open as you shoot.

At full draw, continuously push toward the target with your bow arm and pull away with your string arm as you squeeze the trigger. Follow through smoothly. Try not to move your head, drop your bow arm, or grab too quickly for the bow's handle.

172 PAY ATTENTION TO THE DETAILS

Here are some little things that can make a big difference in how well you shoot. Keep an eye on them and watch your accuracy improve.

SHORTEN YOUR RELEASE If you trip your release trigger with the tip of an extended index finger, quit it. This tends to make you slap at the thing. Instead, shorten your release aid so that at full draw you are able to curl your index finger around the trigger at about the middle joint. This makes it easier to squeeze the trigger smoothly and with better control.

FLOAT THE PIN AND SQUEEZE You wouldn't think that letting your sight pin float on, off, and around the bull as you squeeze the trigger could possibly tighten your groups. But it does, like magic. So stop trying to hold the pin perfectly still on your mark, which is often not possible anyway. Instead, let it float and then squeeze— slow and steady does it.

WATCH THE ARROW Eyeing the shaft all the way to the target through the sight-pin bracket during practice sessions promotes better follow-through and keeps you from dropping your bow arm during the shot.

CHECK YOUR BUBBLE LEVEL The bubble level on your sight reveals the cant and torque you're putting on your bow—both of which are accuracy killers. Always use it on the practice range because it forms good habits. Glance at the bubble as part of your pre-shot routine, adjust the bow as necessary, and your groups will shrink.

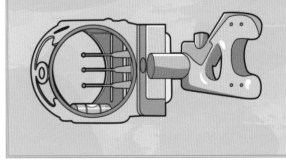

173 GO LONG

Hitting a target at 100 yards with a bow is not so difficult as you think. Try it. Not only does long-range practice make shots at hunting ranges seem like gimmes but it also magnifies subtle mistakes in shooting form. If you mess up your form at 30 yards, you may still be in the kill zone. If you mess up at 100 yards, you'll miss the whole damn target and lose a $12 arrow. This forces you to bear down and shoot well.

WEEK 1 At these ranges, concentrate on perfecting the fundamentals of good form.

WEEK 2 You may have to fine-tune your sight as you move back.

10
20
WEEK TWO
30
WEEK ONE
40
50
60
WEEK THREE
70
80
WEEK FOUR
90

100 YARDS

LAST DAY

LAST DAY Hit a deer target from here, and your confidence will soar at field ranges.

WEEK 3 You don't have to shoot at 100 yards. If you can't hit the target consistently beyond 70 yards, for example, stop at 70. It will still be great practice.

WEEK 4 Way out here, it's especially critical to push and pull through the shot and to make a smooth release.

LONG-SHOT REGIMEN
HERE'S HOW TO HIT AT 100 BEFORE THE OPENER:

WEEK 1
Review the basic shooting tips on the facing page, while shooting three arrows at 20 yards. Step out to 30 and do it again. Now go to 40, take a deep breath, remember the basics, and shoot five arrows. Relax and shoot five more. Do this whole routine two or three times a day.

WEEK 2
Do the same as above, but this time make the distances 30, 40, and 50 yards.

WEEK 3
With your stance, anchor point, and grip perfected, shoot at 50, 60, and 70 yards, focusing on two things: (A) pushing and pulling through the shot; and (B) floating the pin as you squeeze the trigger.

WEEK 4
Same routine, but at 70, 80, and 90 yards. On the last day, replace the block target with a good-size buck target, step back to 100, and double-lung the thing.

174 ACCESSORIZE FOR ACCURACY

No matter what your skill level, the right accessories can improve your shooting. This Hoyt Vector Turbo (35-inch axle-to-axle, 4.2 pounds, 340 fps IBO, 6-inch brace height) is a bow I use both in the field and on the 3-D course. Here's how I set it up:

SINGLE-PIN SLIDER SIGHT One pin simplifies things for beginners and experts alike. If you're an archer who will never shoot beyond 30 yards in the field, you can set it and forget it with many of today's bows. But if you plan to shoot farther, in the field or on the range, a sight like this [A] lets you instantly adjust the elevation setting in single-yard increments and hold dead-on at 120 yards if you so desire.

MATCHED PEEP AND PIN GUARD A round pin guard that perfectly matches the diameter of your peep [B] at full draw helps keep your pin centered and improves your accuracy.

FULL-CONTAINMENT DROP-AWAY REST Yes, nonmechanical full-capture rests were tops for hunting once. But today's best drop-aways [C] completely contain the arrow, instantly fall clear of the shaft upon release for optimum accuracy, and don't mangle your vanes.

STABILIZER A 4-inch stabilizer is a decoration. This 8-inch Fuse Carbon Blade [D] does more to balance my bow, and it also helps to dampen vibration.

NO GRIP It's not as comfortable to hold, but removing the factory grip [E] on some models provides better sensitivity for perfect hand positioning and reduced torque.

NO QUIVER I shoot better with no quiver attached to my bow. Maybe it's all in my head, but it doesn't change the results. Try shooting your bow both ways; if you have a preference, go with it.

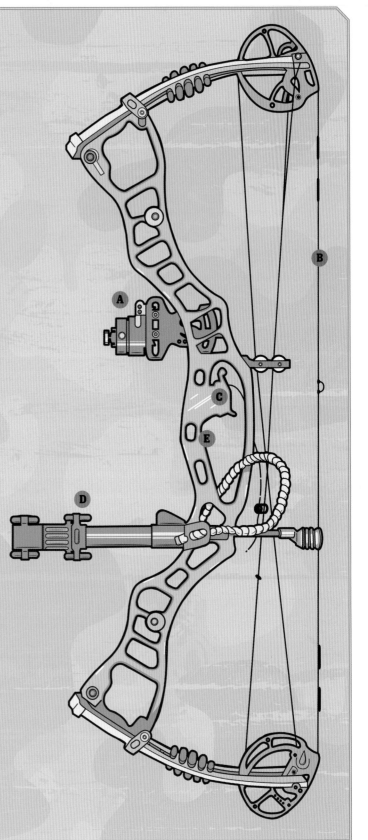

176 MATCH THE ARROW SPINE

Two bows with the same draw length and weight may require different arrow spines for optimum accuracy. Any reputable bow shop will have access to a spine calculator. But if you're buying online, make sure you speak with a tech to match the spine with your bow's specs for optimum accuracy.

175 MAKE THE MOST OF PRACTICE

As with most things in life, the key to getting better at shooting with a bow is practice, practice, and (you guessed it) more practice. Here are a few things that will boost your effectiveness.

PRACTICE IN LOW LIGHT Most bow shots at mature whitetail bucks happen during either the first or the final ticks of daylight, when sight pins dim and your peep sight seems to shrink. So devote some practice time to the opening and closing minutes of legal light in your area to prep for this crunch time and to learn your maximum effective range in low light. And count on it being tighter than you probably expect.

MAKE THE FIRST SHOT COUNT Repetitive practice is fine for perfecting form. But few bucks will give you a second shot, let alone a fifth. About a month prior to the opener, start each morning by shooting a single, broadhead-tipped hunting arrow. Pick a distance, visualize a hunting scenario, and shoot. Then walk away. Increase the difficulty as the season nears, and you'll be ready for that make-or-break shot.

SHOOT FOR SOMETHING A friendly gamble helps teach you to steel your nerves while at full draw. Bet a quarter per arrow with your buddies during backyard practice and let the smack talk flow freely.

177 SHOOT FOR THE HEART AND LUNGS

The heart-lung area, located between and extending behind the front shoulders of a broadside deer, is the deadliest target for the vast majority of shooters. That's because if you make the shot, the deer is dead, period, and because it is the most makeable of deadly shots.

Compared to the throat patch, lower neck, or head (God forbid), the heart-lung area is a larger target—about the size of a rugby ball with its nose wedged tightly between the deer's shoulder blades. Pop it, and you go home with venison.

With a gun and a good bullet you can shoot through the shoulder or brisket to get to those vitals, making broadside, quartering-away, quartering-to, or head-on shots all quite lethal. An arrow, however, may or may not penetrate through the shoulder, and to kill quickly it must either pierce the heart or puncture both lungs. This makes broadside and quartering-away shots the only real high-odds opportunities. Wait for them.

SHOOT THE HEART AND LUNGS

⊕ SHOT WITH A BOW OR A GUN

⊕ SHOT WITH A GUN

GREATEST DEER

"OL' MOSSYHORNS" (THE DEL AUSTIN BUCK)

DATE: OCTOBER, 1962
LOCATION: HALL COUNTY, NEBRASKA
SCORE: 279 $^7/_8$" B&C NONTYPICAL

WHY IT MAKES THE LIST:

Ol' Mossyhorns is more than an iconic trophy; the giant nontyp is also an epic story. When Al Dawson first saw the buck in the fall of 1958, he not only nicknamed him, he vowed to shoot no other. In the five seasons that followed, Dawson had multiple encounters with—and two shots at—the buck of his dreams. Yet Dawson's friend Del Austin would finally become the hunter to tag Ol' Mossyhorns; a 9½-year old monarch that shattered the P&Y world record for nontypicals and held the top spot for 38 years.

178 TAKE THE NECK SHOT, IF YOU MUST

In his book *Shots at Whitetails*, Larry Koller preached the neck shot to gun hunters and proved its lethality by grounding bucks via shots to the throat patch. "Any shot into the upper third of the deer's neck," he wrote, "is so decisive in result that this writer has yet to hear of a deer moving from its tracks after being hit in this area . . . [L]ower neck shots seem to have much the same effect on deer as the quick removal of a head with an ax has on the Thanksgiving turkey." A good neck shot will do the job, but it's a smaller target for the average hunter. If all you have is a neck shot, and it's one you're confident you can make, fine. Otherwise, shoot for the heart-lung area.

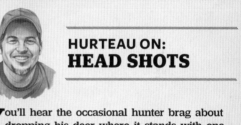

HURTEAU ON: HEAD SHOTS

You'll hear the occasional hunter brag about dropping his deer where it stands with one clean shot to the head. It sounds pretty slick, but don't be too impressed. Head shots are ill-advised. If you miss, even a little, then it's on you that some poor deer is running around with one eye, or half a nose, or a bottom jaw hanging, only to become coyote food or to die slowly of starvation.

179 WATCH THAT FRONT SHOULDER, BOWHUNTERS

I hear a lot of deer hunting stories from fellow bowhunters. Inevitably, a small but not insignificant percentage of them start something like this: "I thought I hit him perfectly, right behind the shoulder . . ." Yet the hunter couldn't have hit the deer perfectly because he either failed to recover the animal or only found it after an arduous tracking job.

Bowhunters need to redefine the "perfect" shot, which has likely been influenced by the 3-D targets we use for practice. Most full-body deer targets sport a neat little 10-ring immediately behind the "animal's"

front elbow, over an area that would result in a heart-shot deer. No doubt, putting an arrow in a real buck here will kill him quick.

But there is something critically wrong with this shot: It leaves too little room for error. And when your eyes are tearing from the cold and your knees wobbling under the influence of buck fever, error is all too common in the field. If you do not make this "perfect" shot perfectly, the likelihood of disaster becomes roughly a coin toss. That is, if you miss too far back, you'll probably be okay. But if you miss forward, your broadhead will

find the shoulder, the brisket, or leg—none of which is at all good.

The solution is simple. Forget the 10-ring on a 3-D target. Erase that "perfect" shot from your mind and replace it with one a few inches farther back—that is, roughly on the center of the lungs, which are about the size of a basketball, perhaps, or even slightly smaller.

If your arrow flies perfectly, your deer is dead. If the shot is a little off, there's a lot of lung surrounding your new 10-ring. Get anywhere close to it with a sharp broadhead and you will find your deer.

180 AGE A BUCK IN THE FIELD

Most beginners look at a buck's antlers and put him in one of three categories: small, big, and holy crap! But if you're concerned about your deer herd's age-structure, you need to study a deer's body size and proportion, too, as these are even better indicators of age. Here's what to look for.

1 ½ YEARS OLD Sometimes called a "yearling," this buck is wearing his first set of antlers, which can range from a pair of spikes to a small 8- or 10-point rack. Either way, the rack will be thin with a spread less than 14 inches. The body is the surest clue: This buck will be slim and long-legged, much like a doe. His neck won't swell during the rut.

2 ½ YEARS OLD In some areas, a 2 ½-year-old buck can carry a Pope and Young record-book rack. But the body will tell you he's still got some growing to do. His belly is sleek with no sag, and he'll still look "leggy" compared to an older buck. Some neck swelling will occur during the rut, but his slim face should tip you off to his youth.

3 ½ YEARS OLD The antlers of many 3 ½-year-old bucks will make P&Y and then some. Though he's well muscled (a common analogy is to that of a thoroughbred racehorse) and has a beefy neck, he doesn't have the bulk of a truly old deer. The biggest tip-off: a distinct junction where the neck meets the shoulders, which seems to get lost in older deer.

4 ½ YEARS OLD This buck is fully mature, with a rack that is wide, high, and massive. During the rut, his neck will swell to meet the shoulders seamlessly, giving him a bull-like appearance. His rounded belly and his chest make his legs appear short. In all but the most tightly managed properties, this buck is the epitome of what a whitetail can be. So quit looking and shoot.

181 SCORE A BUCK ON THE HOOF, FAST

You can estimate a buck's gross B&C score in half a minute simply by judging one side, doubling it, and adding the inside spread. Here's how:

NUMBER OF TINES This side view shows 4 points, which means he's a 10-point (assume the brow tine is there).

TINE LENGTH The distance from the tip of a buck's nose to the corner of his eye is approximately 7 inches. So in this example, the G2 is about 8 inches long, and the G3 matches it. The G4 is about 6 inches. The brow tine is a bit shorter at 4 inches. Give this side 26 inches.

MASS Whitetails get four circumference measurements around the main beam, starting at the base. Use the width of the buck's ear as your frame of reference, about 3 inches at its widest. If the beam looks half as wide as the ear, the buck will have an average of 4 inches in circumference at the measurement points. Add 16 inches.

BEAM LENGTH If the tip of the beam appears to go past the buck's eye, you can assume at least 20 inches. Add 22 inches here.

INSIDE SPREAD If a buck's beams reach to his ear tips, he's 18 inches wide. Give this deer a 19-inch spread.

TOTAL Add up one side and double it: 26 + 16 + 22 = 64; 64 x 2 = 128. Now add the inside spread and you've got the buck at 147 inches.

GREATEST DEER HUNTERS

FRED BEAR
AMERICA'S BOYER

A Detroit native, Bear captured the Michigan state archery championships three times during the 1930s, and sensing the growing interest in bowhunting, began making bows. Bear's "Grizzly" recurve is widely regarded as the first mass-produced bow in history. Today, Bear is one of the leading manufacturers of traditional and compound bows. Fred Bear traveled worldwide, filming hunts that hit local American theatres and primed a generation of bowhunters to follow in his footsteps. Despite hunting from Alaska to Africa, Bear's favorite quarry remained the whitetail deer he pursued in northern Michigan. One of the founders and original board members of the Pope and Young Club, Bear was one of the first inductees into the Bowhunter's Hall of Fame.

182 LEASE A LITTLE BIT OF HEAVEN

At nearly 1,900 acres and located in an area known for big bucks, the farm was a deer hunter's gold mine. When a friend said he could get me hunting permission, I was ecstatic . . . until I heard the catch. I'd have to lease the place. I'd never paid to access land and was hesitant at first.

Five years and eight Pope and Young record-book-size bucks later, I've become totally sold on the concept.

My conversion wasn't just because I've enjoyed great hunting. Leasing not only allowed me to hunt property I couldn't have accessed otherwise, but it also let me enjoy all the aspects of deer hunting—off-season scouting, camera monitoring, creating trails, tweaking habitat, hanging stands, planting food plots, and basically managing our own deer herd—that whitetail freaks who own land can do year-round. Leasing gave my partners and me (none of us wealthy enough to actually purchase hunting ground) a sense of ownership impossible to achieve with any other agreement short of a deed.

The landowner benefits, too. Many landowners view deer as no-value features on valuable property, and leasing converts them to an asset. And of course, lease fees help farmers recoup crop losses caused by deer.

If you decide to lease, think long-term. Short-term leases are nothing but trespass fees. Think about it: You spend hours planting food plots, improving habitat, hanging stands, and doing all the labor-intensive activities associated with managing a property . . . do you want to start all over again on a new place next fall? I don't, and I wouldn't appreciate another group enjoying the fruits of my hard work.

Most of the happy lessees I know have worked out long-term agreements with the landowner; three years is a typical minimum. Many property owners balk at multiyear contracts—the cost of living rises as sharply for them as it does for the rest of us, and their concern that your fee won't keep up with inflation is legitimate. If that's the case with a property you have your eye on, propose a small-percentage increase for each successive season.

183 DO YOUR PAPERWORK

A lease is a business deal, so a formal agreement signed by your hunting party and the landowner is crucial. (Lease agreement templates are widely available on the Internet). Our group combined elements of several samples to draft their own document. Every agreement should contain the following basics. Have all club members and any co-owners of the property sign the agreement. The club stores one copy; the landowner keeps another.

COMPENSATION Explicitly state how much money the landowner will receive and when payments occur.

LIABILITY The landowner should be absolved of liability should a club member (or guest) get hurt while on the property.

CONDUCT Most landowners will want to stipulate where you can or can't drive, which areas are off-limits to hunting and shooting, where to place stands and blinds, and so forth.

EXCLUSIVITY Your hunting party should enjoy sole access to the property for hunting. If the landowner wants to reserve some rights for other activities, clearly spell out the specific details.

TRESPASSER PROTOCOL Will the landowner patrol the property and/or prosecute interlopers, or will your group perform that function?

LAND USE If the landowner agrees to food plots, habitat work, trail creation, and other modifications, indicate clearly where these activities can occur and what they entail.

184 FORM A HUNTING GROUP

Unless you're fairly well heeled, paying for even a modest lease will require one or more partners. Take your time choosing them. Every lease member will be equal parts hunting buddy, coworker, and business partner, and one individual lacking in any category can make for a long and frustrating experience. Here are some guidelines.

SELECT CORE PARTNERS Three to six members is a good, manageable starting point. It's easier to add people if you need or want to expand your group than it is to get rid of a bad egg.

DECIDE ON FINANCES Members should agree on a per-hunter cap on costs. This will help as you shop for ground and decide how to budget for projects such as food-plot seed and equipment like stands, tools, signs, etc.

ESTABLISH GOALS Are you leasing simply to secure access and enjoy an undisturbed hunt, or do you want to manage for trophies? Agreeing on goals ahead of time will establish harmony among members and can help define the size and location of the property you seek.

SET BYLAWS They aid communication and make things fair to everyone. For instance, you'll need to establish workdays for scouting, hanging stands, planting food plots, etc. And you'll need to come up with a guest policy. Will friends or family members be allowed to hunt? How often? How long? Also, some members may have the whole season to hunt; others will have only a weekend or two. Some will want to bowhunt only; others will opt for firearms. Who goes when? And where? Should there be a limit on the number of deer members can take?

185 GO LOCAL IF YOU CAN

If you already live in good deer country, the best lease is often the one that's closest to home, so you won't waste your precious hunting time on travel. Monitoring your property—everything from food-plot maintenance to sweeping for trespassers—is much easier, too. Here are some tactics for securing ground near home.

OBTAIN A PLAT BOOK This atlas of landowners and property sizes (available from the county clerk or recorder) will help you identify properties with the most potential by size and location.

MAKE PERSONAL VISITS Nothing beats a face-to-face meeting with the landowner. An introductory phone call can save time, though, and in the case of absentee owners, may be your only option.

ADVERTISE A classified ad in the local paper can make some property owners come searching for you. Posters placed in stores, restaurants, and post offices can have the same effect. State that you're an ethical, respectful hunter seeking access and willing to pay.

NETWORK Biologists, foresters, and employees of ag-related businesses and agencies can be great resources for any hunter. They're familiar with a range of local properties *and* their owners.

USE A SERVICE A number of websites list properties for lease by state, species, hunting implement, and cost. Some of these website services charge a fee, but you get results quickly. It's certainly worth a little time on Google.

TODAY'S CUTTING-EDGE DEER TACTICS ARE ACTUALLY ANCIENT, ON A FUNDAMENTAL LEVEL. Early Native Americans—Stone Age hunters—pioneered many of the basic tricks we use today, including rattling, calling, decoying, and food plotting. But with the recent whitetail boom, a growing number of deer fanatics now spend every free minute tweaking the basic methods, creating exciting new innovations by the day and making the game more nuanced and fun.

Have you ever rattled in a mule deer? Ever purposely bumped a whitetail buck in order to get in the right spot to tag it? Ever invaded a public-land swamp to ambush the trophy nobody thought lived there?

If you're already taking all the big bucks you've ever hoped to, hey, more power to you. But if you'd like some fresh ideas that will help take your deer hunting to another level, read on.

186 FOLLOW THE EARLY-BUCK RULES

A whitetail buck in August and September is a totally different animal from the one in late October and November, when the rut changes everything. To succeed, you need to understand how early bucks are different and apply that to your hunting plan. Here, you'll find six rules and their exceptions.

RULE #1

EARLY-SEASON BUCKS MOVE ON A PREDICTABLE BED-TO-FEED, FEED-TO-BED PATTERN.

THE EXCEPTION With many prime deer foods coming into season now, bucks can suddenly vanish from a previously predictable hotspot in favor of some other grub.

THE BOTTOM LINE There's no better time to pattern and intercept a feeding buck, but you've got to keep close tabs on him, as well as on the other menu items in your hunting area.

RULE #2

BUCKS HIT EVENING FEEDING AREAS BEFORE DARK, BUT GO TO BED EARLY IN THE A.M.

THE EXCEPTION Several experts we've interviewed estimated that 75 to 80 percent of the bucks tagged now are taken in the evening. But a handful of deer—including some giants—seem to be on their feet only in the morning during the daylight hours.

THE BOTTOM LINE Go in the evening if you can, but don't pass up morning hunts if you can't.

RULE #3

EARLY-SEASON BUCKS ARE UNPRESSURED AND WILL TAKE THE PATH OF LEAST RESISTANCE.

THE EXCEPTION Not all early-season bucks are unpressured. Squirrel hunters, bird hunters, even ginseng hunters can take care of that. Plus, sometimes bucks act the way you'd expect and insist on taking the hard-and-hidden route to where they're going.

THE BOTTOM LINE Sure, scout the obvious trails and funnels. But don't stop there. Look around for a funky little side trail or pinch point where a big, savvy buck can slink unseen.

RULE #4

EARLY BUCKS DRINK ON THE WAY TO FOOD IN THE EVENING AND ON THE WAY TO BED IN THE MORNING.

THE EXCEPTION O.K., this is more of a corollary than an exception—but it's important: If it's very hot out, bucks are likely to get up from their beds several times during the heat of the day to get a drink, often on their way to a shadier, cooler bedding area.

THE BOTTOM LINE This time of year it's as important to know a buck's sources of drinking water as it is to know his food sources. And be sure to scout carefully; that water source may be as subtle as a hollowed-out stump full of rainwater.

RULE #5

EARLY-SEASON BUCKS HANG OUT IN GROUPS, WITH LITTLE AGGRESSION TOWARD ONE ANOTHER.

THE EXCEPTION Seemingly gregarious bucks in velvet use body posture and hoof swats to sort out the pecking order and start sparring as soon as they're in hard antler. Plus, bachelor groups are beginning to break up, and the drifting of bucks into rival territories can mean brawls that have nothing to do with does.

THE BOTTOM LINE If you have a buck's route nailed down, get set up for a silent ambush. But if you need to coax the deer into range, don't hesitate to challenge him with rattling, calling, or a decoy.

RULE #6

BUCKS BED CLOSE TO THEIR PRIME FEEDING AREAS NOW.

THE EXCEPTION Older bucks can be antisocial and bed in odd places away from other deer. Also, as bachelor groups disperse, bucks abandon the bedding areas they've shared with buddies for months, seeking safe havens that may not be on your radar.

THE BOTTOM LINE Expect bucks to bed close to food. But don't assume this is universal—especially as the early season progresses. If you're determined to take a real slammer, you may have to look deeper in the woods to find his core area.

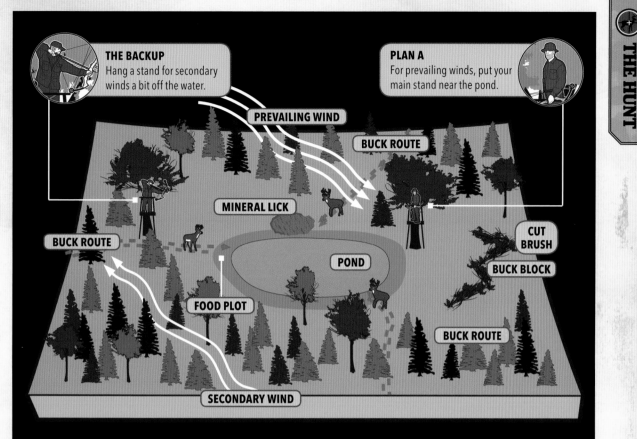

THE BACKUP
Hang a stand for secondary winds a bit off the water.

PLAN A
For prevailing winds, put your main stand near the pond.

PREVAILING WIND

BUCK ROUTE

MINERAL LICK

BUCK ROUTE

CUT BRUSH

BUCK BLOCK

POND

FOOD PLOT

BUCK ROUTE

SECONDARY WIND

187 SET A WATER TRAP

Hunting whitetails near water is always a good idea, but in the warmth of the early season, it just gets better. Thirsty deer tend to visit ponds, creeks, seeps, and springs more frequently now. More important, they hit discreet sources near primary feeding areas like clockwork before heading out for the evening meal—making these spots killer stand sites during the early bow season.

If your property doesn't hold such a water source, dig a small pond in a known staging area a few weeks before the season, let the rain fill it up, and then follow these simple steps.

SWEETEN THE PLOT Plant clover or ryegrass in a small strip around the pond to stabilize the banks and give deer something to nibble on. Spade up some dirt nearby and pour deer minerals in the loose soil (where legal). The lure of a lick wanes as fall advances, but it will attract deer next spring and summer, turning your pond into a regular stop for deer through the year.

DOUBLE UP Hang two stands. The first should offer an easy shot to the pond and be suitable for the prevailing early-season wind. The second should account for a secondary wind and may be slightly farther off the water. Make sure both allow an entry that skirts bedded deer and an exit that avoids the main food source.

DIRECT TRAFFIC Steer deer upwind of your primary stand: Pile brush you cut to block trails that bucks might use as their approach, or as they try to circle directly downwind.

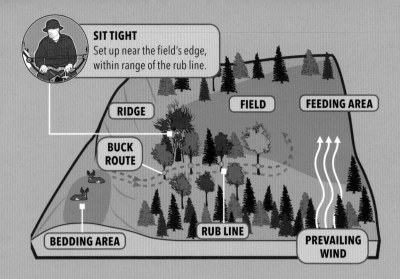

SIT TIGHT
Set up near the field's edge, within range of the rub line.

RIDGE

FIELD

FEEDING AREA

BUCK ROUTE

BEDDING AREA

RUB LINE

PREVAILING WIND

188 RUB OUT WRONG ASSUMPTIONS

Are you convinced, as so many hunters seem to be, that field-edge rubs are made only at night, and that little rubs mean little bucks? Well . . . maybe. The real answer is that it depends on timing. Later in the season, as the rut approaches, all of this is mainly true. The thing is, you can't generalize, because during the early bowhunting season these presumptions can be just plain wrong.

SPY UNDER COVER
Glass from an overlook at dawn to see where a buck beds.

BRUSHY CREEK

BUCK ROUTES

BEDDING AREA

FEEDING AREA

SUMAC THICKET

HIDDEN VISTA

189 FIND THE MASTER BEDROOM

It's easy to oversimplify things when deer are on a late-summer feeding pattern. When a buck is visiting the same dining room every evening, we also assume he beds in the same spot every day. Then again, he might bed in a sumac patch off the east end of a feed field one day, along a brushy creek bed on the north end the next, and on a secluded ridge after that. Guess wrong on any given night in this case, and your ambush is botched. Worse,

SWIRLING WINDS

DON'T BE SHY
If the bucks aren't noticing your deke, rattle so they do.

BUCK ROUTES

RAVINE

PREVAILING WIND

ROCK LANDMARK

HUNTER ENTRY

FEEDING AREA

BUCK DECOY

190 BRING THE PARTY TO YOU

Every early-season hunter hopes to find— and has a good chance of finding before the end of September—a bachelor group of bucks still on a predictable late-summer feeding pattern, hitting the same evening food source well before dark, day after day. Tagging one of these boys can be a simple matter of long-distance patterning, stealthy stand hanging, and patience to wait for the right wind. But the biggest bachelor bucks tend to enter feeding areas at oddball spots with fickle winds, an impossible approach, or lousy stand sites.

The fact is, bucks tend to bed very close to their food sources in late summer and early fall, commonly within 100 yards. So there's little distinction now between a bedding-area rub and a feeding-area rub. And shortly after velvet shed, most fresh rubs are made by mature deer regardless of tree size. Large deer simply start earlier than little guys, and they don't always need a telephone pole for a punching bag.

FIND THE PARTY Walk the edges of early-season food sources, searching for rubs where the debarked side faces away from the food. These were made by a buck headed toward the feeding area for dinner.

STAND IN Hang your stand downwind of the rub line, within bow range of the sign.

SEE AND BE SEEN If you can't find a good tree inside bow range, hang your stand as close as possible to the natural sign and make a mock rub within shooting distance. Choose the same tree species the buck prefers (if available) and blaze a knee-high mark on it with a hand axe or the back of your hunting knife. Bucks are visual critters, and chances are good that your boy will come over to investigate.

---

you'll spook the buck if he approaches or feeds downwind of you. But if you're a turkey hunter, you've already got the skills to kill a bed-hopping buck. You'll need to do your "roosting" in the morning, though. What does that mean in practical terms? Just follow these steps.

BEAT THE SUN Rise well before dawn and drive to a place where you can observe your buck's favorite feed field from a distance. Bucks tend to hit the sack very early now, so you'll need to bring good light-gathering optics.

WATCH THAT BUCK As dawn breaks, glass to find your deer. Stay focused on him until he leaves the field

and note precisely where he exits. Since summer-pattern bucks rarely travel far to bed, it's a good bet he'll enter the field near this spot come evening.

FOLLOW UP Assuming the wind is right, return at midday and find the trail the buck used to exit the field. Now look for any other nearby sign—such as a rub or big track—that indicates where he'll enter. (It may be the same trail.)

TAKE A STAND Quietly hang your stand just downwind of the expected entry point, and you'll have a great shot at tagging that buck in the evening.

SPY ON THEM Glass the field from a distance for at least a week before the opener, looking for the precise spot(s) where bucks enter and their direction of travel as they feed. Time their movements, noting when they reach specific landmarks, like a tree, field corner, rock, or knoll.

STAND ASIDE When the bucks' natural movement doesn't allow for a high-percentage ambush, pick an alternate stand site. In this example, the ravine's swirling winds should keep you away. Find a mature tree upwind of their line of travel (within sight of a landmark that they reach before dark) that allows covert entry and exit.

BLUFF BIG Put out a dominant buck decoy, such as the Flambeau Boss Buck, that will test the ego of the bachelor

group's alpha male. Forget smaller dekes; you don't want Junior moving in and blowing your cover. Position the fake within 15 yards of your stand, facing the animals' normal entry. The real boss will interpret the stare of an unknown "rival" as an aggressive posture and trot over to adjust his attitude.

MOUTH OFF Call to your target buck with a grunt or light rattling if shooting light is running out or it seems he isn't spotting your deke. Once it's clear he hears you, grab your bow fast. He's apt to charge in the second his back hairs bristle. Even if it doesn't happen, there's a consolation: You've set up far enough off the action that you can come back and try again whenever the wind is blowing in the right direction.

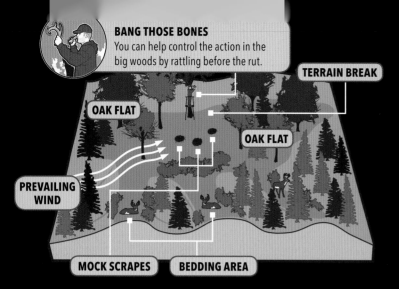

BANG THOSE BONES
You can help control the action in the big woods by rattling before the rut.

TERRAIN BREAK

OAK FLAT

OAK FLAT

PREVAILING WIND

MOCK SCRAPES

BEDDING AREA

191 RATTLE AND HUM

Big-woods hunters chuckle at the complaints of guys trying to refine stand placement over a 50x50-foot food plot they planted themselves. If you want a real head-scratcher, try zeroing in on exactly where an old buck is going to slip into a 500x500-foot oak ridge or old apple orchard. The buck can come from just about anywhere, and if he gets downwind, it's game over. So, what to do?

DON'T GET BUSTED
Set up just downwind of secondary food sources.

BUCK ROUTE

HUNTER ENTRY

APPLE TREES

NIGHTTIME FEEDING AREA

PREVAILING WIND

192 BE A BACK-DOOR MAN

A lone white oak, a clump of two or three apple trees, or any other small, isolated concentration of preferred hard or soft mast surrounded by fresh buck sign is a welcome sight to any bowhunter.

This type of food source, as opposed to a large field or clear-cut, makes it easy to predict exactly where a buck will visit so you can set up a high-odds ambush. And this type of spot is at its best in September or early October. If it were later in the season, you'd set up between

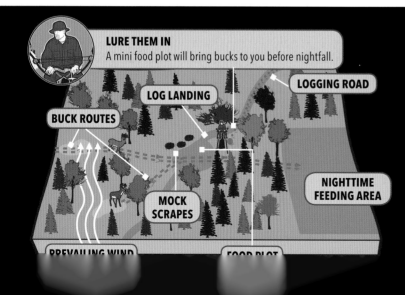

LURE THEM IN
A mini food plot will bring bucks to you before nightfall.

LOGGING ROAD

LOG LANDING

BUCK ROUTES

MOCK SCRAPES

NIGHTTIME FEEDING AREA

PREVAILING WIND

FOOD PLOT

193 SET UP A BUFFET FOR BUCKS

In farm country, early-season bucks lead lives that are divided into two simple compartments: bedding and eating (typically at large agricultural fields). But simple doesn't always mean easy. Though bucks generally hit food sources earlier now, some of the biggest, savviest ones on your property may insist on hanging back in the woods until dark. Others may randomly use two or three different routes to the chow. You can counter these habits

GET YOUR BACK TO THE WALL First, set your stand on the downwind (or quartering downwind) edge of the oak flat or orchard with a terrain-break barrier (such as a ridge or steep creek bank) behind you that will discourage a buck from circling.

MAKE A SCENE Before climbing into your stand, make a semicircle of three or four mock scrapes just upwind and within easy bow range of your tree. You don't need scent, and forget the licking branch. These aren't for long-term scent marking. Like rubs, scrapes hold a visual appeal for whitetails, and the mere sight of the dirt can bring a buck in those last few yards.

REV UP Get in your stand, pull out your rattling antlers, and make some noise. Start with some light clacking that's just enough to tempt a buck bedded nearby.

DON'T HOLD BACK Wait a second! You're not supposed to call aggressively in the early season, right? That's some accepted wisdom you can discard. As soon as a buck sheds velvet, he's ready to rumble. Some of the most brutal fights take place during the early season. That doesn't mean you should rattle on every September hunt, but this is the perfect situation for it. So put some muscle into it. Then wait till you see that bruiser trot in and spot your scrapes—you'll swear you're hunting the rut.

the buck's bed and this grub to increase the odds that the deer will reach your stand during shooting light.

But you don't have to worry about that with early-rising summer-pattern bucks, especially when the food source lies within the security of the woods. They'll show. And that lets you create a nearly fail-safe setup.

Here's how to pull it off.

SCOUT THE GRUB Inspect these secluded feeding areas now and then for early fruit or mast and any fresh sign that reveals the direction from which feeding deer come. Rainy days are best, as the rain washes away your scent.

GET AHEAD Return at midday, approaching from the opposite side the deer do. Don't walk all the way to the food. Instead, hang your stand 15 to 20 yards ahead of it. This way, you minimize the chances of bumping a close-bedding buck, and you leave no scent between the deer's bedroom and kitchen.

STAY PUT When your buck waltzes in, all that's left to do is to make the shot. Even if you don't loose an arrow, stay there until full dark and watch which way the deer head after feeding. As long as they don't get downwind, you can keep sneaking back to this stand with almost no way of getting busted, until you do seal the deal.

by luring bucks to a specific spot where they'll feel safe during shooting light.

LOG ON Find a small opening in the woods—a logging trail, a log landing, the void left by a large blowdown—that's between a bedding area and a quality food source and that also has good deer trails nearby. Hang your stand just downwind.

CLEAN UP A few weeks before the season, clear the area of grass, leaves, and debris. Scarify the soil using a weed whacker (or a heavy steel rake if you're young and tough). Once as much dirt as possible is showing, cast pelletized

PUT DOWN ROOTS Sow clover, wheat, or ryegrass after 24 to 48 hours, and then wait. Within days after the first rain, tender green stuff will begin popping up in your hidden mini food plot, and even savvy bucks will start dropping by before heading to the big field after dark.

MAKE YOUR MARK Make a line of mock scrapes with the rake or weed whacker while you're at it, ensuring that each has a licking branch overhead. These will attract bucks, too, whether or not your seeds sprout in time for the opener. The rut may be weeks away, but mature bucks won't be able to resist checking out the new sign in the neighborhood and will walk right under your stand to

194 DEAL WITH THE BREAKUP

Bachelor groups are like young lovers and rock bands. Just when they've got a good thing going, they break up. Then you're forced to go find the singles. There's no sugarcoating this: Relocating these bucks after they disperse is hard work. The key is food. Start by scouting the top food sources in the area, checking for newly opened rubs and scrapes. If you have trail cameras, set them up on these areas and check them at midday, switching them to new spots if they don't snap a pic of your buck. Meanwhile, abandon hunting for a few days and glass remote fields and food plots in the evenings. One or more of those bucks is still in the area; with effort you'll soon be back in the game.

195 GET STAGE READY

As the early season progresses, bachelor bucks are less likely to enter an open feed field during daylight. Unless you know they've switched food sources, scout for a staging area just off the main food source. Staging areas are places where bucks bide their time, waiting for the light to dim before hitting a field or food plot. To find this honey hole, simply visit the food source at midday, and start walking trails back toward the bedding area. You won't go far before you find a cluster of rubs or scrapes where bucks are working off steam as they ready themselves for dinner. Hang a stand in midafternoon, and stay on red alert, as bucks may show up long before dark.

1:00:38 AM   M 1/3
ERT

196 CHALLENGE THE BOSS BACHELOR

When you see half a dozen bucks hitting the same field day after day during the early season, it seems like tagging one should be a cakewalk. But bachelor groups are notorious for entering fields from unpredictable points—usually not close enough to your stand tree. So steer those bucks right under your perch by making a mock scrape. Mature bucks are anxious to lay down the first scrapes of the year to show their dominance to other members of the bachelor group. Your mock will punch the dominance button of the boss buck by introducing a "stranger" with the cojones to make a scrape on his turf. The dominant buck and his buddies will soon take it over and start hitting your scrapes routinely when they visit that field. And if for some reason the mock scrape isn't enough of a challenge to pull those bucks close, stake a buck decoy right next to it.

197 HUNT IN THE HEAT

Every early-season hunter who has walked away from his stand sweaty and empty-handed knows that high fall temperatures are all too likely to turn whitetails into slugs. Still, you can score in beach weather, if you follow these hints.

SHADE If you hunt hilly or mountainous terrain, focus your efforts on shaded north slopes; if your hunting grounds are chalkboard-flat, on the other hand, concentrate on areas where a dense canopy of mature trees provides plenty of shade.

WATER Wooded creek and spring corridors are significantly cooler than surrounding uplands. What's more, they provide whitetails with the extra drinking water they typically need in hot weather. The same is true of lake, pond, and swamp edges, which often feature dense, shaded bedding cover nearby, as well as convenient foods.

TIMING Dawn and dusk are the best times of day, of course, but pay special attention to subtle changes in the weather. A breezy day, a slight drop in temperature, or an overcast sky can make a big difference. And if the forecast calls for a light rain or drizzle, grab your rain suit and hit the woods. Nothing gets sluggish bucks moving like light precipitation—even if the mercury remains high.

APPROACH Hot-weather whitetails move less frequently and cover less ground when they do move. This makes setting up tight to a buck's bedding area (without invading it) almost mandatory—which in turn makes an unobtrusive approach critical. If you're hunting near a water source, as you should be, use a stream course as your entry and exit trail, or paddle a canoe across a lake or pond instead of bungling in to your stand from the uplands. When hunting north-slope timber, use the ridges to hide your approach. Once you're in a promising location, don't give up on it just because your buck doesn't show up on the first day. The following day's forecast, even if it is only slightly different, could be different enough to put that deer in your sights.

198 SEE A GOOD MOON RISING

Early-season bucks routinely trade between bed and feed, making this a great time to pattern a trophy. The big question is, when will the buck you're after be on his feet during daylight? The answer, according to Knight & Hale pro Chris Parrish, is when the moon rises in late afternoon. So convinced is Parrish of this that he limits his early-season bowhunting to a single five-day stretch when the moon is right.

"Lunar activity is 100 percent critical after deer shed their velvet," says Parrish, who tagged 140- and 170-class bucks in the past two years on afternoon moonrises. "There's no better indicator of when big bucks will be on their feet and feeding before dark." So, the $64,000 question is: How do you learn to hunt like Parrish? Here are the crucial steps.

STEP 1 In September, when it gets dark between 7:30 to 8 P.M., wait until you see the moon in the sky from 3 P.M. on. An early moonrise now will have deer—especially mature bucks—hitting feeding fields way before dark. A good moon table can help you pinpoint exact moonrise times for your part of the country. In states where seasons open later in the fall, the next afternoon moonrise often takes place before the middle of October—still early enough for this approach.

STEP 2 Since you're locked into this rather unforgiving schedule, be prepared to hunt no matter what. Have backup plans in case of shifting winds, high temperatures, or changing food sources. If a hot spell hits, Parrish hunts near water sources he's identified ahead of time or on travel routes between water and food. He also scouts fruit and mast production, which can change deer patterns. "Set enough stands that you cover every possibility, because waiting until next week to hunt the right moon is not an option," he says.

Also, because you're counting on the deer to feed earlier than they normally do, you can hunt closer to the grub than you otherwise might.

STEP 3 Stick to your mission. Parrish believes so strongly in this approach that he avoids the temptation to stretch out his hunt if he fails to put a buck on the ground. "Hunt intelligently those five days and then back off until later if it doesn't pan out," he advises. "There's no reason to hunt deer that early if all you're going to do is educate them." Instead, catch them flat-footed when the next rising-moon cycle comes.

GREATEST DEER HUNTERS

LARRY KOLLER
THE COMPLETE HUNTER

Any one hunter might routinely outsmart deer. Another may shoot them expertly with gun or bow—even with a bow of his own making or a gun of his own smithing. A few are gifted taxidermists, others skilled butchers, or fine cooks when preparing venison. But Larry Koller (1912-1967) was all of these things. And he could write about it with great deft. Jack O'Connor called Koller's *Shots at Whitetails* the "best book on deer hunting since Van Dyke's *The Still-Hunter*. A far more complete guide, the former has become the better-known classic. What little of Koller's tome is not still of practical use today is a window into a time when deer were not behind every bush and tagging a good one every year required uncommon skill. When "experts" actually had to prove themselves, Koller was the real deal.

199 FIND THE PERFECT SPOT FOR YOUR STAND

Some stands offer little more than a view, while others produce bucks year after year. Here are the 10 components of a whitetail hotspot.

4. BUCK STOP

A perfect stand is worthless if you miss the shot. Increase your odds by positioning your stand within easy range of a place where a deer will slow down or halt for a brief time. For example, a buck will stop for a quick bite at an isolated food source such as a fruit tree, pause to drink from a small pond or pool, and hesitate before jumping over a fence. Lacking these, consider digging a small pond, putting in a mineral lick (where legal), or making some mock scrapes.

1. DEER HUB

All the most likely travel corridors—in this case, the two wooded ridges, the upper field's fencelines, the creek, and the wash—point to or lead past this stand. Whether bucks are moving from bed to feed or roving unpredictably for does during the rut, they're bound to pass this spot. In the big woods, look for intersections of ridges, old logging roads, skidder trails, creeks, and habitat edges.

2. SCENT BLOCKER

Position your stand so there's a sharp decline straight downwind; this way, the prevailing breeze carries your scent above any deer that approach from that direction, or circle your stand in response to calls or rattling. (Just don't expect it to work when thermals are falling on dead-calm days.) The next best thing is to set up where an open field, a steep bank, deep water, or other obstruction discourages bucks from getting downwind of you in the first place.

3. HARD FUNNEL

All funnels are good—but hard funnels are best. A low brushy swale or a line of dark timber may encourage bucks to travel in a certain direction. On the other hand, a deep river, rock face, or sheer dropoff pretty much requires it. This steeply cut wash is a good example; it just about forces deer toward its head—where your stand is located.

FAR RIDGE

UPPER FIELD

NEAR RIDGE

STAND SITE

POOL

THICKET

5. TRAIL'S BEND

A buck that can travel into the breeze is more likely to move during daylight . . . but you and your buck can't both have the wind, right? If you look hard, though, you can sometimes find a bend in a buck's route that allows you to have it both ways–or at least close enough. A buck that beds on the far ridge quarters into the wind as he descends, but once he turns toward the pond, you have the advantage. Likewise, a buck returning to the near-ridge bed from the lower feed field can expect to have the wind once he gets past your stand. But he won't get past your stand.

6. EASY IN, EASY OUT

No stand can even approach perfection unless you can get in and out of the area without spooking deer. Here, a farm road leads to the back side of the hill behind your perch. It could just as easily be a creek bed, an irrigation ditch, a skidder trail, or a four-lane highway. The road leads to where you can quietly slip in and out, avoiding all bedding and feeding areas and leaving no residual scent anywhere deer are apt to travel.

7. CHECK STATION

A stand located on a hub of funnels is likely to see good rut action, but if that same stand is also downwind of prime doe bedding and feeding areas, you may have the hottest spot in the November woods. Note the upper field's northeast corner. Rutting bucks love to scent-check open feeding areas for hot does just downwind of places like this. In the big woods, look for similar scent-checking locations off clear-cuts and beaver-pond openings.

8. DAY TRIP

Lots of stands are either morning or evening hotspots, but the perfect stand is a great place to sit early, late, or all day long. The key is to set up so the prevailing wind blows perpendicular to the basic line of deer travel. This not only lets you sit any time of day–it means that does or smaller bucks that walk past your stand don't get directly downwind of you, where they might otherwise spook and alert that big buck that's about to step into range.

9. SOUND EFFECT

If you like to call and rattle, position your stand well above the deer, where sound will travel well. This stand, for example, is a great spot for rattling in the morning. The noises from your fake fight will fall into the lower field, where deer will be grabbing their last few bites; as well as into the doe bedding cover below, where bucks will linger looking for hot does.

10. NASTY COVER

It doesn't matter whether it's composed of tangled blowdowns, brier thickets, cattail sloughs, or dense conifers. Big bucks find comfort in heavy cover, especially as hunting pressure builds through the season. That doesn't mean they're going to live in it 24/7. But they'll be close, and you should be, too.

WASH

LOWER FIELD

200 HAVE AN EXIT STRATEGY

More hunters get busted by deer when leaving their treestands than at any other time. Why? Because while most of us are ultracareful getting to our ambush sites, we have a tendency to forget about stealth once the hunt is over—potentially ruining our best spots. Here are eight dos and don'ts for when you leave your perch.

DO have more than one exit trail to account for changes in wind direction and deer movement patterns. Make sure your trails are clear of low branches and any debris. Mark trails with tape or tacks.

DO wear a face mask and gloves as you leave to avoid glare, even in moonlight. Deer have excellent night vision, and the human face is a danger signal.

DO sneak out using a stop-and-go cadence to sound like a deer or squirrel moving through the woods.

DO use a GPS or compass to help you navigate a long, convoluted exit trail. You can't afford to get turned around and go stumbling where you might spook deer.

DON'T talk on a cell phone. If you need to send a text, hold the phone inside your jacket so the screen's light is hidden.

DON'T be sloppy about lowering gear and climbing down. Be careful not to clank the stand, ladder, or steps with your bow, harness buckles, or other hardware.

DON'T try to sneak out of your evening stand if any deer are still feeding nearby, and always avoid crossing open feeding areas in the evening.

DON'T use known deer trails to exit the area. Avoid letting your scent drift into suspected feeding areas at night, or bedding grounds during morning or midday.

201 GET IN, BE QUIET

One of the surest ways to ruin a hunt is to alert deer to your presence as you walk to your stand or blind. Here are 10 proven tips for a covert entry.

MORNING HUNTS

SET YOUR ALARM Get to your hunting area early so you can walk in slowly, quietly, and sweat-free. It's better to be in your stand an hour early than a minute late.

GET ORGANIZED Have all your gear laid out and accessible in the vehicle, which eliminates needless clanging and banging as you get prepared in the dark.

HUSH UP Turn off the radio of your vehicle before you park, and close all doors quietly. No talking at the truck or on the trail into the woods.

FOLLOW THE LIGHT Have your entry trails marked with reflective tacks or tape (or follow a GPS bearing) to avoid crashing through the brush.

BLOW BACK If you spook a deer on the walk in, wait until you hear it stop, then imitate a deer snort. Deer bumped in the dark often don't know what spooked them, and the snort will make them think it was just another deer.

AFTERNOON HUNTS

MAKE A PRIVATE PATH Clipping an entry path to your afternoon stands makes for quiet walking, but you don't want deer walking on it and catching your scent. Block the trail with a branch that you can quietly tip to the side as you enter.

CARRY A SMALL STICK Use it to vary your step cadence as you walk in so you don't sound like a two-legged predator. Or scratch the leaves like a feeding turkey.

YELP YOUR WAY IN Cluck, purr, and yelp softly with a diaphragm turkey call as you walk in.

GO UP THE CREEK A steep-banked creek makes a great covert route to your stand; sneaking along a brushy fencerow or the back side of a hill works, too.

SOCK IT TO 'EM When you're creeping close to a bedding area for an afternoon hunt, mute your clunky boots by slipping a pair of socks over them. And walk s-l-o-w-l-y. You're trying to beat a buck's ears, not a stopwatch.

CREEK

HUNTER A

40-60 YD.

HUNTER B

TO BEDDING AREA

WIND

BUCK ROUTE

TO FOOD SOURCE

202 USE THE BUDDY SYSTEM

For bowhunters, most camaraderie occurs around the campfire. That's because we typically hunt alone. But there are some situations in which hunting with someone is more than helpful; it's critical to success. This is especially true when you're rattling, calling, or decoying. Experienced hunters know all too well that deer have an annoying habit of hanging up just out of bow range or circling downwind before approaching a caller or decoy. For a solo hunter, either maneuver can spoil the hunt. Two hunters working together, however, can counter these moves.

Whitetail bucks are especially notorious for circling downwind in response to calls and rattling. To account for this behavior on an evening hunt, grab a buddy, slip into the woods and set up so that Hunter A is closest to the suspected bedding area, along a travel route leading to a feeding area.

Hunter B should take a stand 40 to 60 yards slightly downwind and to the side of the buck's typical travel route. Ideally, Hunter B can place some terrain feature—such as a creek, a pond edge, or a steep rock face—at his back that will help keep a circling buck in front of him. Hunter A should be the primary caller and rattler. An approaching buck might charge right in to his efforts, but if the deer pulls around in a circle, Hunter B gets the shot.

GREATEST DEER

THE MEL JOHNSON BUCK

DATE: OCTOBER 29, 1965
LOCATION: PEORIA COUNTY, ILLINOIS
SCORE: 204 $^{4}/_{8}$" TYPICAL

WHY IT MAKES THE LIST:

Nearly 50 seasons have passed since Illinoisan Mel Johnson shot the world record typical bowkill. Johnson, hunting from a ground blind and shooting a recurve, kept his composure as he watched the giant whitetail walk 300 yards across a soybean field and into easy bow range. Literally thousands of typical whitetail bucks have been entered in the Pope & Young record books since 1965, but none have seriously threatened Johnson's "Beanfield Buck."

203 LOAD YOUR STAND BAG

You already know to bring clothes, binoculars, and snacks, right? Here are 13 other items you need on every treestand hunt.

1. BACKUP RELEASE Bowhunters, sooner or later, you will drop your primary (or find that you've forgotten it). This way, you don't have to climb down.

2. BOOK As long as the leaves are dry and crunchy, go ahead and read. You'll hear deer coming.

3. EXTRA TREE STEPS They prove handy in so many ways, but in particular: Ever try to climb into the stand of a friend whose legs are twice as long as yours or whose family tree (it becomes obvious) is swinging with orangutans?

4. TWO PULL-UP ROPES One so you always, always have a pull-up rope. The second in case you lose the first, or you want to pull up a stand and then a bow or gun.

5. TWO HANGERS One so you always, always have a bow or gun hanger. The second for when you forget to unscrew the first one and put it back in your pack.

6. BIODEGRADABLE WET WIPES So much better than TP. Plus they're great for cleaning up after gutting your buck and wiping blood off your deer for field pictures.

7. CELL PHONE For safety's sake. But also to silently text with your buddy on the other side of the farm. And to take and send pictures of your buck.

8. DRAG ROPE I bring a 25-foot length of $^3/_8$-inch-thick braided rope for dragging because it has so many uses, such as pulling up a heavy stand more easily.

9. DUCT TAPE Because you shouldn't go anywhere without duct tape, but especially to secure your saw to the end of a long stick to cut that one annoying branch you forgot to trim when you hung the stand.

10. WIND CHECKER The wind at your stand may not be what it was where you parked or what weather.com said it would be.

11. FOLDING SAW I use this to trim shooting lanes, to fashion a handle for my drag rope, to open a buck's chest cavity . . . and that's just for starters.

12. ALLEN WRENCH For those rare but otherwise hunt-ending in-field bow or gun repairs.

13. PACK RACK I always carry a grunt tube and bleat can, but this innovation is handy because it means I don't always have to lug my heavy, awkward rattling antlers.

204 KNOW WHEN NOT TO USE A DECOY

There are situations in which you really don't want to use that decoy. These include the following.

NO SURPRISES When you're not able to put the fake in a highly visible area, don't use it; bucks don't like to be surprised by decoys.

SHY BOY When you know you are dealing with a shy, nonconfrontational buck, leave the deke at home.

FEW TARGETS When your area has few bucks, don't risk running one off by intimidating it with a buck decoy.

205 BE READY FOR THE WIDE-CIRCLING BUCK

Early in the season, a buck is likely to waltz right up to a buck decoy or circle tightly. The pressured bucks I've hunted, on the other hand, almost always circle cautiously downwind on a wide arc— at least 10 to 15 yards. In this case, if you stake your decoy 12 to 15 yards out, like most archers, that buck is going to wind up at the base of your tree or behind you, making for difficult shooting.

If you are most comfortable shooting out to 30 yards or more, stake your fake between 20 and 25 yards from your stand. This way, an aggressive buck that walks right up to the decoy is still in easy killing range, and a wide circling buck will cross right in front of your stand at about 10 yards.

206 FOLLOW THE FAKE-DEER RULES

Most deer will show at least some curiosity about any decoy they see. But whether a buck will close in to bow range and give you a good shot usually comes down to your setup. Here are five rules— and their exceptions—for staking a fake.

USE A SUBDOMINANT BUCK Doe decoys tend to attract does, which can hang around long enough to bust you. A subdominant buck decoy, on the other hand, tends to attract larger bucks looking to assert their dominance.

Two exceptions: When specifically targeting a giant buck, you may need to bust out a dominant deke. Also, it can pay to play the jealousy card during the rut by using a doe decoy or adding one to your buck setup.

FIND AN OPENING Keep your decoy in relatively open cover so that bucks can spot it easily. Decoys placed in brush, tall grass, or dense timber can surprise—and spook—an approaching buck.

PUT IT 15 YARDS UPWIND Most interested bucks will approach the fake and circle tightly to get a few yards downwind, putting them only about 10 yards from your stand—an easy chip shot. A few bucks will walk right up and face your fake. This setup puts them in easy range, too.

FACE IT QUARTERING TO YOU Even circling bucks will eventually approach your deke face to face. With your fake quarting to you, he'll likely offer a perfect quartering-away shot.

One exception: When using a doe decoy, face it quartering away from your stand—because deer will likely approach this fake in just the opposite way, from the backside.

ELIMINATE ODOR You've seen what dogs do when they meet a new pup on the block. Deer are the same. Your deke is going to get a thorough sniffing. So it's critical to eliminate (or at least mitigate) odors on the fake, whether it is human scent from carrying it in or exhaust from it being in the bed of your truck. My last step before I get into my stand is to spray my decoy down head-to-tail with scent-eliminating spray.

207 STAKE A FAKE ALL SEASON

Don't make the mistake of thinking decoys are just for the rut. Use these four setups all season long.

EARLY SEASON

Bucks are working out a pecking order now and will be curious about any intruder. Stake a fake with a small- to medium-size rack in a feed field, facing toward the most likely entry trail. A big buck will interpret the fake's steady stare as a challenge.

PRE-RUT

With bucks covering more ground, now is the time to stake a buck decoy in a known travel corridor and then rattle or call cruising bucks in for a look. Set up upwind of a barrier (fence, creek, cliff) that will prevent an incoming buck from circling downwind.

RUT

Right now, bucks pay attention to other bucks only when a doe comes between them. So place a bedded doe in a visible spot with small buck decoy standing nearby. Snort-wheeze to challenge incoming bucks.

POST-RUT

It's mostly about food now, so set up a buck-and-doe feeding pair in a hot food source like a picked corn or soybean field. This will give an approaching buck confidence that the field is safe, and if he still has the breeding urge, he'll move in to challenge your "buck."

208 BLOW A BLEAT

I bleat a lot. In my opinion, this vocalization has the greatest upside and the smallest downside. As opposed to a grunt, growl, or snort-wheeze and unlike antler rattling, a bleat won't send a shy buck packing or run off a doe I might want to put in the freezer. And so, I always carry a can-style bleat call, which is easy to use and doesn't take up much space.

The one and only downside to a using a can call is that it's not very loud. So here's a trick. When you need a little extra volume—such as when your buck is off in the distance or shuffling through noisy leaves—instead of covering the hole with a fingertip, as usual, blow into the call. This not only allows for more volume; it lets you put some emotion into the call. Now you can make a loud, urgent-sounding bleat when you really need to get a buck's attention.

HURTEAU ON:
CALLING

This happens a lot: Someone says, "Well, he just never came close enough for a shot."

I ask, "Did you call to him?"

"Nope," he answers, like it never crossed his mind at all.

Honestly, it's a head-scratcher.

Sure, it's always best to call to a buck before he has started to leave. But don't let him walk out of your life without saying something. Hit him with a grunt, a bleat, a snort-wheeze. It won't work most of the time. But once in a while, it will turn him–into burger.

GREATEST DEER

THE MIKE BEATTY BUCK

DATE: NOVEMBER 8, 2000
LOCATION: GREENE COUNTY, OHIO
SCORE: 304 $^{6}/_{8}$" NONTYPICAL

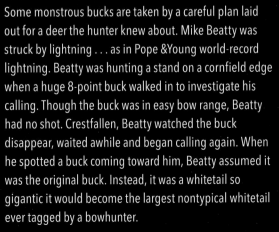

WHY IT MAKES THE LIST:

Some monstrous bucks are taken by a careful plan laid out for a deer the hunter knew about. Mike Beatty was struck by lightning . . . as in Pope &Young world-record lightning. Beatty was hunting a stand on a cornfield edge when a huge 8-point buck walked in to investigate his calling. Though the buck was in easy bow range, Beatty had no shot. Crestfallen, Beatty watched the buck disappear, waited awhile and began calling again. When he spotted a buck coming toward him, Beatty assumed it was the original buck. Instead, it was a whitetail so gigantic it would become the largest nontypical whitetail ever tagged by a bowhunter.

209 BANTER LIKE A BUCK

What do you say to a whitetail you've never met? Naturally, it can be a bit awkward, for both of you. But once you've broken the ice with a grunt or a little antler rattling, the key is to interpret the deer's body language to gauge his personality and attitude. Read his vibe correctly, and you'll have a much better chance at talking him into range. This chart details how.

SITUATION	TRANSLATION	YOUR MOVE
You make a grunt to a walking buck, but the deer continues walking, head down, ears set.	He can't hear you, thanks to distance, his own breathing, or crunchy leaves.	Amp it up before he walks off for good. Grunt loudly until he acknowledges you, by stopping or by swiveling his ears. If that doesn't work, tickle the rattling horns to get his attention.
You grunt to a walking buck. He stops to stare but then tucks his tail and keeps his head down low.	This guy has no desire for male company. He either has a meek manner or is licking his wounds from a recent fight.	Be quiet and let him relax. Then switch to soft bleats, cupping a gloved hand over your tube or can call to muffle the sound slightly. He should be more receptive to subtle girl talk.
You grunt to a feeding buck. He lifts his head to stare your way, and then flicks his tail and resumes feeding.	He knows there's a deer over there, but he's not letting the prospect of a little company spoil his dinner.	Be persistent. Grunt at him again. Typically, he'll look up and go back to feeding. But as long as your calling doesn't seem to irritate or unnerve him, he should eventually come over for a look.
You rattle blindly. A buck trots in and pauses out of range to thrash a tree and make a scrape.	He's pinpointed the fight but is posturing to show off his stuff before getting involved.	Play it cool. If this guy really felt like the king of the woods, he'd be under your stand already. So don't challenge him. Instead, grunt softly to steer him in for the kill.
You rattle to a buck chasing does. He stops and stares your way, with erect back hair and laid-back ears.	He's ticked off enough to see who proposes to spoil his love triangle.	Don't let up, or he'll remember those does. Once his gaze veers away, hit him with a snort-wheeze or growl. Get him to think there's a new stud on the block that deserves a whupping, and you'll have him.

210 TOTE A RACK

Real antlers pack more volume and produce a better sound than rattle bags, but toting a couple of main beams is inconvenient and noisy. Solve these problems by making a simple strap that lets you carry the antlers quietly and comfortably around your waist. Here's how.

STEP 1 Start with a rack that has at least three fighting tines on each side and is cut off (or shed) at the base. Brace one antler in a vise. Then, using a ¼-inch bit, drill a hole about 1½ inch deep into the bottom of the main beam.

STEP 2 With the antler still in the vise, screw a ¼x2-inch eye screw (available at hardware stores) into the hole. Use a sturdy pair of pliers to bend the eye of the screw open slightly to create a gap. Repeat steps 1 and 2 with the other antler.

STEP 3 Lay both antlers down on a bench or table. Slide the elastic section of a 24-inch bungee cord into

the gap you made in the eye of each screw. Bend the eye closed again with the pliers.

STEP 4 Your antlers are now ready for the field. During bow season, tote them around your waist, stretching the bungee cord around your midsection like a belt, or use the bungee cord to lash the antlers to the outside of a day or fanny pack. (Make sure they're hidden during gun season.) When in your stand, wrap the cord around the tree trunk to store the antlers, or use the hooks at each end of the cord to hang your horns on a nearby branch, where they'll be right at your fingertips.

211 | GET HIM OUT IN THE OPEN

During gun season, your objective in calling isn't to bring deer right to the base of your tree, but to get one out in the open where you can make a clean shot. Take advantage of the buck's tendency to circle downwind of the caller.

GET EDGY Set up within gun range of a hard edge—that is, a lakeshore, river, pond, steep bluff, or any feature that a buck will not or cannot cross. Make sure the wind is blowing parallel to the obstruction. When you call, an approaching buck will be funneled along this edge as he tries to get downwind of you. But he'll never make it that far.

USE THE WIND Take a stand in a field corner with the wind blowing out toward the open ground. Now any buck that wants to get a whiff of you has to step into the field. As long as your scent is drifting toward the middle of the opening and not the edge, you're set. Just be ready to shoot before he can get directly downwind and bust you.

212 | GET A SOUND SETUP

Hunting without a decoy? The single most important thing to understand as you decide where to set up to call in a buck is this: If the deer can see the area at the source of the calls, he doesn't need to come in to check it out. Get in position so that he is already in range when he sees that there's no deer.

RISE UP Use a rise in the terrain close to your stand to hide the source of the calling. At 20 feet up, you can see the buck, but he can't see the area near your stand. When he comes over the rise to see what's there, you've got him.

SCREEN BACK Situate your stand so that a screen of brush or tall grass separates you from the buck's approach. A buck will bust through a narrow patch of thick vegetation to get to the sound of a hot doe.

213 | TALK UP A MULEY

Mule deer bucks may not respond as aggressively to rattling and calling as their whitetail cousins— but they do respond. The best time to talk one into range is during the rut. Here's how.

FIND HIM Mule deer bucks aren't hard to spot during the rut. They are constantly moving, checking does, and looking for intruders. Gain a vantage point, glass from a distance, and shop around for a big, aggressive-looking buck.

GET IN POSITION Use the wind and cover to get within 200 yards. Set up in a final calling location that offers good cover behind, shooting lanes, and a clear view of the buck you're calling to.

HIT THE HORNS In open country, you need the sound of your rattling horns to carry, so pack a sizable set of real antlers and hit them hard. Watch the buck. If he starts walking your way, stop calling. If he only stares, keep up the ruckus. It often takes several sequences to get a wise brute to start coming in.

KEEP HIS INTEREST Once he does, drop the rattling horns. Start calling again only if he pauses for longer than 30 seconds or veers off course. If he starts looking back in the direction from which he came or begins milling from side to side, use a standard whitetail doe bleat tube or can-style call. The sound of a hot doe is often all it takes to bring him those last few yards. As the buck steps into bow or gun range, take your eyes off his headgear, take a few extra breaths, pick a spot, and shoot.

214 LISTEN TO A LEGEND ON CALLING BUCKS

Whitetail bucks are rarely more visible than just before or during the rut. This creates a common problem: You see a good buck in the distance, with no way to know whether it will move in for a shot. Do you call to this deer? If so, what calls do you make?

No one is better able to answer these questions than noted whitetail calling expert Mark Drury. "Over many years of observing whitetails' reactions to every type of calling, I've found that the mood and personality of an individual buck have a huge influence on how he'll respond," Drury says. "Being able to see the deer you're hunting is a big advantage, but only if you take a moment to judge its demeanor and let that dictate if and how you call."

HOT BUCKS Bucks exhibiting aggressive rutting behavior are particularly susceptible to calling. When Drury sees a buck come charging into a field, chasing other deer around, he stands a good chance of calling him in. With a buck like this, he'll start with light estrous-doe

bleats or tending grunts. If that doesn't get his attention, he'll increase volume by going to the rattling horns or even to the snort-wheeze call, a loud *phh-phh-phhht* sound that bucks use to challenge one another.

HUNGRY BUCKS If Drury spots a buck acting less aggressively, such as one that enters a field and begins to feed, he tones things down. "This buck may just need to fill his belly, so I'll let him eat. As soon as the deer's head comes up and he starts looking around, I'll hit him with some soft grunts and bleats. The key is to just get this buck's attention. If you can manage to raise his curiosity even a little, he may change his mood in a hurry."

TENDING BUCKS A buck that's tending a doe is one of the most difficult to call. When paired up, a buck isn't likely to move toward your stand on its own. If the doe happens to lead it toward you, there's no need to call. Otherwise, you've got nothing

to lose, and only aggressive calling will do the trick. Sometimes a challenging, in-your-face call is more than even a tending buck can stand. If you see a mature buck with a hot doe and the pair is surrounded by lesser bucks, rattle hard at him.

SHY BUCKS Some bucks frustrate even the most skilled callers. "If I see a clean-looking mature deer—one with no marks on his coat or broken tines from fighting rival bucks—and he's just slipping through the timber, I assume he's going to be difficult to call," Drury says. "Some bucks are just shy. I feel they're either nonbreeders or simply afraid to challenge other bucks." They might come to a call out of simple curiosity, Drury notes, but they're almost certain to circle downwind of you en route. Here, it may be best just to cross your fingers and hope the buck moves into shooting range. "Most of the time, I won't even call to a buck like this," Drury says. "I don't see any point in educating a deer. They're smart enough as it is."

215 GET REAL (OR NOT)

You've heard the standard advice for realistic rattling: Rake the antlers against a tree; then clash the horns for three 60-second bursts every 20 minutes; finish with a series of deep grunts. Well, forget it!

Okay, don't totally forget it. There are definitely times when this sort of ultrarealism is not over-the-top—namely, when you know a buck can hear you. In those cases, by all means, be the deer.

Otherwise, the gospel according to outdoor writers doesn't warrant a literal reading on this topic. First, the basic premise is flawed. Raking branches, for example, is not necessarily more realistic. For those who insist it is, I invite them to explain this to the countless bucks that have skipped that step during a fight. Point is, buck battles are extremely variable.

Second, bucks do not read outdoor magazines. They don't hang back listening for some deviation from the accepted rules of rattling before deciding whether or not to commit. They hear you and are interested, or hear you and are not interested, or just don't hear you.

In a great many situations—especially during the rut, when buck movement is unpredictable—you do not know that a buck can hear you. Rather, you are trying to get one to hear you as he passes through the area. So it makes no sense to conform to any particular rules of timing. Instead, keep it simple: Start out quiet in case there's a buck close and then rattle loud and rattle often.

When you're not smashing horns, focus on watching and listening for responding bucks—not fiddling with grunt calls and bleat cans and tree-raking. You can't be sure a buck has heard your rattling at this point, so why would you expect one to hear much quieter calls? Instead, save the subtlety for when you can actually see that a buck has responded, is close enough to hear softer calls, and needs extra coaxing to come into shooting range.

Until then, just bang the horns together.

216 GET THE BIG BUCK

To ambush a megabuck, you need to hunt each spot when it's hottest, and only when the wind allows. To that end, here are 10 killer big-buck stands and how to get the most out of each. Keep in mind, your ridges may be 500 feet lower than our hypothetical 600-footers, and your refuge may be a six-year-old clear-cut rather than our swamp. No matter. Apply the general principles here to the specifics of your ground, and you'll have a better shot at your dream buck.

1. RIDGE END

WHEN TO HUNT Early season, pre-rut; evening.

WHY IT WORKS Big bucks love to bed on the ends of ridges like this one, where they can escape danger by bailing straight downhill toward the swamp, or down either sidehill. Small bucks will travel the ridge's spine to feed, but a bruiser will parallel it off to one side.

TIP Look for a trail, rub, or scrape to tell you on which side of the ridge to hang your stand.

2. TURKEY FOOT

WHEN TO HUNT Early season, pre-rut, rut; any time of day.

WHY IT WORKS The ultimate terrain funnel, a turkey foot occurs where three (or more) ridges meet, eliminating the need to pinpoint which one your monster runs on a given day.

TIP It's a great spot on a calm day, as the natural thermals set up perfectly for both A.M. and P.M. hunts.

3. HIDDEN FOOD PLOT

WHEN TO HUNT Early season, pre-rut; evening.

WHY IT WORKS Mature bucks won't make it to the big cornfield until dark, but they'll hit this small, hidden food plot with plenty of shooting light left. Plant something other than conventional farm crops.

TIP Steer deer toward your stand by piling brush or felling trees.

10. BENCH BED

WHEN TO HUNT Pre-rut, rut; all day.
WHY IT WORKS This bench is both a travel route and a perfect big-buck bedding area, especially if you leave it alone in the early season. Then, when bucks start chasing does, sneak up here and hunt all day.
TIP Hang one stand on the bench's uphill side for rising thermals, another on the downhill side for falling thermals.

9. CRP SENTINEL TREE

WHEN TO HUNT Pre-rut, rut; morning and evening.
WHY IT WORKS CRP land, or any tall grassy field, is likely doe-bedding cover. In this case, it's also a perfect transition from the timber to the cornfield. Big bucks will almost invariably gravitate toward a sentinel tree, fenceline, or isolated patch of cover.
TIP This is the perfect spot for a buck decoy. Bring rattling antlers and a grunt tube to attract a cruising buck's attention.

8. SWAMP SANCTUARY

WHEN TO HUNT Rut; all day.
WHY IT WORKS Leave this tangled swamp as a sanctuary through the early season and pre-rut, and it will become an almost guaranteed big-buck refuge when gun season starts. Wait for a favorable wind then sit all day.
TIP Expect your buck to bed on a high spot within the swamp.

7. CATTAIL SLOUGH

WHEN TO HUNT Late season; morning.
WHY IT WORKS When big bucks get pressured, you can expect to find them where most hunters wouldn't look, like this cattail slough behind a farm.
TIP You may have to sit on a stool within the marsh or wear a gillie suit.

4. DARK TIMBER

WHEN TO HUNT Early season, pre-rut, rut, late season; evening.
WHY IT WORKS Big bucks will readily cross the CRP field to get to the standing corn, but they'll stick to cover as much as possible. Expect them to approach from these dense conifers.
TIP Before the rut, big bucks may move less during daylight, so wait for a cold front or drizzly rain to hunt this spot.

5. CREEKBOTTOM FUNNEL

WHEN TO HUNT Pre-rut, rut; any time.
WHY IT WORKS Brushy creekbottoms are big-buck magnets because they offer the security of thick vegetation along a natural travel route. Plus, they're a convenient source of drinking water for hard-running bucks during the rut.
TIP Look for a rub line to indicate where a buck parallels or crosses the creek, and hang your stand accordingly.

6. CORNFIELD EDGE

WHEN TO HUNT Late season; midday and evening.
WHY IT WORKS Big bucks are usually different, but the one exception is in winter, after the rigors of the rut, when they'll waltz right into this cornfield during daylight to feed. Hit this spot after an extended cold snap or snowfall.
TIP Sacrifice a day of hunting to learn exactly where the deer enter this field.

217 DIG IN FOR BUCKS

When you want to fool bucks that have seen it all, sometimes you need a whole new approach. Rick Kreuter of RK Outfitters and *Beyond the Hunt*, (and, with his wife, Julie, half of a hot TV hunting couple) digs a hole. "Making a shallow pit blind lets you get on bucks quickly and quietly. It's a different approach that has really worked well for us."

STEP 1 Go to any hardware store and buy a spade. "You want one that's short, light, and really digs," Kreuter says.

STEP 2 Go to where you are planning to hunt and pick a spot with good background cover. "If there's no cover to be had, say in wide-open farm or prairie country, use the dirt you dig to build up the back side of the blind. Also, pick a spot uphill of where you expect deer to show, if possible."

STEP 3 Check the wind and the sun. Obviously, you want the wind in your favor, Kreuter says, but it's also important to keep the sun behind you; the shadows cast by your background cover will help to keep you better hidden.

STEP 4 Get digging. For one person, make a wide, shallow, bathtub-like pit. Pile the dirt up around to add depth. Leave a few low spots as shooting lanes, and recline the back.

STEP 5 Put native plants, grass, or branches on top of the dirt to make it blend in. Now get in, sit down on a portable cushion, and wait. "If you're in the right place, bucks will walk right up to you."

218 FOLLOW THE DEER-PEE PLANNER

Urine is a big deal with deer. It's one way they communicate. So to get the most out of urine-based deer lures, you have to make sure you're sending the right messages at the right time.

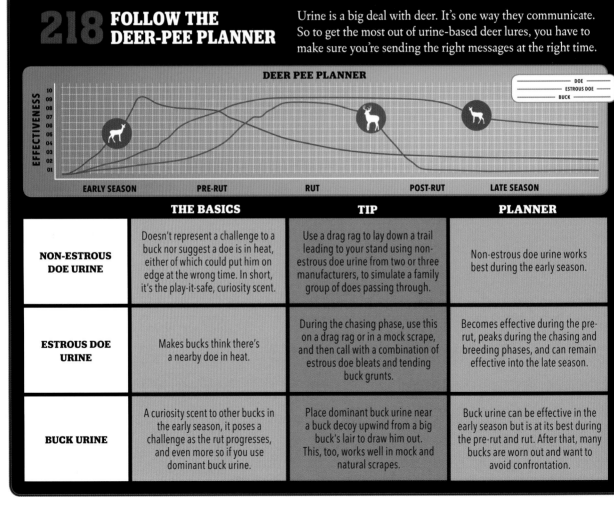

DEER PEE PLANNER

EFFECTIVENESS — EARLY SEASON / PRE-RUT / RUT / POST-RUT / LATE SEASON

Legend: DOE — ESTROUS DOE — BUCK

	THE BASICS	TIP	PLANNER
NON-ESTROUS DOE URINE	Doesn't represent a challenge to a buck nor suggest a doe is in heat, either of which could put him on edge at the wrong time. In short, it's the play-it-safe, curiosity scent.	Use a drag rag to lay down a trail leading to your stand using non-estrous doe urine from two or three manufacturers, to simulate a family group of does passing through.	Non-estrous doe urine works best during the early season.
ESTROUS DOE URINE	Makes bucks think there's a nearby doe in heat.	During the chasing phase, use this on a drag rag or in a mock scrape, and then call with a combination of estrous doe bleats and tending buck grunts.	Becomes effective during the pre-rut, peaks during the chasing and breeding phases, and can remain effective into the late season.
BUCK URINE	A curiosity scent to other bucks in the early season, it poses a challenge as the rut progresses, and even more so if you use dominant buck urine.	Place dominant buck urine near a buck decoy upwind from a big buck's lair to draw him out. This, too, works well in mock and natural scrapes.	Buck urine can be effective in the early season but is at its best during the pre-rut and rut. After that, many bucks are worn out and want to avoid confrontation.

219 GO GILLIE

Illinois whitetail expert Marc Anthony has arrowed three net Booners at eye level. His ground game is simple. He dons a gillie suit and slips within bow range of giant bucks. The hard part for the bowhunter, he says, is realizing you don't need to be 20 feet up in a tree. "Like most archers, I started as a stand hunter. But bucks were always passing out of range. One day, after watching a huge buck feed out into a beanfield, I got out of my stand and crawled toward him. Suddenly he turned around and fed back at me as I kneeled there. I drew and killed him at 30 yards. That was it. I knew I didn't need to be confined to a stand anymore."

He starts, like anyone, by working good cover. "I like wooded areas off field corners and especially hillsides. In my experience, bucks rarely walk the top or bottom of a hill. I focus on faint sidehill trails, which have been a big key to my success."

With a gillie suit and a slow approach, Anthony sneaks right up on bucks. "It may take me a couple of hours to move 80 yards. But if I see a buck, I just move right toward him." Breezy days are ideal, he says, when the ambient noise and movement help cover his own. "If there's a little bit of wind, I can draw on a buck at 10 yards, and he'll never even raise his head to look at me."

Anthony never sits. If he wants to wait a while in a promising spot, he usually just stands next to a tree that's at least as wide as his torso. "This hides my silhouette but not my draw. In most cases, I let the buck walk slightly past me before I pull the bow back. I never shoot deer beyond 30 yards, and most of my shots are 20 or under."

220 GET DOWN

Call it freestyle ground hunting—a retro tactic that has a growing number of bowhunters rediscovering the excitement of a nearly lost craft: fooling whitetails using nothing more than stealth, skill, and camo. No stand, no ground blind. Fred Bear would smile.

Here are four tips for getting close, getting drawn, and making the shot on an eye-level whitetail.

SEEK COVER Remember the handy saying: Cover behind makes the best blind. In practical terms, this means that to ambush a buck from the ground, you should set up so you have mostly unobstructed shooting in front and good cover to the rear that breaks up your silhouette. I killed an Iowa 8-pointer years ago by backing up against a blowdown. Two years ago, I arrowed a doe from in front of an upturned root ball.

BLEND IN Use 3-D leaf camo or a gillie suit (see above) if you plan on doing as much stalking as sitting. Otherwise, standard camouflage will do.

SIT TIGHT Bring a portable stool or seat. It's more comfortable than sitting on the ground and makes it easier to pivot, draw, and shoot. If you're still-hunting or stalking, shoot from your knees, which makes it harder for deer to recognize your form.

LOOK CLOSELY When setting up an ambush, mentally mark the spots—a wide tree trunk, some low brush—where a buck's vision is obstructed enough for you to draw your bow. You may need to draw early. On the other hand, if a buck surprises you, let him walk past, and double-lung him as he's quartering away.

221 CANOE FOR YOUR DEER

Some wilderness bucks die of old age without ever catching a whiff of a stinky human. That's because getting into their backcountry haunts on foot is a formidable task. So go by canoe instead.

FLOAT AND HUNT Quietly slip down a river's edge or glide along a lake's irregular shoreline to catch a big buck flatfooted as the canoe swirls around a bend (check local regs). Only the hunter sitting in the bow should be allowed to shoot from the canoe. The stern-man's job is to paddle slowly and quietly and choose a route that offers the person in the bow the best opportunity at a shot. Wear gloves to keep the paddle from whacking the side of the canoe and pad the gunnels and thwarts with a blanket or old carpeting.

TAKE A STAND As you float, keep an eye out for water crossings littered with fresh tracks. These make good ambush sites, so grab the stand you were smart enough to bring and set up.

GO FOR A WALK Look, too, for that magic line that separates mast-producing hardwood ridges and the security of lowland conifers, as float hunting provides the perfect opportunity to make several short still-hunts in the best-looking places.

MAKE NOISE Or grab your rattling antlers. Clashing the horns can be very effective for wilderness bucks just prior to the peak of the rut. Slide your canoe ashore, rattle on and off for no more than a half hour, and then move on.

GO FOR A DRIVE Because big bucks routinely feed and travel along the edges of waterways, float hunting can provide a great opportunity to stage a simple, effective hopscotch drive. Just drop the bowman off and the paddle downstream a half mile or so. The bowman can then still-hunt toward the canoe, or both hunters can walk slowly toward each other.

And don't forget perhaps the biggest advantage to a canoe: No matter how you bag your wilderness buck, you can use the canoe to get him out.

GREATEST DEER HUNTERS

LARRY BENOIT
THE TRACKER

Growing up on a hardscrabble farm in the mountains of Vermont during the Great Depression, Larry Benoit (born 1924) learned to follow the biggest deer track for one reason: it meant more food on the table. Soon he had an unparalleled record of bagging huge bucks in the big woods of northern New England. In 1970, he was named "The Best Deer Hunter in America" by *Sports Afield* magazine, and his 1975 book *How to Bag the Biggest Buck of Your Life* turned generations of stump-sitters into active hunters. He co-authored several more books with his sons Lanny, Shane, and Lane. But they take a back seat to their pop, who is widely considered the best tracker of all time. His legacy can be can be seen today on November mornings across the North Woods, when legions of hunters take to the woods clad in Benoit's signature green-checkered wool jacket and carrying his signature Remington pump rifle. They are looking for a large, fresh track to follow, but they are also following in Benoit's footsteps, using skills he passed on and a hunting style he popularized.

222 WAYLAY HIM IN A WASH

Although washes (ravines gouged into hills by runoff) are well-known deer funnels, not all have the right stuff to influence deer travel. Here are features to look for and strategies to funnel a buck into your sights this fall.

WHERE TO SET UP YOUR STAND

From the top of your wash to the bottom, there are a number of advantageous spots.

AT THE TOP
You can hunt from a flat area at the top of a wash [1] from the seeking phase to season's end because it's a favorite morning travel route for does, and once big bucks start tailing them, your odds soar.

IN THE MIDDLE
While most deer are likely funneled to the top and bottom of a wash, big bucks may use this subtle, covert soft spot [2] as an early-season crossing. Look for fresh tracks or rubs, and then set up a stand.

AT THE BOTTOM
When the wind is wrong at the top, or when the sign tells you deer travel has shifted to the bottom, sit here [3] to catch a cruising buck.

WASH FEATURES

PINCH POINT
A field edge running perpendicular to and near the top [A] and/or bottom of the wash is a huge plus, as it pinches deer through an even narrower corridor.

DEER CROSSING
Soft spots—areas where the walls of the wash become less steep—are readily used as crossings [B] and diminish the funneling effect. One is okay, but two or more are too many.

WALLS
To funnel deer, a wash must be long enough and deep enough and have steep enough walls that deer would rather skirt it than cross it. Rough terrain at the bottom [C] helps, too.

223 GET UP A CREEK

Flowing water is a powerful whitetail magnet. Here are four great stand sites; you can likely find one or more of these hotspots on any creek in your area.

INTERSECTION CROSSING Any creek crossing can be a decent ambush point, but one where several trails and funnels merge [A] is a place you really want to be for maximum opportunities.

OXBOW BENCH Oxbows always seem to hold deer. Trees and brush flourish in the fertile soil, providing abundant browse and bedding cover. It's tempting to set up right in the heart of the oxbow, but a better spot lies at either end of the elbow [B]. Cruising bucks will shortcut the oxbow and scent-check for does from this transecting trail; meanwhile, you stay out of the bedding area.

CANYON CROSSING Whitetails often carve a crossing into a very steep bank, but the trail is not the best stand site. Deer tend to be on high alert here, and, if the creek banks are steep enough, they can create swirling winds that help whitetails bust you. Better to back off to one of the flats above, where the wind is true and you can cover multiple trails leading to the crossing [C].

OAK RIDGE Many creeks have finger ridges that abut the stream corridor and drop sharply to the bank below. The tip of the finger [D] is a surefire bedding site, and a fantastic spot to catch a buck returning to his lair in the morning. If there are oak trees growing on top, even better, as bucks will grab a bite to eat before lying down. Wait for a wind that is blowing out across the creek, and no deer can bust you.

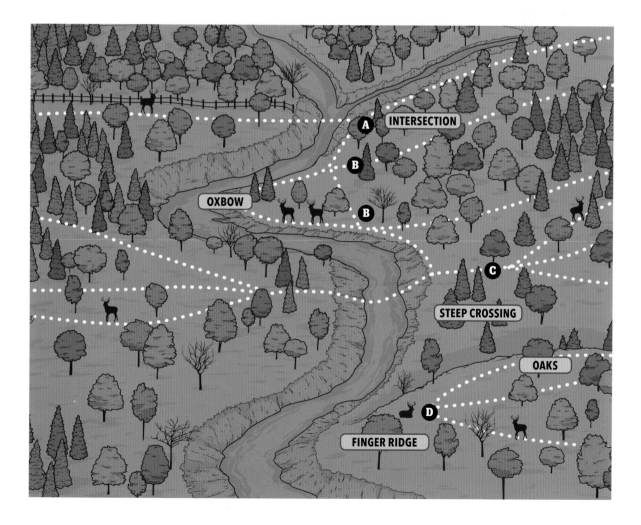

224 HUNT THE FRUIT STAND

Biologists call apples "deer candy" because these fruit offer little in the way of nutrition—yet whitetails find them irresistibly sweet. Little wonder, then, that apple trees are early-season hotspots: Bucks love their fruit, albeit primarily as a snack before the real meal. This makes overgrown orchards, as well as individual trees along the woods' edge, killer evening staging areas to catch an unsuspecting buck noshing while there's still plenty of shooting light.

FIND THE TREE Some trees drop their fruit earlier than others, and deer prefer certain apples over those from nearby trees for mysterious reasons. So, look for abundant tracks and partly chewed chunks to reveal the favored spots. Look for buck sign, too. Low-hanging apple branches incite scraping, and rubs may appear on nearby saplings.

NAIL A BUCK TRAIL Several trails may lead to the fruit. Follow each for a short distance until you find one with large tracks, rubs, or scrapes. Although few apple trees will accommodate a tree stand, many orchards abut mature timber. If there's a suitable tree within easy range of the buck trail, hang your stand.

STAY LOW Lacking such a site, set up a ground blind within shooting distance of the buck trail or the hottest tree. Hide it well with brush and give deer a few days to accept the odd shape before you settle in to hunt. Another option is to nestle a tripod stand into the crown of a nearby apple tree, cutting just enough limbs for a clear shot.

When the season starts, get to your stand or blind in early afternoon. The deer are not yet heavily pressured at this time and may head to the orchard several hours before dusk. Be there waiting, and you'll have venison in the freezer before the season even gets into full swing.

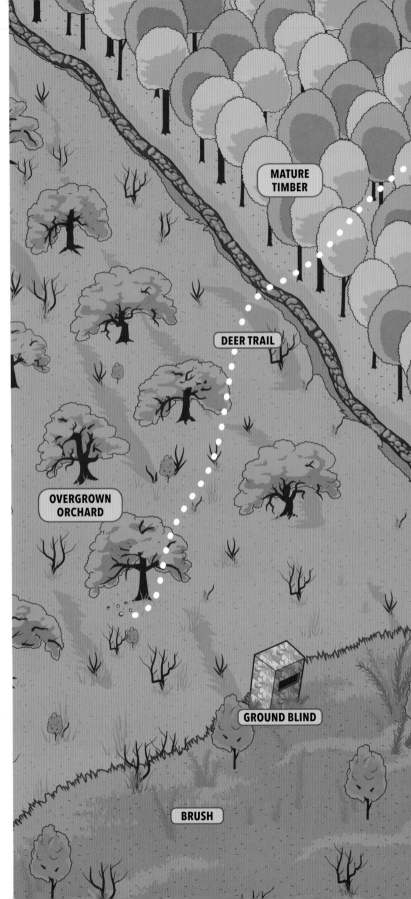

225 KNOW YOUR FIELD POINTS

Sure, a deer can step into a field from almost anywhere. But here are the top spots. During the early season—when hunting field edges is most productive—look to these features to help you determine where best to set up.

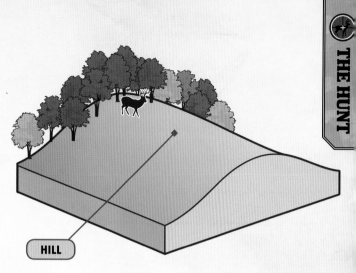

HIGH AREAS Older deer seldom enter a field without checking things out first. They often do so by scent-checking, but they look with their eyes, too. Vantage points—high places around the field's edge with quick escape routes—always have a lot of whitetail traffic.

HILL

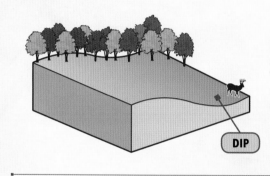

DIP

SWAGS AND SADDLES When you don't see good sign in the field's high spots, check the low spots. These are places where a secretive buck can enter unseen. These areas also attract a lot of doe traffic, which eventually attracts bucks.

NECKDOWNS Deer that are feeding on one side of a field or plot will routinely cross through the neckdown to reach the other side, making it a great place to be waiting in a treestand or ground blind for a close shot. Deer often enter and exit fields near neckdowns as well because these areas provide fast access to cover on both sides.

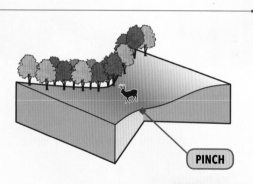

PINCH

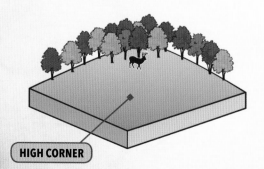

HIGH CORNER

CORNERS Field corners also offer the security of cover on two sides, and they form a natural intersection. But some corners are better than others. Look for sign, but also pay particular attention to corners that are combined with some other type of attractive terrain feature. If a saddle or creek draw funnels deer through the woods toward a particular corner that also rises to a good vantage point, your chances of taking a buck there are that much better.

226 GET YOUR BUCKS IN A ROW

An unharvested cornfield is one of the best places to find early-season bucks. That said, tagging one there can be tough. There are two keys to success in hunting the early-season stalks. First, you'll want to find a relatively small field that has adjacent cover and good structure, like a fenceline or ditch, amid the corn. Second, use the low-impact tactics below to catch a trophy by surprise.

WALK THEM UP Still-hunters should wait for a wind that's strong enough to rattle the cornstalks. The rustling will cover the sound of your approach, allowing you to get closer to your quarry.

With a south wind, crosscut the breeze. Poke only your head into the first row of corn and look left and right for bedded or feeding deer. If you don't spot a buck, slide your bow or gun between the stalks, then follow with your body. And repeat.

Any deer that you spot may be bedded, or may be facing directly toward or away from you. If your shot angle is poor, simply wait for the buck to move. Otherwise, you can slip back two rows and sneak directly toward the deer to change your angle and ensure a clean killing shot.

TAKE A STAND As bucks begin to seek does, they will be cruising any

brushy fencelines that run through or adjacent to the corn, especially when those fences connect to a different habitat type where does may feed or bed [A1 and A2].

Bucks can enter a cornfield almost anywhere, but they usually choose a low spot, like this wet, grassy swale, making B1 a perfect evening setup. If there are no suitable trees, sneak into the cornstalks and set up a portable stool at B2.

Corners [C1 and C2] make for excellent ambush sites because bucks gravitate to the corners of edge cover, especially where there's a nearby travel corridor, such as the creek. The waterway also allows stealthy access.

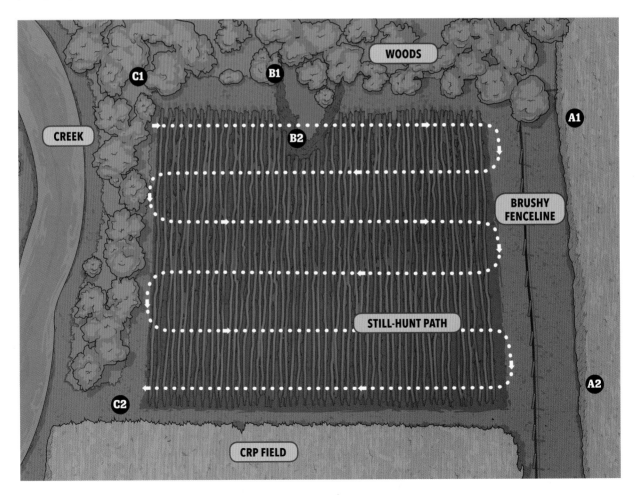

227 CREEP IN FOR THE KILL

You've heard this old saw: "The first time you sit a spot is the best time to kill a buck." Actually, I've had more success on the second or third sit. Why? Because many times a buck will leave just enough sign to let you know he uses an area, but not enough to pinpoint the one key place to tag him. If you get too aggressive on your first setup and bust the buck, your odds of tagging him there nosedive. So creep in instead, using your first setup primarily as a scouting location. Here's how.

SCOUT THE AREA Look for buck sign to determine two or three potential stand sites.

HANG BACK Place your stand in the least intrusive of these sites. Generally, it will be the one farthest from the bedding area and gives the buck the least chance of seeing or winding you—all while providing you a safe exit route. Ideally it also offers the best visibility; you want to see that buck if he makes a move.

HUNT THE SPOT If the buck comes through and offers you a shot, great. If not, don't worry. Odds are you'll spot him within a couple of sits. When you do, watch closely to pinpoint the perfect ambush point on his route.

RELOCATE If you saw the buck on a morning hunt, wait until you're sure he's bedded, then move your stand. If you saw him in the evening, come back the next day and hang the new set just prior to your hunt and wait for him to show.

228 TRY THE EASY OAK HUNT

Ironically, smack in the middle of one of the season's toughest times (the October lull) is one of the season's easiest opportunities. You can miss it completely if you're not paying attention. But if you are, if you monitor the oaks closely and are quick to notice when deer suddenly shift their feeding focus to acorns, acorns, acorns—then you are in for a simple, high-odds hunt.

When deer start hammering the oaks, they tend to favor a single tree or clump of trees above all others. It's not hard to see. Leaves are turned over, pawed, and indented with heavy tracks. The area is littered with droppings and partially eaten acorns. And this is key: Bucks often open brand-spanking new rubs and/or scrapes nearby—and at a time when only larger bucks are making such sign. The plan is simple. Hang a stand right over the best sign in the afternoon and wait.

229 HUNT THE HOT SIGN

If the October lull gives you fits no matter what you try, take heart. All you have to do is wait. In many areas, the last week of the 10th month brings an obvious uptick in rubs and scrapes. As the rut nears and testosterone rises, bucks go on a sign-making spree, and suddenly you don't have to guess where they are—because they are showing you.

One excellent way to take advantage of this activity is to forget your pre-hung stands (particularly the ones from which you haven't been seeing squat for deer), grab a lightweight climbing stand, and go hunt the very hottest buck sign.

Head to a prime feeding area at midday and walk the perimeter looking for smoking-hot buck sign—a just-obliterated tree trunk or a stinky scrape with big hoofprint in it. Basically, if the sign doesn't make you think, "Good Lordy, I need to hunt here right now!" then you should move on.

When you do find that eye-popping field-edge sign, quietly follow the rub or scrape line back into the woods a little ways, find a good setup where you don't have to do a lot of noisy trimming, climb up, and wait. If you don't kill a buck that night, do the same thing in a different area the next day, and the next. Once you're onto a few good bucks, hunt them in rotation, slipping a little closer to the suspected bedding areas each time until one of them goes home with you.

230 BEAT THE LULL

Telemetry studies prove that buck activity steadily increases through the fall. So if you have trouble during the so-called October lull, it's mainly a you problem. Here, then, are seven things you can do differently to score.

FIND THE FOOD The No. 1 reason why hunters see fewer deer in early October is because of changing food sources. While you're watching the edge of a bean or alfalfa field, the deer are eating the apples that just started dropping in the woods or the waste grain in the cornfield the farmer next door just combined. So, when you stop seeing deer, take a day to scout new food sources. And do yourself a favor: Start with the oaks. Eight times out of ten, acorns are the answer.

MOVE A LITTLE Another reason could be that the deer simply have

your stand pegged. In this case, deer often make just a subtle shift to avoid you, like a rising trout that sidles closer to the far bank when you wade in. Do some speed scouting to find fresh sign, and quietly move your setup.

WAIT FOR WEATHER Yet another reason could be that warm weather in early October has winter-coat-clad bucks moving only at the very edges of daylight (and at night). A slight dip in temperature or a misty rain can get these bucks moving during shooting hours. Watch the weather and act fast.

TRY A MORNING HUNT Many hunters avoid mornings because bucks tend to hit the sack too early to catch them during shooting light. But dawn is cooler than dusk; a warm-weather buck might linger at a morning food source, making him a little late for bed.

HIT THE WATER If your choices are to hunt hot weather or don't hunt—then hunt near water. When temps are up, evening bucks are apt to get a drink before feeding. A pond or creek near a staging area is good choice now.

GET CLOSER Another option for late-rising bucks is to simply get closer to the bedding area. Find a faint trail or rub line, slip along it to the suspected lair, and set up as close as you dare. It's risky but can really pay off.

HUNT LIKE IT'S THE RUT When standard tactics aren't working, you have little to lose and a lot to gain by getting aggressive instead. A handful of does come into estrus about a month early, and the biggest bucks know it. Rattling, calling, decoying, and using doe-in-heat scent can pull in a monster now.

231 SAY HAY

Whether it's a muley come down from the badlands or a whitetail stepping out of the neighbor's posted woodlot, early-season bucks often walk into the wide open to feed on lush alfalfa and clover fields. But where do you hide? The answer is right in front of you: The crop itself, when baled, makes the perfect cover for your hayfield setup. Scout the field to find where deer enter, and then build the blind.

With square bales, start by placing three in a line and then stack three more on top for the base. Add two more, separated with an opening to shoot through. Lay 2x4s over the opening and then put three bales on top to complete the front. Now build walls on each side, four bales high. Finish with a partial wall on the back, leaving an opening for your entrance.

With round bales, by contrast, you'll want to push two together in a V-shape so they almost meet, leaving just enough room to shoot between them. Then fill in above and below the hole with extra hay.

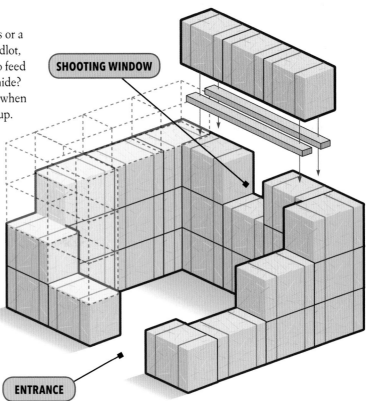

SHOOTING WINDOW

ENTRANCE

232 TIME THE PRE-RUT

Like every whitetail nut, prize-winning Adam Hays of Columbus, Ohio, knows that the last two of weeks before the primary rut is one of the best times to tag a big buck. But he focuses his efforts to just a few hours of a few days within this period. He's taken several trophy bucks then, including three giants that grossed more than 200 inches.

In his area, these narrow big-buck windows open during the last seven to ten days of October, says Hays, when bucks are primed for the rut but still following regular feeding and bedding routines. Scouting at every opportunity, he first figures out where a big buck beds. Then he walks nearby creekbottoms, wooded funnels, and fencelines to find the rubs and scrapes that reveal the buck's travel route to its feeding area.

Hays selects a tree along this path that's about 150 yards from the bruiser's bed and is situated so the approaching deer will quarter into the prevailing wind without catching his scent. Then he leaves . . . and waits for the perfect wind and a rising afternoon moon.

When conditions are right, Hays sneaks out to his chosen tree in the early afternoon and quietly hangs his stand. Once that's done, he doesn't get serious about luring a buck until the last half hour or so of shooting light. Just before dusk, he grunts softly. Then he waits 5 to 10 minutes and rattles for 15 to 20 seconds, trying to mimic a pair of bucks sparring. "If you rattle just before that buck would normally get out of bed," Hays says, "he'll come right to you."

233 MAKE A DATE WITH A SCRAPE

The problem with hunting scrapes, plenty of hunters will tell you, is that bucks visit them mostly at night. "That's true," says Bill Pyles of Ohio Bowhunting Outfitters. "But there's a very important exception in October."

Pyles maintains 26 trail cameras year-round. His photos show that 90 percent of overall scraping activity happens outside of shooting hours. But, five to seven days after the October full moon, daylight scraping activity heats up.

"Suddenly, about 40 percent of scrape visits occur during the day," Pyles says. "And we're talking visits by 140- and 150-class bucks." Still, he warns that not just any scrape will do. "Look for a big scrape back in the timber, near thick security cover," he says. You'll also want to be

looking for large rubs nearby. The best hunting lasts about 10 days. "It's a short window," says Pyles. "You have to get it right."

Guys who set up right on top of a scrape are wasting their time, according to Pyles, because mature bucks are routinely circling downwind to scent-check the sign. Instead, position your stand 75 to 150 yards away from the scrape in security cover to intercept a circling buck.

With no time to waste waiting out unfavorable winds, Pyles rings each scrape with three to five treestands. "Put your primary stand between the buck's bedding area and the scrape, if possible," he says. The rest should circle the scrape like spokes on a wheel. "This way, you've got a chance to score no matter which way the wind blows."

234 GET A SWAMP BUCK

A sea of cattails on public land probably doesn't look much like a good spot to hunt deer to most people. That's why big bucks bed there—and that's why Wisconsin's Dan Infalt, who has taken more than two dozen Pope & Young bucks, has those big deer all to himself. "The woods and fields surrounding marshlands look great," he says, "but the biggest bucks don't go there until nightfall. To tag them, you've got to get your feet wet." Here's his step-by-step plan.

STEP 1 Find tiny islands within the marsh with enough dry ground to support brush and a few trees. This is where trophy bucks bed. Large tracks and copious rubs confirm the spot.

STEP 2 Because a mature buck won't leave his sanctuary until near dark, you need to find a tree on the marsh island where you can hang a stand just downwind of the buck's exit route. Often that means setting up only 50 or 60 yards from the buck's bed.

STEP 3 When it's time to hunt, Infalt slips into his stand at midday while the buck is dozing and sets up silently. He rarely climbs higher than 10 feet; otherwise a buck so close is apt to spot him from its bed. "Just get high enough to shoot over the cattails and underbrush," he advises. Then settle for a long wait. Finally, just before dark, get ready for that big swamp buck to finally stand up and step into easy shooting range.

235 HUNT THE RUT RIGHT

The rut is dynamic, ever-changing, and downright confusing. You need a plan—like, say, two good strategies for each phase of the rut.

SEEKING PHASE	CHASING PHASE	PEAK BREEDING	POST-RUT
MAKE SOME SCRAPES Bucks will hit just about every scrape they see now, so mock up several in a transition area between feed and bed that's already peppered with good buck sign. Quietly hang a stand in the early afternoon and get ready for a monster to work over your creation.	**BEAT A BUCK TO BED** Now's the time to slip into a buck's bedding area and catch him coming home late from a night of girl chasing. Pack in a light climber or hang-on and set up in the dark. If your stand placement isn't perfect, calling will coax him in.	**STAY IN THE SADDLE** Almost every buck in the area has better things to do than walk by your stand. Almost. You're looking for that one big guy who's between does and looking for his next mate. The way to find him is to sit in a terrain funnel (like a saddle) and just hang in there all day. And call. A lot.	**RETURN TO RUBS** Mature bucks often revert to their old bed-to-feed travel routes marked by their pre-rut rubs. Watch for one or more to get freshened now, and then hang your stand within shooting distance.
SIT THE SIDE TRAIL You can find big-buck gold now not more than 20 to 60 yards off a prime feed field. Look for a faint trail or rub line that parallels the edge. Bucks will follow this discreet path to scent-check every trail leading to the field.	**FAKE HIM OUT** Bucks run to just about every deer they see right now, so exploit that weakness with a doe-and-subordinate-buck-decoy combo set up on a food-source edge.	**CHECK OUT THE VIEW** Find a breeding pair by setting up in an area where you can see a bunch of country, such as a fenceline or high spot, and just wear out your optics. When you spot a breeding pair, get down and make a stalk.	**HUNT THE GRUB** Bucks have been running big for a month, and they're hungry. And if they're looking for does, guess where they're going to find them? Right, the hottest food source. Focus on acorns, waste grain, cereal grains, and young clear-cuts.

236 HUNT THE HIGH WIND

"A stiff breeze is the kiss of death for hunting on most days," says Tim Walmsley, an Illinois whitetail expert. "But during the rut, I make sure I'm in the woods on a blustery day. Big deer will be moving."

Why would a rocking wind get bucks rolling? "First," says Walmsley, "high winds typically usher in a cold front following hot weather, offering physical relief for deer. Second, pre-estrous does tired of being harassed by bucks figure they can escape their suitors more easily when wind covers their movement and noise, so they're up and about. Bucks start catching whiffs of doe scent all over and run around trying to find the females. This builds on itself until you get a kind of chaos."

Meanwhile, gusty conditions make it harder for deer to hear and easier for hunters to go undetected. What's more, windy-day bucks tend to take refuge in predictable places, making them simpler to find. "They head to a valley, bowl, creekbottom, dense timber, or the lee side of a hill," Walmsley says.

"When the wind is pushing hard in one direction, I head straight toward these spots," he adds. Walmsley has found that it's helpful for him to listen to a radio to learn when the wind will hit. "As soon as it does, I pile out of my stand and nearly run to get closer to protected bedding cover, expecting bucks will move. I settle in until the action stops or I stop a buck."

237 HUNT RUT RUBS AND SCRAPES

You've heard many times that bucks abandon rubs and scrapes once the breeding season kicks into full swing. That's largely true. But there are some important exceptions that can help put a rutting buck in your sights now. They are as follows.

CORE-AREA SIGN Most of the rubs and scrapes that buck made in and around his core area during the pre-rut are ignored now. But even at the peak of the rut, a buck will make regular return visits to his core area—and he may freshen those rubs and scrapes, or make new ones.

DOE-AREA SIGN Rutting bucks will also open new rubs and scrapes just off prime doe feeding and bedding areas. This sign may be active for only for a short time, but it can draw visits from multiple bucks when a member of a doe family group is nearing or in estrus. Remember to keep an eye out for steaming hot rubs and scrapes to tip you off that bucks are active in the area right now and to help pinpoint that activity. This can be a great place to hang a stand or to still-hunt if the wind is right. As with core areas, use trail cameras or speed-scout at midday to check for freshened spoor. With bucks preoccupied with does and moving unpredictably, you can get away with more intrusions—and hunting that fresh sign as soon as you find it can really pay off.

238 DON'T GIVE A SCRAPE UP FOR DEAD

We've all seen scrapes go dead during the rut, and one that has been covered by leaves for days on end must surely be dead, right? Actually, not according to Patrick Willis of Kentucky's Buck Country Outfitters. Early in the rut one recent fall, a rainstorm soaked and littered a field-edge scrape line. Guessing that bucks would quickly freshen the sign, Willis hung a trail camera. Several days later, the dirt was still scattered with leaves. "We assumed the scrapes were dead," he says. "But then we saw the pictures." Seven different bucks visited the scrapes. Not one pawed the dirt, but all hit the licking branches. Willis and his clients eventually killed 130- and 145-class bucks on that scrape line. So don't assume a scrape is dead. Instead, go in at midday, hang a camera, and get proof.

239 WAIT. THEY'LL CIRCLE BACK

The latest research in doe behavior offers a key insight that can help you fill your buck tag during the chasing phase of the rut: Does are homebodies.

GPS studies prove that does have much smaller home ranges than bucks and that they cling to their turf more stubbornly. And so, they tend to circle within their home area when bucks chase them during the rut—just like rabbits chased by hounds.

Bottom line? If a buck chases a doe past you within shooting range but you don't get a shot, stay put and ready yourself for the return trip. If the action takes place out of range, take advantage of the commotion to position yourself in the perfect spot to hold out for the return trip.

GREATEST DEER

THE KEVIN PETRZILKA BUCK

DATE: NOVEMBER 19, 2010
LOCATION: SAUNDERS COUNTY, NEBRASKA
SCORE: 202 $^{6}/_{8}$" B&C TYPICAL

WHY IT MAKES THE LIST:

There have been millions of typical whitetail bucks shot in North America since B&C started keeping records in 1830; only 15 have scored 200 inches or better. Kevin Petrzilka's giant Nebraska buck not only entered that exclusive club, it landed in 7th place. Petrzilka was making a drive with his sons, Mason and Dillon, on their family farm when the buck jumped up and offered Petrzilka a single, running shot. The buck shattered the Nebraska typical whitetail record by more than 8 inches and was the largest typical shot on U.S. soil in decades.

240 GET A JUMP ON THE CHASE

The chase phase is the most exciting stage of the rut and a time when bucks are highly vulnerable. But it's all too brief and will be over before you know it if you don't pay strict attention and get ready to react.

WATCH AND LISTEN Ideally you'll see bucks dogging does. But finding kicked-up leaves or pine duff that reveals multiple sets of running tracks is another reliable indicator. You can also hear chasing: Hooves scampering over dry leaves, sticks breaking, a buck grunting, even a doe snorting or bawling. In short, it sounds like a deer stampede.

HANG WHERE IT'S HOT You can expect that area where you've identified chasing activity to stay hot for several days. So go back there with a climber or featherweight hang-on and set up for an ambush. Where exactly should you sit? Favor thick doe bedding cover, any natural travel lanes, or pinch points within the general area.

JOIN THE FRAY Another good option is to get even more aggressive, especially if you're gun hunting. If you see or hear a chase happening nearby and it doesn't seem like the deer will come your way, hurry over and get involved. Remember, bucks are going nuts and does are in a panic, so they often won't notice you. Try to cut in front of the deer to get a shot. Or, just wait.

241 CALL THE CHASE

In that frantic period just before the peak rut, when does are running from prying noses in every direction, calling bucks away from their hard-to-get girlfriends may seem like a tall order. In fact, the chase phase is one of the best times to talk a trophy into shooting range.

Not quite ready to be bred, does bolt away when suitors get too close. Invariably, some bucks temporarily lose contact with the female. Suddenly alone, they use all their senses to relocate the doe, making your estrous bleats and contact grunts potentially deadly.

Don't have a grunt tube or bleat call handy? Simply scuff the leaves to imitate the footfalls of a nearby doe. Lone bucks will react to the sound of another male, too, thinking he may be with a doe. So another good trick is to rub a dry stick against a sapling to imitate the sound of a buck taking out his frustrations on a young tree. Or rake leaf litter to sound like a buck making a scrape. I always toss the duff high into the air, as the sound of debris pelting the forest floor seems to bring these bucks running. Just remember, when a wild-eyed bruiser charges your position looking for love, you'll want to either shoot or run. So be ready to shoot.

242 HAVE A GREAT WEEKEND

It's tough to pattern pre-rut homebody bucks from far away, but once those deer start roaming during the rut, intercepting a good buck can become a routine matter with the right plan. Try this Friday-through-Sunday rut-hunt itinerary.

▶ FRIDAY

1 P.M. Arrive at your hunting property in time to scout and set up for Saturday morning.

1 P.M. TO 4 P.M. Hit the field, looking for well-used trails between bedding cover and food with both fresh doe and fawn tracks. Pick the spot with the hottest sign and hang a stand nearby to waylay bucks checking on these family groups on Saturday morning.

4 P.M. TO DARK Glass feed fields until dusk, looking for doe-and-fawn family groups and/or bucks to determine where you should place your ambush for Saturday afternoon.

EVENING Review the lay of the land in maps and aerial photos. Identify cover and terrain funnels specifically for Sunday's hunt.

▶ SATURDAY

PREDAWN TO 11 A.M. Get to your morning stand about a half hour before sunrise. When shooting light breaks, grunt several times and wait. If there's no response, hit your rattling antlers hard to attract cruising bucks.

11 A.M. TO 2 P.M. Climb down from your stand and go prepare for Sunday's hunt. Speed-scout the funnels you previously located on the map, and then hang a comfortable stand where two or more good travel

corridors intersect in the vicinity of both food and thick cover. Bucks will cruise here, looking for does.

2 P.M. TO DARK Hunt the afternoon. If yesterday's glassing paid off, you'll know right where to go. Bring along a climbing stand and set up in a staging area just off the field where you spotted deer.

▶ SUNDAY

PREDAWN TO NOON Sit the funnel stand. On your way in, trail a drag rag soaked with doe-in-heat scent from a boot, freshening it every 75 yards or so. If you're hunting with a bow and the terrain is fairly open, stake a doe decoy just upwind of your stand and hang the drag rag nearby.

NOON TO 2 P.M. Take a break, have lunch, Make sure there are no deer in sight, and then stand up, stretch your legs, have a sandwich . . . but stay alert.

Mature rutting bucks are notorious for cruising corridors around midday.

2 P.M. TO DARK. Get settled, refocus, and hunt until it gets too dark to hunt any more.

AFTER DARK Pack up and leave in time to say good night to the kids when you get back. Drive home. On the way, justify the money you'll spend on getting that monster trophy in the bed of your truck mounted.

243 GET IN THE BEDROOM

With rutting bucks frantically searching for females, it makes perfect sense to camp out in prime doe feeding and bedding areas now. And with does spending most shooting hours on their bellies, it makes sense to start in the bedroom. Here's your three-step plan.

FIND THE BEDS Start at a prime food source and walk into the woods, concentrating on gentle brushy knolls or benches, overgrown pastures, pines, and tall grassy cover. Look for groups of oval depressions of differing sizes. Mark as many such bedding areas as possible on a topo map. Then study your map for travel corridors that connect them, such as creek beds, gullies, or thick cover.

SET UP Mature bucks will scent-check a group of does from the downwind edge of the bedding area, making this a prime spot to hang a stand. As the rut progresses, bucks will constantly move from one doe bedding area to the next along connecting travel routes; hang stands here, too.

ROTATE Does come into estrus at slightly different times. If the does in a group seem nonchalant and mostly interested in eating, find a more active group. If you spot a large doe that's particularly active, pacing around, and glancing over her shoulder, that doe is ready for a mate, and you should focus on her group. Check the first group again in a few days—unless you already got your buck.

244 LURE A RUTTING BUCK CLOSE

If you've watched many hunting shows, then you've seen one big-racked whitetail after another march up to a buck decoy and kick its plastic rear end. What you rarely see, however, is how effective doe-decoy setups can be, especially during the rut. Try these three.

FUNNEL FAKE-OUT It's common knowledge that funnels and pinch points make good stand locations any time of year. The trick, of course, is getting a buck to travel through the particular funnel you happen to be hunting. Spray down a standing doe deke with scent eliminator and place it in the pinch point about 20 yards upwind of your stand. Make sure it's in a spot where cruising bucks will be able to see it. Walk a scented drag rag to the decoy from the direction you expect bucks to approach and hang wicks with doe-in-heat urine in a circle around your stand.

WOODS WAYLAY Rutting bucks love to cruise open hardwood flats to check for does nibbling browse or chomping hard mast. But with few edges or terrain breaks to funnel deer, these areas are tough to hunt with a bow. Stake a feeding doe decoy over the grub and run a drag rag with doe-in-heat scent 100 yards to each side. Hang your stand just downwind of the fake and call with a combination of tending grunts and doe bleats.

THE BEDROOM SCENE When the seeking and chasing phases of the rut are over and bucks are actually breeding does, the tactic of targeting known doe bedding areas can be the deadliest decoy setup in the woods. Bucks may be lying down with the does now, so don't barge into the bedding area. Instead, place a doe decoy in plain view off the downwind edge of the bedroom. Hang your stand nearby and call using doe bleats.

245 FOLLOW THE BREEDER

Can't find a good buck track to follow after a fresh overnight snowfall? No problem. Get on the right doe trail, and bucks will actually come to you.

DOES IN HEAT When you find doe prints, follow them and look carefully for rose-colored urine stains in the snow. This is a dead giveaway that she's in heat. Also, look to either side for the tracks of a flanking buck or two. If she's close but not quite ready to stand, bucks will zigzag her trail like skiers running a slalom course. You can't miss it.

THE SOLO DOE When you find only the rose-colored stains, and it's clear the doe hasn't caught the attention of a buck yet, follow her trail, being careful not to spook her. And keep an eye on the flanks. Eventually, a passing buck is apt to spot her, move in to check out her breeding status, and give you a shot.

THE CHASE If the tracks tell you that your doe already has an admirer or two, follow her trail, staying far enough back to not spook the bucks, and wait for an advantage. Or if the doe seems to be circling, then your best bet may be to have a seat. The doe will eventually return to the area, suitors in tow. Just don't shoot at the first forkhorn that prances into view. It's usually going to be the biggest buck that brings up the rear.

246 MAKE A TWO-MAN LOCKDOWN STALK

During the lockdown, tending bucks commonly push does out into open farm country, which presents a prime stalking opportunity if you can recruit a buddy to help.

STEP 1 Mount a good spotting scope on your vehicle's window with a clamp. If you don't have a spotting scope, quality binoculars can work in a pinch. Then, with your buddy along, drive the back roads, carefully glassing open areas near known deer hotspots. The first hour of daylight is the best. Take the time to visually pick apart small bits of cover, such as fencerows, grassy waterways, weed patches, brushy clumps, and terraces.

STEP 2 Carefully plan your approach. The wind is the most important factor; the lay of the land is second. Be sure to choose a backup route because things can look different once you're out there. Pick some features as reference points and a destination feature from which to take your shot. Finally, work out a system of hand signals that your buddy can use to help guide you.

STEP 3 Now grab your gun or bow and get stalking. But don't rush it. The deer will likely stay put for the majority of the day. So take all the time you need, and use binoculars to check your buddy often for hand signals. This is not an easy way to bag a mature buck, but it can be one of the most exciting.

247 KILL A MIDDAY GIANT

Many hunters have found that midday hunting can be good during the rut, but whitetail expert Pat Hailstones of Cincinnati, Ohio, is fanatical about it: "Hunting early and late in the day is practically a waste of time now," he says. "I see plenty of little bucks then, but not the big boys. When the rut kicks into high gear, I usually sleep late." Don't think Hailstones lacks motivation. His passion for big bucks has helped him tag more than a dozen Pope & Young whitetails, including a pair of Booners. Most of them have fallen between 10 A.M. and 2 P.M.

"In 30 years of hunting, I've seen the same thing in every state I've hunted, including Ohio, Illinois, Kentucky, Missouri, and Kansas," he says. "Trophy bucks don't run helter-skelter early and late in the day like younger bucks do. The does are moving then, which makes them harder for bucks to find," Hailstones explains. "The bigger, smarter bucks wait for does to lie down for the day; then they rise and circle downwind of bedding areas to scent-check for does that have come into estrus." Hailstones intercepts midday bucks by setting treestands along overgrown fencerows and other funnels that connect doe bedding areas. To prevent the bucks from getting wise to his setups, he doesn't go near these stands until the breeding season begins. "Even at the peak of the rut, there will be days when you don't see anything at midday," Hailstones says. "But when a buck does come by your stand, it's going to be a good one."

248 LEARN 5 LOCKDOWN SECRETS

Steve Snow doesn't sugarcoat the challenge of hunting the peak-breeding period, known by many as the lockdown. "It's godawful horrible for about a week every fall," says the Iowa expert. But Snow, a 41-year-old bowhunter with some 40 P&Y bucks to his credit, isn't giving up; some of his most memorable bucks have come in a week that stymies many hunters.

START OVER Your first job is simply finding the deer. They might be just about anywhere, Snow says. To find them, you need to scout almost as if it's the preseason again by doing a lot of glassing and sitting in observation stands.

LITTLE BUCK = BIG BUCK Snow isn't after young bucks, but he doesn't ignore them. "Any time a mature buck has an estrous doe pinned down, there will usually be several smaller bucks nearby," he says. "If you watch them carefully, one will eventually wander too close to the big guy, who will stand up to warn him off and then lie back down."

WALK RIGHT IN If the habitat isn't good for glassing, Snow recommends scouting to find bucks. "Once you start jumping does or small bucks you can set up a stand nearby or begin still-hunting the area immediately with a decent chance of getting lucky."

GO CRAZY With whitetails using offbeat covers, Snow isn't afraid to experiment. "For several years, I noticed bucks hanging near a lone maple in a CRP field during lockdown. I finally decided to hang a stand there, and I felt completely foolish doing it. Now I call that spot 'The Magic Tree.' Give me an east wind during peak breeding, and I just know I'll see a monster there."

TAKE IT TO 'EM When you do find peak-breeding bucks, quietly setting up and hunting a stand in the area can lead to a shot. But in the right conditions, Snow may sneak into bow range instead. "If you keep the wind in your favor and move slowly, you can get right in on them."

249 WALK ON BY

When I lived in Grayling, Michigan, I had the honor of meeting legendary bowhunter Fred Bear. He pointed out that deer were quick to react to hunters who skulked through the woods but often stood still for humans who appeared to be out for a walk. The trick, he said, was to avoid eye contact and wait until you had passed the deer before turning smoothly to draw your bow. I never became proficient enough to take a deer with an arrow this way, but the trick has put more than one deer in my freezer when I had a rifle in hand.

250 GO STRAIGHT AHEAD

How many times have you seen a deer and attempted to work to one side for a shot, only to have the animal bolt the moment you moved? Rocky Miller, one of the West's preeminent deer hunters, believes that deer are less able to perceive a hunter heading very slowly but directly toward them. He's had great success by advancing straight at whitetails and mule deer that he can see. His method requires tremendous patience, but on numerous occasions he's been able to get within yards of unsuspecting deer.

251 LISTEN TO A LEGEND ON STILL-HUNTING

Master still-hunter Ken Petrie has bagged more than 50 bucks on public forest lands in the Northeast. He regularly tags mature animals in the Adirondack Park's High Peaks region, one of the toughest places to hunt whitetails in North America. Here are his top five lessons.

COVER GROUND You can't spend all day crawling along in the mountains or you'll never find deer. I go fast until I find fresh sign. Then I slow down.

TAKE PATHS TO SUCCESS I follow deer trails as much as I can. They take me to deer. They're easier and quieter walking, and deer are used to seeing movement on trails.

READ TERRAIN AND COVER Passes, saddles, shelves, ledges, and the heads of beaver ponds are all hotspots—travel routes and funnels that concentrate deer. I also like to hunt in and out of the high, green edge where the spruces and firs meet the hardwoods.

HAVE SOME SCENTS I don't worry about the wind. In the mountains, it's going to do what it's going to do. But I keep a big, stinky tarsal gland from a previously harvested buck attached to my belt, and I use Tink's 69 buck lure on my boots. I don't think it attracts deer, but it might confuse them long enough for me to get a shot.

BE VOCAL If I find fresh buck sign, I'll cold-call with an estrous can and grunt tube. And if I bump a buck that moves off blowing, I'll blow back and then use the can and tube. He'll often come right back.

252 FOLLOW THAT FLAG

Here's another great still-hunting trick from Maine guide Randy Flannery, who says too many still-hunters think their luck is up when they see a flag. "They figure, 'I blew it' and go to another spot," he says. But why go somewhere else when you know a deer is close?

"First off, I guarantee you'll improve your luck tenfold if you cross-cut the wind instead of still-hunting into it, whether you jump a deer or not. But if you do jump one and he doesn't blow, open the action on your rifle and run forward at a 45-degree angle toward the downwind side about 75 to 100 yards. Then drop to one knee and wait 10 to 15 minutes. When that buck circles downwind to see what spooked it, you'll often get a shot within 30 to 60 yards." If the buck does blow, Flannery says, run right at him 100 yards or more. "He'll be running at the same time, so he won't hear you. Then, usually somewhere between 75 to 200 yards, he'll slow to a trot or even stop as he starts to swing downwind. If he makes that swing early, there's a good chance you'll tag him."

253 HEAD INTO THE DITCH

When the late season serves up rain or snow, Indiana Hunter Brian Bice knows where big bucks hole up. "They'll stay bedded during the bad weather, so there's no point sitting in a stand," he says. "But with the ground so damp, you can slip quietly along a stream bank or swale and get very close to a big buck."

The hunkered-down deer typically face downwind, says Bice, so he prefers to hunt with a crosswind, which lets him approach from the side, away from the deer's line of sight. Also, if he jumps a buck and doesn't get a shot, he can swing downwind 100 yards or more to meet the deer as it circles to get a whiff of what spooked it.

Bice zigzags through the cover, throttling down as he approaches brushpiles, blowdowns, and clumps of tall grass. Wherever possible, he tries to spot his quarry first. "But I'm also looking to kick a buck up to get a jump shot." He carries a quick-handling gun with open sights at port arms and is always ready to make a quick decision and a good, fast shot —which is just what he did on a rainy November day in 1992, when he bagged a 27-point, 256-1/8-inch colossus. Two snap shots and the 6½-year-old giant was down 30 yards away along the water's edge.

HURTEAU ON:

WHY I LOVE STILL-HUNTING THE BIG WOODS

When you are still-hunting well–when the sound of your footfalls sinks into the duff and you are not moving too fast, for a change–you feel like you deserve to see a deer. You sense not just that you could see one at any moment (a rare enough feeling in the hinterlands) but that you should.

But the big woods quickly cure you of such nonsense. You don't deserve anything. You get what you get. And you usually get zip, and more zip, and then some more of the same, maybe for days on end.

Then suddenly, impossibly, there's a buck. Poof. Like magic.

When I hunt farmland I expect to see deer. No big deal. But when I see a deer in the big woods, it's always a surprise–almost a shock– and it never gets old.

254 WALK LIGHTLY

In all of deer hunting, there's nothing so challenging and rewarding as walking up a big wilderness buck. In a treestand, you all but deny a buck its eyes and ears. Following a track, you know there's a deer at the end. On a drive, you have your buddies to thank.

But when still-hunting the big woods, you usually walk alone. You don't know where the deer are—the nearest buck could be right in front of you or a mile away. And it's you, as much as the deer and often more, who is skulking and slinking and throwing shadows and rustling leaves and brushing branches. Seeing a buck before it sees you is a serious challenge.

It's a near-insurmountable one if you don't know how to be stealthy. Here are two basic ways.

WALK QUIETLY With few exceptions, the only time you can truly walk quietly in the woods is when the woods are quiet—when the forest floor, damp with rain or melting snow or dew, absorbs the sound of your steps. But even here, drier leaves can rustle and sticks can crack loudly underfoot. Take short, balanced steps. Keep your weight on your back foot, using your lead foot to probe the ground ahead for noisy sticks or litter. Once you find a quiet footing, gradually shift your weight to your lead foot and repeat. Find the quietest footholds of moss, rocks, or bare earth; use rolling terrain to stay hidden; time your steps with gusts of wind; and stay in shadows— lurk just inside the edge of thicker cover, where your movements are screened but you can see out clearly.

WALK LIKE A DEER On a dry forest floor, it's impossible to still-hunt silently—so don't try. Instead, walk like a deer, which after putting a front hoof down immediately follows with the opposite back hoof, in a step-step, pause, step-step cadence. Most still-hunters mimic this by stepping down sharply with the toe of the lead foot, and then bringing the heel down. Step-step. Then repeating with the other foot. Step-step. I find it more comfortable and just as effective to jab my heel down first, then drop my toe.

Pause frequently at odd intervals, like a deer does. Go ultraslow in the most promising areas, and use a grunt tube or fawn bleat to further the illusion. The deer will hear you coming, but as long as they think you are one of them, they'll often let you get close enough for a good shot.

255 SPOT A RACK FROM ABOVE

Author of *Still-Hunting Trophy Whitetails* and an *F&S* contributor, Bill Vaznis has killed some 75 deer from the ground. When the foliage is down, spotting a bedded buck becomes easier—especially if you focus on finding his rack, says Vaznis. "A bedded buck moves his head in response to subtle changes in the wind. He looks side to side at squirrels, birds, or leaves kicked up by a breeze. When that rack swivels, you pick it right up. Yes, you should look for a black nose, a white throat patch, the horizontal line of a deer's back. . . . But if you key in on the rack, you'll spot that movement through the bare branches of even dense thickets."

One of the best ways to spot a rack now is to get above the deer in the morning when thermals are rising. "Late-season bucks love to bed on south-facing slopes, typically about a third of the way down from the top near a blowdown or thicket, usually facing downhill," says Vaznis. "If you work slowly along a ridgetop, sidehilling just down from the crest to keep from being silhouetted, you can glass downhill to spot the rack of an unsuspecting buck. Pay special attention when you get near the end of the ridge, as bucks love to bed there."

You may already be in rifle range of the deer when you see that rack swivel. But if you're carrying a bow, as Vaznis often is, he recommends moving to put a large tree trunk between you and the buck. "Then just slip straight up to that tree and repeat until you're in bow range," he explains. "Finally, peek around the tree and picture your shot. Using the trunk as a shield, come to full draw. Then you just have to go for it: Take a step out and shoot."

256 BAG A BLACKTAIL

Donny Warren of Backbone Creek Outfitters and his clients annually shoot trophy class bucks from the rugged mountains of northern California. Follow his tips to score on these elusive trophies.

START EARLY "Start scouting in late spring and early summer. I'm finding bucks at 7,000 feet as early as May."

TAKE A PICTURE "I put cameras pointing down well-used trails and water holes and springs in the timber. It's hot here in summer and bucks are drawn to water."

GO HIGH WITH A BOW "When archery season opens in August, the good bucks are all in the high country. I set up my camp as high as I can get, so I can get into my good glassing spots before first light."

GET BEHIND THE GLASS "I try to find a spot where I can glass a brushy bowl, a grassy hillside, or open timber where bucks like to feed in the morning."

KEEP COVERT "There's a lot of thick timber here that bucks like, but if you try to still hunt that stuff, all you do is bump the deer you could stalk later."

KEY ON THE MIGRATION "When we start getting some cold weather in the high country the bucks will start moving to lower elevations on old migration routes. Get on one of these deeply rutted trails and just wait. You might sit all day and not see a deer, but the next morning you'll see two dozen by 10 o'clock."

FIND LOW-HANGING OAKS "When bucks migrate from the high country, one of their favorite places to winter are oak thickets at low elevation. I scout black- and pin-oak thickets and focus on spots where l I find good feeding sign."

FLEE THE CROWD "Elevation and thick cover intimidates most hunters, but one of my favorite low-elevation oak thickets is a simple 1-mile hike on a logging road. But that road is gated; if you can't drive to a spot, most hunters aren't interested."

257 HUNT THE SWAMP, TWO WAYS

In wilderness areas, many of the biggest bucks feed or chase does in the hardwood ridges at night and then move down into thick, evergreen growth of swamps and flowages to bed and rest up during the day, says veteran Maine guide and friend Randy Flannery.

He suggests you check the wind in the morning and then study the drainages on your topo map. What you're looking for is a creek, a beaver flow, or a linear swamp that (a) connects two roads and (b) lets you crosscut the wind as you work its length.

Next, grab a buddy and drive two vehicles to the area. You park at one end and, in the case of a flow, begin paralleling upstream. Your buddy parks at the other end and works down the opposite bank. "A buck bumped by the upwind hunter is apt to circle downwind into the other's sights. And a buck that's been bumped by either may well follow the natural funnel of the flowage or swamp right to the other hunter."

When you meet, shake hands and keep going to the other end of the area. "You can drive your buddy's car home, and he'll drive yours. Or you'll both drive one car to the other, after your friend helps you drag out your buck."

If you're hunting alone, you'll want to do the same things but plan on reaching your farthest point at midday, and then work the opposite side back in the afternoon, as bucks begin returning to the ridges to feed. Whether it's a swamp, flow, or creek, remember that the water's edge acts as a travel corridor for bucks, so keep it within sight and gun range as much as possible.

Flannery will occasionally work the high side of slopes in the lowland terrain to stay above traveling or bedded deer. As you hunt, expect a buck to jump up from every blowdown you see. "You may catch a buck on his feet, but he'll likely spring up from his bed 20 feet in front of you. And it's going to happen fast. You need to be ready to shoot."

258 TAKE THE WHEEL

"Most deer drives are designed to push deer into open cover," says northern Wisconsin expert Tom VanDoorn, who has taken 30 big-woods bucks age 2 ½ years or older, including a 160-class P&Y. "But pressured bucks don't want to expose themselves. Rather, their instinct is to circle and hide." To counter this, VanDoorn employs a tactic he calls the wagon-wheel drive. "It's a drive in name only," he says. "You're not trying to push whitetails anywhere in particular; you're just bumping them up and letting them do what comes naturally."

First, grab a treestand. (Don't worry; nobody sits for long.) Then grab a buddy and walk to a clear-cut, swamp, or grown-over beaver pond where a stand tree offers decent shooting. Hang the stand, have your buddy climb in, and then you walk straight away from him on a line toward the most likely bedding cover, such as a clump of brush, a dry hummock in a swamp, or tall grass along a stream. "When you bump a buck, he'll run straight away to avoid the danger at first," says VanDoorn. "But then he'll circle back, potentially giving your buddy a shot."

Once you reach the edge of the thick cover, just double back, switch roles with your partner, and repeat the process. Viewed from above, the paths of the drivers would look like spokes on a wagon wheel.

259 TAKE DRIVING LESSONS

How can you improve your driving skills? Pay attention to the following 10 lessons.

KEEP YOUR MOUTH SHUT Barking like a dog, whooping, or banging pots usually hurts your chances because it gives your exact position away. It's better to have a big buck guessing where you are. Plus, when he does move, you want him walking past the posters—not hightailing it because he's scared out of his wits.

STOP Instead of yelling or barking, simply halt in your progress when you come to a promising thicket. A skulking buck will think you've seen him, get nervous, and get moving.

USE THE WIND Everyone knows to post blockers downwind and drivers upwind. But you can actually use a breeze to your advantage before you even start the push. Have drivers get in position and just hang out upwind for a while. Their scent may be all it takes to nudge deer slowly past the posters.

FIND FUNNELS Funnels are fundamental to stand hunting, but deer also follow them when fleeing drivers.

KEEP OUT One of the surest ways to increase your driving success is to put a few choice areas of security cover off limits from day one. Bucks pressured elsewhere will move into your sanctuaries—and be there when you're finally ready to push it.

DRIVE IN REVERSE When you have a draw or a finger of woods that juts out from the main cover, try driving into the wind. That is, slowly still-hunt toward the narrow end of the draw or finger as another hunter or two posts downwind, just inside the main cover, to catch bucks slipping out the back door.

FIND NATURAL BLOCKERS Take advantage of any natural features that look likely to block bucks from fleeing in a given direction, thus helping steer them toward your posters.

POST BLOCKERS EARLY Sensing distant noise or movement, heavily hunted deer sometimes realize a drive is being set up and sneak out before it even starts.

WATCH THE WEATHER When it's snowing sideways, raining buckets, brutally cold, or unusually hot, bucks tend to hole up in thickets, making drives especially productive.

YELL AT A BUCK Finally, if a driven buck comes screaming past you too fast for a good shot, try yelling, "Hey, buck!" You've got nothing to lose, and he may pause to look or at least slow down, offering a better shot.

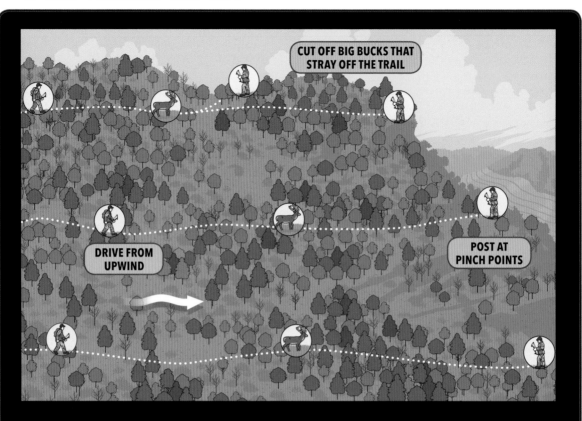

CUT OFF BIG BUCKS THAT STRAY OFF THE TRAIL

DRIVE FROM UPWIND

POST AT PINCH POINTS

260 DRIVE A HILLSIDE

Bucks love to bed on hillsides and ridge ends in steep country. Bob Borowiak, a Minnesota whitetail expert who's taken more than 20 Pope and Young bucks, suggests some ways to get those deer on the hills up and moving.

THE THREE-MAN DRIVE TEAM Three drivers start pushing from upwind to get the deer moving through the woods. "The hunters should stay on the best whitetail trails," Borowiak advises. "Bucks will not be far off of these trails, and with the wind at the driver's back, he should be able to kick out most of the whitetails ahead of him."

THE CONCEALED POSTERS Three to four posters should set up downwind. "Good camouflage is an absolute must, because you will be on eye level with deer," says Borowiak. "I like to watch from several feet behind good screening cover. I often grunt to stop the deer, since they're usually moving."

THE ESCAPE ROUTES If you don't push the deer too hard, most of them will take the major trails toward the ridge end. "Typically, there's a good trail running along the top of the hill, another trail at the bottom, and one somewhere in the middle of the hillside," says Borowiak.

THE PINCH POINTS In order to significantly increase your chances of being in range of one of the passing whitetails, don't set up just anywhere on the escape routes. Take a stand at a pinch point, such as the head of a wash or a bench, that will steer the bucks right past you.

The biggest bucks may stay on the main trail, but they are still more likely than other deer to try to slip out the side of the drive. "If you're going after a mature buck, cover these routes," says Borowiak. "Posting in a saddle along the ridge, for example, is a smart move."

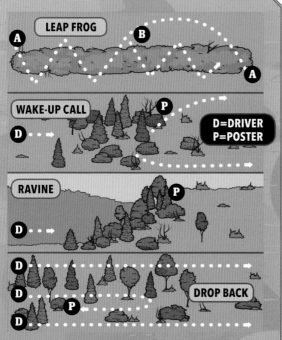

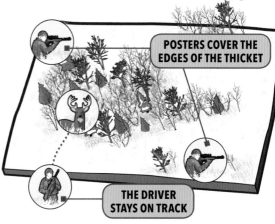

261 DRIVE ON, FOUR WAYS

Deer drives don't have to be big or complex. Any one of these small, simple drives can put a buck in your trunk.

LEAPFROG DRIVE Wooded stream corridors and hedgerows are good areas for two hunters to take turns driving and posting. Hunter A pushes in a zigzag pattern to Hunter B, then circles ahead to become the poster. Hunter B then pushes to Hunter A.

WAKE-UP CALL Here, you need to know the location of a bedding area and of any connected deer trails leading to escape cover. Drivers (D) push through the bedding area, and posters (P) set up along the trails.

RAVINE DRIVE A wooded ravine that runs uphill through a saddle is an ideal area to put on a drive. It works especially well for mule deer. Pushed deer will usually stay in the wooded ravine and move uphill to cross over the ridge. Drivers push from the bottom toward posters at the top.

DROP-BACK DRIVE In almost any area, some driven deer will try to slip back behind the drivers. Here, as the drivers near the end of the cover, one of them drops back and becomes a poster to cut off backdoor deer.

262 TRACK AND DRIVE

You may not have access to enough property to track a buck for miles. But with good bedding cover and snow, you can employ the same tactic that put Milo Hanson's name atop the B&C record book. On an arctic-cold December day in 1993, Hanson and three neighbors found large, just-made tracks entering a willow thicket. They drove the buck out, and Milo put him down.

So the formula for a world record goes like this:

After a new snowfall, grab some buddies, and search the edges of bedding areas until you find a single ember-hot set of large tracks leading into cover, but not out. Next, position the posters to cover key escape routes, such as a finger of vegetation or lane leading to the next closest pocket of heavy cover. Then send in the driver. "He should carefully follow those tracks until he pushes out the specific buck he's trailing," Hanson stresses. And he should work slowly. Finally, it's up to the posted hunters to shoot straight. That said, with fresh tracking snow you may get more than one chance: Hanson took down his famous buck on the group's third such drive.

263 BUMP AND HUNT

Pat Willis of Buck Country Outfitters stages late-season drives, but he doesn't tag his buck until a day or two after he bumps him. Willis starts by pinpointing likely bedding areas, saying "late-season bucks love to hole up near a prime feeding area in a thick, low spot protected from the wind." Then he puts a buddy downwind of a promising bedding area and moves in from the upwind side.

264 LISTEN TO A LEGEND ON DRIVING

One of archery's most accomplished and popular hunters, Barry Wensel has produced six deer hunting videos with his twin brother, Gene, including the classic *Bowhunting October Whitetails*. "Driving deer has been around forever, but it's a tactic that few bowhunters consider, and that's unfortunate," says Wensel. "A well-planned push can work whether you're carrying a gun or a bow. I hear all the time that you can't kill a good buck on a push, and that's total B.S. Any deer will move. The challenge of hunting this way, of deciding where a big buck is going to go before he knows it himself, is one of the great thrills of whitetail hunting."

FIND THE SAFETY ZONES "You can't force a deer where he doesn't want to go; you can only encourage him to move in a certain direction to where he already feels safe. When planning a drive, locate the nearest security cover and assume deer will flee there."

GO QUIET AND SLOW "The usual approach, in which drivers push deer down—or crosswind toward standers, works best in linear cover, such as a riverbottom. Drivers should move slowly, so as not to panic deer. If you jump one, drop to one knee and wait; the deer will relax some and move slowly toward the posters."

PICK YOUR SPOT "Standers should set up with good cover at their backs, in a place where a deer is likely to stop or pause. One of my favorites is where thick cover gives way to thin."

LET HIM WALK "Standers should resist the temptation to set up right on top of trails or funnels. Position yourself 15 to 20 yards from where you expect a buck to appear. If you're bowhunting, let him walk past you, then draw. Try it when he's broadside, and he'll get you every time."

TRY A NUDGE "Try this when you have a block of cover surrounded by open terrain. The deer will be bedded on the downwind side of the cover, their backs to the wind. Two guys walk slowly to that side. The deer see and hear you coming and move toward the upwind side. The stander gets in place, preferably in a premade ground blind. The driver then makes a big circle to the upwind side, where he does nothing more than let his scent blow into the timber. The deer smell him and move back to the downwind side—the place they just left and feel safe, where the shooter is now waiting."

265 TRACK ESCAPE ROUTES

Paul Payton of Nebraska Trophy Whitetails has had tremendous success staging late-season, late-morning drives. The key to that success, says Payton, is historical data about the deer's escape routes. "I can't say enough about how important this is. We've been driving late-season deer for 14 seasons, and every year is better than the last because we have more hard information about how deer escape the cover we're pushing." Payton recommends that hunters consult a good aerial photo or satellite image as a group to study potential escape routes before each hunt. Then reconvene after the hunt to note exactly where deer actually did flee.

"In three seasons, you'll really have something," he says. "You'll confirm the expected routes, like fingers of brush and hedgerows—but you'll also uncover the subtle little dips, ditches, and wisps of cover the smartest deer use to disappear in plain sight. "Two years in a row, we missed a big buck that ran along a shallow ditch with no cover in it; all you could see were the tips of his antlers," he says. "We'll have someone looking right down into that ditch this year."

266 LISTEN TO A LEGEND ON TRACKING

Vermont's Benoits are the first family when it comes to whitetail tracking. Here, Lane Benoit gives his top 10 hints on pursuing deer.

BE PERSISTENT "You've got to have a kind of dogged determination. If you weren't born with it, it's time to make yourself have it."

BE CONFIDENT "The successful tracker believes he is going to catch up to that buck. If you don't believe in your heart that it's going to happen, then chances are it won't."

DRESS LIGHTLY "If you wear heavy clothing, you will overheat, and you'll never catch up with your buck. I wear a light wool jacket and pants, a lightweight shirt, and a T-shirt. That's it."

BE QUIET "If you're sneaking up on a bedded buck, you've got to be totally silent. Wear wool or fleece, and get rid of anything that makes noise."

GET ON THE RIGHT TRACK "Find a big, flat-footed track with the toe tips squished out, showing it's a heavy deer. The tracks should also have a wide stagger between prints, to show the deer has a sizable chest. Hoof marks outside the track left by hind legs swinging out widely mean an old, mature buck."

KNOW WHEN TO GO FAST "If a track leads in a mostly straight direction or following a trail, you've got to go as fast or faster than the buck to catch up. Don't worry about making noise.

KNOW WHEN TO GO SLOW "If the track suddenly turns hard and heads toward a ridgetop or hummock, the buck is ready to lie down. His strides will shorten, and you'll see a bud nipped here and there. Slow down, and look hard for him, because he's right there."

DON'T RUSH IT "Take a half step at a time, slowly sliding your foot forward in the snow, feeling for every branch and twig. Don't move until you've thoroughly looked everything over."

LOOK FOR PIECES "You won't see the whole deer; look for a buck's nose, or a horn sticking out, or the horizontal line of its back, or the white patch on its throat."

PRACTICE SHOOTING "Learn to shoot off-hand and fast. Practice with a deer gun or a .22 as much as you can. If you hunt deer with a pump, then do your bird hunting with one. You'll be just as quick with a .30-06 in your hands."

MYLES KELLER
THE TROPHY ARCHER

When Myles Keller started bowhunting in 1962, most hunters considered themselves lucky to tag any buck, and a trophy big enough to qualify for the Pope & Young record books was a veritable lightning strike. Keller, a modest Minnesotan, changed all that in a big way. An expert at reading sign, observing behavior, and patterning a specific buck, Keller used those tactics to fill the P&Y books. By the early 1980's, he had over 30 whitetail entries, including an 8-point goliath that measured 175-5/8" and reigned as the Wisconsin state record typical bowkill for 13 seasons. Accomplished at hunting other species—he has black bear and elk listed in P&Y—Keller perfected a blueprint for whitetail hunting that he developed long before the boom in whitetail numbers and technologic advancements like trail cameras.

267 TWO-TRACK A BUCK

"After a fresh snow, I like nothing better than teaming up with my son Scott to track a buck," says veteran Maine guide Randy Flannery.

The Flannerys get up before dawn and drive logging roads to find the dark imprints of deer tracks crossing under the beam of the headlights. "Once we find a fresh buck track, we make up our minds to either kill that deer or run out of daylight."

Randy follows the track, straddling it; Scott flanks him 50 to 60 yards away on the high side. "When a buck beds down or circles to check his backtrack, he'll usually J-hook on the uphill side, giving the flanker the best chance." Still, Flannery says, the tracker shouldn't stare at the ground. "Follow the prints with your eyes as far as you can, then walk to that point while looking for the buck out front and to the sides."

When the trail indicates that the buck has started going up and down grades and zigzagging between thick evergreens and blowdowns, he is getting ready to bed. "Slow way down," Flannery says. "Expect a J-hook coming up, and if you can, hand signal to your flanker to stay on his toes." With a little luck, your hunting partner will see the buck still lying down or just getting up from his bed and will get an easy shot. Otherwise, both hunters should be ready to shoot at a moving target.

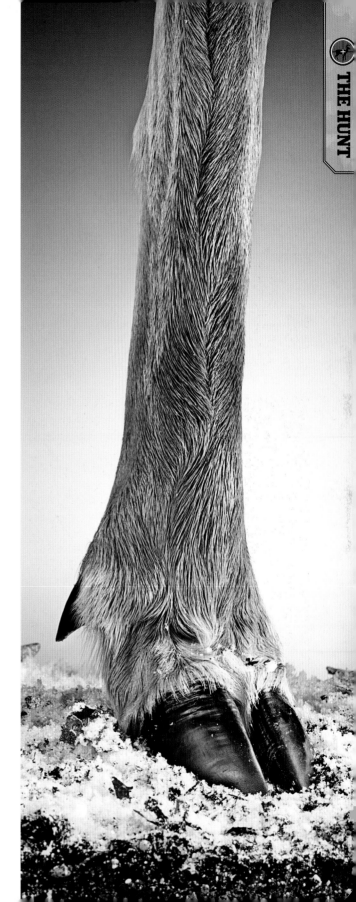

268 TRACK TO CALL

In tracking, the toughest part is the last bit—slipping in close enough for a shot without the buck seeing you. Dave Hentosh of Smoldering Lake Outfitters just skips that step.

"I follow the same basic tracking strategy many hunters are familiar with," Hentosh says. But when the track shows a buck has bedded down or is milling just ahead—when most trackers will try to sneak in for a shot—he stops to study the terrain. "I look for a small opening or a low ridge where I can see well out in front." Then he sets up and makes estrous-doe bleats on a call. "When it works right, the buck believes that the doe he's been covering miles to find is right behind him.

"I've shot bucks that virtually charged me. Others walk in more cautiously. But the important thing is that I'm almost always getting an easy, quick-killing shot at a buck that's coming to me, as opposed to a snap shot at a buck that's moving away because I've busted it out of its bed."

269 TRACK TO AMBUSH

You don't have to be a big-woods hunter to get pumped about 4 inches of fresh snow. And you don't need vast tracts of public timberlands or a rifle season to track a buck. You can instead follow fresh buck prints in a way that (1) avoids spooking the deer that made them, and (2) lets you figure out the best spot to set up an ambush.

Late in the morning, cover ground to pick up a fresh buck track and follow it backward away from the most likely bedding areas. This will tell you where the deer was feeding at dawn, where it bedded at night, and perhaps where it fed last evening. You may find the perfect spot to ambush the buck this very afternoon.

If not, come back to that track after dark with a flashlight. This time, follow it forward to find your buck's empty daytime bed—and get ready to meet him there early the next morning.

270 FAST-TRACK A LATE-SEASON BUCK

"Tracking is all I do," says well-known Adirondack hunter Joe DiNitto, who in the last 15 years alone has tracked and killed 14 bucks averaging more than five years old. "I can't think of another way to hunt that consistently gets more and more exciting as the day goes on and gets me so close to a mature buck so fast."

DiNitto prefers to track bucks after the rut. "They're more interested in putting weight back on than in chasing does far and wide. So they're catchable now." He hits the woods in the morning and quickly covers ground on foot to locate a track. "I don't hunt and I don't worry about being noisy," he says. "I just go until I find a large set of prints showing a wide gait, or stagger. At first, I follow them slowly in case the deer is close, but if the tracks are beelining through the woods, I pick up the pace," he says. "I want to catch up to the buck as quickly as I can."

Once the track veers hard to the right or left, however, he slows to a crawl. "In the late season, bucks heading to bed act just like you do coming home from work," DiNitto says. "You get on the highway and go straight until you reach your off-ramp; then you make a few quick turns, and you're home."

And just like you, bucks will often do some snacking before they hit the couch. "When I see them start meandering—nipping a few buds or pawing around for beechnuts—I know I'm in their house," he says. He stays on the track, but goes ultraslow, taking short, careful steps, each followed by several minutes of motionless watching. "One of you is going to see the other move first," says DiNitto, who wears soft, quiet fleece in snow-camo to break up his outline. "Make sure it's the buck that makes the mistake."

271 PUNCH THE SNOW

How fresh is that buck track? A good way to tell is to punch the snow next to a print. Your ungloved fist transmits a little heat, just like a deer's hoof. Jab down quickly and come up and out with a slight forward motion. Now compare. If the edges of each are about equally sharp, if the walls of both are fairly soft to the touch, if the texture of the snow sprayed out in front is similar . . . you've got a fresh track. Go get him.

272 BREAK A STICK

When the track you're following mingles with a bunch of others, break a stick exactly equal to the width of your buck's print. Then keep it handy as a measuring device to stay on the right track.

273 HUNT THE LATE SCRAPE

After the peak rut, scrapes become major meeting points for late-cycling, unbred does and the big bucks seeking them. If you're after a trophy, scrapes can be even better now than they were during the pre-rut. They are, however, fewer and farther between. Speed-scout for fresh scrapes at midday just off doe feeding areas, bedding areas, and along transition corridors between the two. The best time to look is after a new, light snowfall. Bucks will be eager to reopen the blanketed sign and, once they do, the dark, bare earth will pop against the white background.

If you find a late scrape in semiopen cover, find the buck's approach route, backtrack 75 to 100 yards, and then hang your stand. If the scrape is farther back in the woods, near doe bedding cover or in a transition corridor, hang your stand or erect a simple ground blind directly downwind. Use a doe bleat or occasional contact grunt to entice any nearby bucks.

274 GO NUTS

Many hunters think of acorns as an early-fall food. But after the rigors of the rut, with winter weather moving in, late-season whitetails seek acorns because they provide lots of fat; are easily digested; and, unlike corn and bean stubble, are located within the security of the woods—which is key to pressured deer now. In some heavily forested habitats, acorns may be the only substantial high-energy food source this time of year.

Once you remember that acorns are a prime late-season food source, too, the rest is simple. If there's no snow on the ground, look for disturbed leaves, bits of half-chewed acorns, and fresh deer droppings to identify a hot oak ridge or flat. Then set up downwind, overlooking the hottest tree or trees. If there is snow, abundant tracks and dug-up leaf litter will make the hotspot obvious.

Here, however, you should identify the largest hoofprints and backtrack them a short ways off the feeding area toward thicker, bedding cover. This will give you a better chance at intercepting a late-rising buck while there's still shooting light.

Every winter, state wildlife agencies field phone calls from people concerned about overpopulation because they see 30, 40, 50, or more deer feeding in single field. What they are seeing, in fact, is a prime agricultural food source that draws hordes of hungry whitetails from miles around. A "superfield." At first glance, superfields look like easy pickings. But big herds pose big problems for hunters, says whitetail researcher Grant Woods. "Fifty deer bring 50 noses and 100 eyes to bust you with," he says. "But that doesn't mean you can't score."

FIND THEM Simply drive around and look for big groups of deer hitting prime crops such as corn or winter wheat. Also, call a regional biologist who fields calls from the public. Getting permission can be easy, because when hordes of deer are ravaging one of their fields, farmers can be very obliging.

SCOUT THEM When you locate a superfield, scout it from afar. "If the deer catch your scent," says Woods, "you'll have instantly turned that field into a nocturnal feeding site." Instead, glass the area from a distance to pinpoint where the deer are entering the food source. "Then wait for plunging temperatures or an approaching storm to move in for an ambush." If you play it right, you should have dozens of deer heading your way with light to spare.

276 CROWD A BUCK

"If I can't kill a late-season buck at a food source, I'll get aggressive and move in closer to his bed," says Tom Ware of Bucks BeWare Outfitters in Illinois's Pike County. "But I want to know that buck's every move before I make mine."

And for that, he has a plan: First, scout the field edge for big tracks and mount trail cameras to confirm exactly where a good buck enters the feeding area. That done, follow the buck's trail into the timber, placing cameras in promising spots, such as a secondary food source, a pinch point, or a fresh rub or scrape. Start out cautiously, penetrating only halfway or less to the buck's suspected bedding area. If you don't get pictures in the first two or three days, there's still time to move closer.

Keep hunting the field edge, as before—you might get lucky. But check your cameras daily, starting with the one closest to the field. "It's a big help to have a unit or an accessory that lets you view photos in the field," says Ware. "This way, you don't move any closer to the bedding area than you absolutely have to." All you need is one picture of your buck moving

through a given spot during shooting light, morning or evening. "Once you get it, forget the other cameras. Just go get a stand, put it up, and hunt it at the first opportunity. If he came through there once during daylight, there's a great chance he'll do it again."

277 HIDE IN THE CORN

The one place guaranteed to draw winter deer is a standing cornfield, says David Schotte of Kansas' Blue River Whitetails. One of his favorite tactics is to drive around at midday to find a uncut field, get permission, and sit right in the crop with a pop-up blind. "These fields sustain lots of deer damage," says Schotte, "and farmers will usually let you hunt if you're willing to take a doe before shooting your buck."

Schotte looks for a field that abuts a wooded south-facing slope where deer will bed. Then he pinpoints the heaviest trails entering on the north side and sets up right in the stalks near the hottest feeding sign. "If there's one place where you can get away with setting up a blind and hunting it immediately, it's standing corn."

Use stalks already flattened by deer to completely camouflage your hideout. Then just sit back and wait for a hungry buck to show up.

278 WAKE UP BUCKS

If the tactics above don't work, or if the bucks sleep so close to a food source that they can see it from their bed, try this radical tactic: Barge right into the bedroom and scatter deer like a flock of turkeys. Sounds crazy, but I know of some hardcore hunters who make it work. They purposely bust late-season deer out of dense bedding cover and then set up an ambush for their return. This tactic works because when deer find a thick bedding area that keeps them safe through the heart of the season, especially one that has food close by, they don't leave it for long. The key to success is to make as light a scatter as possible. Approach the bed like you're hunting, with the wind in your favor. If the deer don't smell you, especially if just one deer's escape spooks the others, there's a great chance a nice doe or even a trophy buck will walk right back in and help you end the season right.

279 GO SNOW BLIND

You know, you don't have to freeze your butt off in a late-season treestand. Here are five reasons to hunt from a white or snow-camo ground blind this winter:

COMFORT Blinds block the wind and offer space to move around, store extra clothes or a blanket, and even fire up a small portable heater.

EASE Setting up a blind is far easier, quieter, and quicker than hanging a stand.

PROXIMITY Sometimes the only way to get a shot at a deer is to set up in a feed field itself, which you can do with a snow blind (but not a treestand).

BLENDING IN A white blind has no visible outline against a white background, as long as you don't skyline it in an open field. So it doesn't need to be brushed in or set up days in advance for deer to get used to.

MOBILITY Winter deer congregate around prime late-season food sources, which they typically enter from multiple directions. A snow blind gives you the mobility to keep up with the hottest trails or instantly react to other sign or sightings. And that's how you zero in on a late-season buck.

280 PLAY LEAP-FROG

"Late-season bucks may travel a mile or more to get to a prime evening food source," says Joel Snow of Hunt Masters Lodge, who hunts across Ohio, Missouri, and Illinois. "But, there's usually no telling exactly how far away they bed. If that's the case, I try a leapfrog hang-and-hunt strategy."

Key to this approach are south-facing slopes, which bathe deer in sunshine and are therefore the prime bedding sites. Snow's initial move is to follow a good deer trail away from the feed and hang a stand near the first south-facing slope he finds. Each subsequent day, he moves farther up the trail to the next south slope, and so on. "If I see deer stand up and stretch, I've obviously gone far enough," Snow says. "Otherwise, I glass up the trail to see exactly where the deer are coming from. And if a good buck doesn't show during shooting light, I move in that direction the next day." Meanwhile, he stays on stand well past dark to let the deer get past him before he leaves.

If he hasn't got his buck by the last hour of the last evening, he sends a friend upwind to make a controlled bump. "I don't want the deer to see or hear him—just catch his scent, so it'll just move out a little earlier to feed. And that's all I need."

281 KNOCK ON THE BEDROOM DOOR

When winter bucks don't make it to the feeding area before dark, you need to break a rule of late-season hunting and set up tight to the bedroom. Just remember, you'll have to be extra sneaky. Bucks are apt to be bedded on south-facing slopes, facing downhill with a view out front and falling evening thermals at their backs. The key is to find a little wrinkle in the topography or a line of cover that will let you slip in from the side and set up within range of a trail leading toward the grub. If you know you're well hidden, carefully hanging a stand can work. Otherwise, just put on a gillie suit or snow-pattern leafy camo and slowly still-hunt into position. Find a blowdown or stump and settle in for an ambush.

282 GET A SNOWBOUND BUCK

When deep snow blankets the landscape, bucks seem to vanish. Ironically, there may be no easier time to find them if you know what to look for. Here's your three-step plan.

STEP 1 The secret is to locate green browse. Thickets dotted with honeysuckle, galax, smilax, and certain species of rhododendron, mountain laurel, and greenbrier provide whitetails with protective cover and food when nothing else is available. Bucks love them.

STEP 2 Once you've located a promising thicket, expect a buck lay-up in the thickest, lowest-lying part of it. Now look downwind from there for green browse, as well as fresh droppings, tracks, and trails. Set up and sit until dark.

STEP 3 If your buck doesn't show up on that first or second evening, increase your chances by inching closer to the low-lying bedding cover, looking for several trails that converge and lead directly toward the buck's lair. You are dangerously close now, so don't try to hang a stand. Just sit in a spot where you have a good vantage point but are also well hidden. If you busted that buck, you'll have to find a new thicket tomorrow. If you didn't, you'll have to find a taxidermist.

283 GO FIELD HOPPING

Normally, Dr. Keith Chaffin watches just one prime feeding area during an afternoon hunt. But when the season is winding down, this Texas whitetail fanatic often checks several in a matter of hours, an aggressive approach that has produced some big bucks for him, including a 228-inch nontypical giant.

"The key is to have two or three choice evening feed sites located fairly close together," he says. Wheat, oat, or rye fields, food plots, and recently harvested cornfields are your best bets. And don't forget open oak flats and recently-logged sites where treetops provide browse.

The trick is to follow ditches, hedgerows, or brushy fence lines that allow you to sneak toward one feeding area unseen, glass it thoroughly, slip away, and ease up to the next. Once you spot a good buck, simply slip in close enough for the shot. After a long season of sitting in one spot, Chaffin says, it's a great way to have a more active hunt and up your odds of getting within range of a late-season bruiser.

284 MAKE A COLD CLASH

When the secondary rut rolls around, most young bucks are out of the breeding race and many does are already bred. Competition for remaining females is concentrated among big bucks, and the confrontations get very intense. "Bucks lock horns and really go to battle now," says Jim Carpenter, a Texas guide who's rattled in hundreds of deer. "They'll run over anything out there—including you." Late season means prime time to rattle in a trophy.

CARRY A BIG STICK Carpenter recommends using the largest set of rattling antlers you can get your hands on. "The sound carries farther, and I believe that bigger antlers draw bigger bucks."

CREATE A FIERCE BATTLE Carpenter rattles long and loud in the late season. "If you've ever watched deer fight, they don't stop for anything; neither should you." Shake tree limbs and stomp undergrowth to simulate the collateral damage of a buck fight.

GET 'EM CLOSE "Even if you see a buck, as long as he doesn't see you, keep clashing the antlers." The Texas guide has rattled bucks in close enough to touch them this way—but getting a big one within easy gun or bow range should be near enough for you.

285 MEET BUCKS FOR A COLD LUNCH

The late season is a prime time to catch a big buck on its feet during the middle of the day. Hungry, worn-out post-rut bucks are more apt than usual to conserve fuel during the coldest parts of the day and feed heavily during the warmest—and have learned that they encounter fewer hunters at midday. Finally, does tend to feed early too, including late-cycling yearlings and fawns sure to draw the attention of the biggest bucks. For good feeding activity at midday, you want three things.

COLD Wait for a significant and preferably sustained drop in the mercury.

SNOW A snowfall really helps. It seems to strike panic in the deer, and they feed with abandon—often right through the middle of the day.

FOOD A concentrated, high-carb food source is essential. In farm country, this means mostly corn or soybeans but also newly seeded alfalfa. In the big woods, hit clear-cuts, oak stands, and treetops from freshly logged areas.

If you can put these three things together, the hunt plan is about as simple as it gets. Pinpoint the best feeding sign. (If you have snow, this should be a piece of cake.) Then simply set up between the grub and the most likely bedding cover, such as a nearby south-facing wooded slope. Finally, get to your spot well before the noon whistle. If you wait for the dinner bell, you'll probably be too late. Then just settle in and wait for a buck to show up for your lunch date.

GREATEST DEER HUNTERS

BILL JORDAN
THE SHOW MAN

Bill Jordan has tagged a pile of big bucks, and he led the "camouflage revolution" in the mid-1980s. But that's not why he's here. Early on, he harnessed the power of television, video, and celebrity (tapping the likes of Dale Earnhardt and Jeff Foxworthy) to make Realtree a household name. In the meantime, Jordan, as much as anyone, spawned the modern deer hunting entertainment business. Today, "Realtree Outdoors" is one of the longest-running hunting shows on TV. But if you really want to understand Jordan's relationship to today's deer-hunting showbiz? Think of this fact as a metaphor: Michael Waddell, unequivocally deer hunting's top current entertainer, started out as Bill Jordan's camera assistant.

286 SHOVEL UP A BUCK

Clearing snow doesn't have to be a thankless chore. The trick is to bag the driveway and focus on your hunting property. Seriously, clearing trails through deep snow can help deer reach vital, dwindling food sources—and it can put a late-season buck in your lap. Simply clear some walking trails. Start at a feeding source and try to get within 150 to 200 yards of a good bedding area. That's close enough that deer will quickly pick up the trail, yet far enough that you're not apt to spook them. I've used an ATV or small tractor with a blade, a snow blower, leaf blower, shovel—even my feet. Then just set up an ambush. With dense whitetail populations in many areas, winter kills can be severe after deep snows. If I can help 20 or 30 deer reach a vital food source in difficult conditions and possibly harvest one mature buck out of those, I don't feel bad about it. You shouldn't either.

287 FLUSH A PRAIRIE BUCK

"Every year I jump bucks out of little sloughs and cattail swamps while pheasant hunting," says Ron Spomer, Western deer hunter and costar of the *Winchester Whitetail Revolution* TV show. "When deer season comes, I go back and jump them again. Everyone visualizes prairie deer hunting as full of long-range rifle shots, but I've killed some great bucks at 20 yards."

Spomer starts at a high spot at daybreak, glassing small wetlands, sloughs, creek beds, and brushy draws for bucks heading back to bed. "The key for late-season deer is to focus on the small or odd patches of cover overlooked by other hunters." Once he spots his buck, Spomer goes right after him. "I never hunt with a chambered cartridge, so I just shoulder my pack and start trotting toward the buck."

If he can get a shot before the deer beds, he takes it, of course. Otherwise, it's decision time. "In some situations, it's best to settle in and wait for the buck to get back up. But if I know where he's lying, if he's big enough that I'll recognize him if other deer get up, and if the surrounding cover is open enough for good shooting, then I'll just walk directly at him. Odds are he's going to sit tight—just like a pheasant—until I'm right on him. When he gets up, I find him in the crosshairs and take him."

288 LISTEN TO A LEGEND ON STALKING

"Stalking is one of my favorite techniques," says G. Fred Asbell, renowned archer and the author of five books, including *Stalking and Still Hunting: The Ground Hunter's Bible.* "In my opinion, stalking is the essence of hunting—of being a true predator. I believe that we all have the instinct, ability, and skill to do it well." Here's how to get started.

RELEARN HOW TO WALK
"When you stalk, you need to go slow and place your feet toe to heel. It requires total balance and feels unnatural. I practice in my house, standing on one leg, keeping the center of balance on my hips."

FEEL WITH YOUR FEET "Place your toe down first so you can feel ahead for sticks, rocks, or other obstructions and move your foot to one side if necessary so it won't make noise. Any soft-soled footwear with little or no heel will work; in warm weather a pair of Converse All Star sneakers is a perfect choice."

MOVE STRAIGHT AHEAD "In most cases, moving directly toward the animal you're stalking is best. Once you turn sideways or move laterally, it becomes instantly easier for deer to spot you. Think of it this way: Is it easier to spot an airplane flying directly at you, or moving left to right against the sky?"

USE COVER WHEN STALKING
"This is usually not going to be a problem in whitetail habitat. Mule deer habitat is more open, however, and this forces you to use less-obvious cover. Remember that shadows are cover, too. It's much easier for deer to spot you when you're highlighted by the sun."

REDUCE YOUR SILHOUETTE
"When there's no cover, you have to present a smaller profile, which means getting down on your hands and knees, or even crawling on your belly. I've long said that in order to kill a lot of mule deer with a bow, you're going to have to wear out some belt buckles."

289 TAG-TEAM MULEYS

Arrowing an open-country mule deer is one of deer hunting's toughest challenges. But it's a lot easier, says veteran guide Al Bousley of Central Montana Outfitters, with two hunters— one stalker and one spotter.

STEP 1 This is a really easy one—sleep in! "I rarely go out before 9 A.M.," Bousley says. "I want the majority of deer bedded when I start."

STEP 2 To find bedded bucks, Bousley drives two-lanes, stopping at vantage points to scope it out. If that's not an option for you, hike to a ridgetop where you can view a lot of ground. "Nothing beats time behind your binoculars," Bousley says. "When glassing, look for structure and shade. I find most bucks bedded

against a rock face or ledge, on the edge of some brush, or down in a swale."

STEP 3 "You need to find a buck bedded in a vulnerable spot—one that you can approach from downwind and behind its field of vision. The stalker also has to be able to see the spotter, who will guide him to the deer from afar."

STEP 4 Make a wide loop around the buck, and then glass back toward the spotter for directions. "I use a flag or rag tied to a pole for signaling because it's highly visible," Bousley says. "The signals are simple: A straight-up flag means the stalker walks directly toward the spotter. A sideways flag means he should correct left or right. A flag that's straight down means the buck is

dead ahead and very, very close. Basically, the spotter is saying: 'You're right on the deer now, and on your own."

STEP 5 The final steps are so critical they usually make or break a stalk. "Most of my hunters either remove their boots and go the final yards in stocking feet or slide on felt booties for silence and protection from rocks," Bousley says. For hunters who prefer not to shoot a bedded deer, Bousley tells them to toss a stone 20 to 30 yards past the buck, which will stand to investigate the sound. "I tell them, 'Don't whistle, grunt, or make any other noise. That will usually blow the deer out of there. As soon as you toss the rock, draw your bow.' In my book, there isn't a more heart-stopping hunt out there."

290 WALK IN CIRCLES

Only when you have exhausted hope of finding the next drop of blood in the immediate vicinity of the last should you risk leaving the main blood trail. And even then, you should do so little by little. First, clearly mark the last blood, and starting there, slowly walk in a gradually expanding cloverleaf pattern, looking for any sign of your deer. What you really want to find is more blood, so you can pick up the trail. Short of that, look for hoofprints, scuff marks, broken branches—any hint of your deer's direction of travel.

291 GET A FRIEND

The worst-case scenario when trailing a hit deer comes when you've searched hard, long, and ultimately in vain for the next drop of blood and you find no other clear indications of where your deer went. While it's not a bad idea to have a buddy along from the beginning of the trailing process, it is especially helpful at this point to get a friend or two. Line up—close together in thick cover, farther apart in thin—and methodically comb the area, looking for the deer. Pay special attention to blowdowns or thickets where a hit deer is apt to lie down, as well as any low areas, as mortally wounded deer tend to run downhill and often seek water. If all else fails, there is one friend to consider: man's best. Where legal, specially trained blood-trailing dogs can save the day and your venison. Call your local wildlife agency for details.

292 STAY ON THE BLOOD

Your hit deer most likely lies at the end of the blood trail. This would be obvious to anyone under normal conditions. But shooting a deer can cause your adrenal gland to squirt gobs of high-octane liquid goofiness—or epinephrine—into your frontal lobe. So instead of staying on the blood trail, way too many hunters go bumbling out ahead, muttering things like "I'll bet he went on this trail" and "He's probably going to water" and "Are those scuff marks in the leaves up there?"

Listen to me: If in the excitement and stress of trailing a hit deer you can only remember one thing, remember this: Stay on the blood.

Even when the blood trail seems to end, stay on it. This is important: When you're standing over the "last drop" and wondering where the deer went, nine times out of ten the answer lies not somewhere out in front of you but somewhere near your feet. Look closer. Get on your hands and knees. The deer may have taken a hard turn or doubled back some. Comb the area, for a half hour if needed, to find that next drop. It may lead to another, which may lead to your deer.

HURTEAU ON:
BUCKING UP

If you've done the right thing and taken a high-percentage shot, you will most likely find your deer. But, and I hate to bring this up, sometimes you won't. I don't know a single experienced deer hunter who hasn't lost a hit deer. It's a tough thing. When friends in this situation reach out to me for consolation, here's what I tell them: Nothing goes to waste in nature. In the immortal words of the outlaw Josey Wales, "Buzzards got to eat, same as worms." We are imperfect predators, just like bears and wolves. If you did your best, with the right intentions, and didn't do anything wantonly stupid, buck up and get back out there.

293 FIELD DRESS A BUCK IN MINUTES

You want to see someone unzip a deer in a damned hurry? Watch a seasoned guide. I've watched a bunch, and while there are many different ways to go about the job, all of the fastest-gutting guides do it the same way. And you don't need a special tool. Just get your knife and do the following.

STEP 1 Grab your buck by the tallywhacker, the Johnson, the schwanz—what, do I have to paint a picture? (Fine, see illustration at right.) Make an incision under the penile sheath and slice toward the anus, cutting away the whole package from the abdominal wall until it is attached only by the urethra. (For a doe, do the same, but start with the udder.)

STEP 2 Pull down on the urethra with one hand while making careful cuts to free it—without severing it—just above the anus.

STEP 3 Now cut all the way around the anus and do a thorough job of it; put the blade in deep and take a few trips around the barn. (For a doe, cut around the anus and the vagina.)

STEP 4 Make an incision at the base of the belly, being careful not to puncture the guts. Making a V for "victory" with your off hand, stick those two fingers in the incision, using upward pressure to open some space between the abdominal wall and the innards. Then run your knife—blade up—between them, opening the gut all the way up to the sternum.

STEP 5 Cut away the diaphragm. Do this thoroughly, or you will have trouble later.

STEP 6 Now reach up into the chest cavity with your off hand—far enough to get your elbow dirty—and grab the windpipe. Carefully slip your knife hand up in there and, without mutilating yourself, cut the windpipe free. Then carefully retract your knife hand.

STEP 7 Pull down on the windpipe, grabbing any guts as necessary, and flop/slop the whole lot of it up and out of the cavity.

STEP 8 Finally, pull the rectum and urethra under the pelvic bone and out, cutting away any connective tissue as necessary. There. You're done.

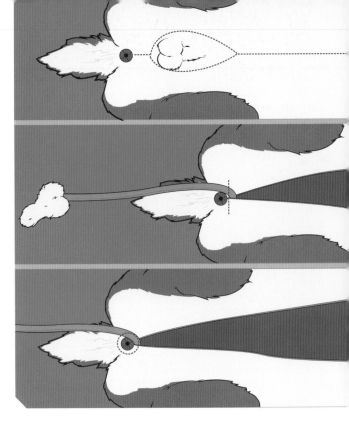

GREATEST DEER

THE DOUG BURRIS BUCK

DATE: OCTOBER, 1973
LOCATION: DOLORES COUNTY, COLORADO
SCORE: 224 $^{6}/_{8}$" B&C
TYPICAL MULE DEER

WHY IT MAKES THE LIST:

Another iconic trophy, the Burris Buck has reigned as the world record typical mule deer for 40 seasons now. Burris, a Texan, had made three previous–and successful–trips to Dolores County to hunt the region's trophy mule deer before he and his buddies arrived for his fateful hunt. On the third day of the hunt, Burris spotted a pair of bucks feeding when a third, even larger, muley joined them. Burris made a stalk through oak brush and downed the giant typical with one shot from his Winchester .264 Magnum.

294 GET YOUR BUCK OUT

You've probably heard that the real work of deer hunting doesn't begin until your buck is down. But with good planning, getting your deer out can be relatively painless. The first thing to do is carefully map out the easiest way back to your vehicle or camp. Keep in mind that this is rarely the straightest path. Use the terrain and available trails to your advantage. If you expect the drag to be difficult, remember: This is why you have hunting buddies. Any of these three tools can help, too.

DRAGS The simplest commercial drags are basically a 9-inch rubber-coated handle attached to a loop of braided nylon. Wrap the loop around the base of a buck's antlers, pass the handle through the open end, and pull. Deluxe models may use an adjustable shoulder harness of 2-inch webbing, leaving your hands free to carry a gun or bow.

SLEDS Less compact but far more helpful are sleds. The best are constructed of smooth, durable plastic that rolls up into a packable, lightweight scroll. When unrolled and loaded down with a deer, they make bare ground feel as slick as snow and snow as slick as ice.

CARTS Wheeled game carts are the heaviest and most expensive haulers, but on relatively level ground, they provide the easiest going, and most fold up into a comparatively small and lightweight package that you can carry on your back into a wilderness base camp. With any luck, you'll be wheeling it out.

295 SPLIT THE BREAST-BONE, NOT THE PELVIS

Some folks split the pelvic bone to make it easier to remove the rectum and urethra. But if you do a good job on steps 1, 2, and 3 (see item 290), there's really no need. On the other hand, if you have a game saw handy, splitting the breastbone and opening the chest cavity doesn't take long and does indeed make it easier to grab and cut the windpipe without slicing your off hand to ribbons. Your call.

296 SKIN YOUR DEER

I hang my deer head down from a gambrel for cooling and aging, which keeps the blood from draining into the best meat. And I skin it that way, too, using these steps.

STEP 1 Lower the carcass so the hams are roughly eye level and the head is touching the ground, which helps keep the critter from swinging as you work.

STEP 2 Starting at the groin, slip your knife's point under the skin, blade up, and cut a long slit up from the bottom of one ham past the knee. Repeat on the other side. (Don't worry about hair on the meat during the skinning process, rinse it before trimming.)

STEP 3 Loosen the skin around each knee and cut all the way around each joint. Grab and peel the skin off the back legs and down to the tail.

STEP 4 Sever the tailbone and then keep peeling all the way down to the front shoulders, using your knife when necessary to help free the skin.

STEP 5 Cut the front legs off at the knee. (Sharp lopping shears are handy for this.)

STEP 6 Starting at the chest opening, slip your knife under the skin and cut a long slit along the inside of each front leg to the severed end. Peel the skin off the legs, then over the shoulders, then all the way down to the base of the neck, using your knife as necessary.

STEP 7 Slice through the meat of the neck with a knife and cut through the spine with a saw.

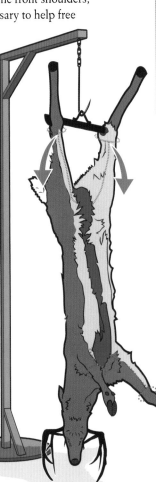

297 GET THE GOOD CUTS

Many processors offer bone-in cuts, but most do-it-yourselfers totally debone their meat instead. Here's what works for me. Start with two large, clean pans. One is for meat we'll categorize as "good"—the tougher, fattier, more sinewy portions that will become burger, sausage, jerky, stew meat, and pot roast. The second is for "best"—the larger, leaner, more tender cuts for steaks, dry roasts, and kabobs. Set that one aside for now.

STEP 1 Detach the front legs by pulling one away from the body while slicing between the leg and the rib cage. Continue cutting around the leg, eventually between the shoulder blade and the back. Repeat on the other side and set front legs aside.

STEP 2 Remove neck meat, brisket, and flank and toss into the pan. Since this will all be scrap meat, it's not important that you get it off in one nice piece. Hack it off the best you can.

STEP 3 Remove the shank meat on each hind leg. Now grab and remove all the meant from the front legs, putting it all, as well as any remaining edible meat on the carcass, into the good pan. Later, you can separate the best of it for stew meat and jerky.

298 BONE OUT THE BEST CUTS

After you've separated out the good-quality meat, it's time to grab that "best" pan. Start by removing the backstraps. For each, cut long slits from the rump to the base of the neck—one tight along the backbone, the other tight along the top of the ribs. Make a horizontal cut across these two slits at the base of the neck and lift the backstrap while scraping along the bone beneath with your knife to collect as much meat as possible.

On the rest of the hindquarter, natural seams of silverskin run between large muscles. Separate these muscles as much as possible by working wetted fingers into the seams. Then just cut the muscles off the bone to get largely seamless hunks of meat.

299 TRIM THE FAT

Deer fat can taste gamey. If you don't like that flavor, trimming is a critical step: It can spell the difference between mild and bold meat. When the trimming is done, many folks steak their best cuts. Don't do this. Instead, try this routine.

First, sharpen your fillet knife. Grab the Good pan, and take any piece of meat and assess it. It's O.K. to have some silverskin and a small amount of fat in what will become burger or sausage. But you want very little to none in your jerky and stew meat. So if the piece you're holding can be easily trimmed into a small hunk of clean, lean meat, trim it and toss it into a pile designated for jerky or stew. If not, trim the fat as best as you can (don't worry about the silverskin) and toss it into a second pile for burger and sausage.

Now take your Best cuts and trim every last bit of fat from each. If you expect your venison to be in the freezer for longer than six months, leave the silverskin for now and trim it later, as it can help protect the meat from freezer burn. Otherwise, take it off.

Cutting the backstrap and parts of the hindquarter into steaks now limits how you can prepare the meat later. Instead, cut the backstraps into 10- to 12-inch-long sections, leave the individual muscles and muscle groups of the hindquarter whole, and freeze it all like that. When you take a package out to thaw and cook, you'll still have the option of making ¼-inch-thick medallions, 1-inch-thick steaks, 5-inch-thick fillets, or whole dry venison roasts.

GOOD CUTS

BEST CUTS

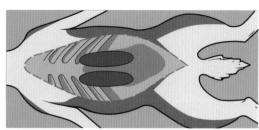

300 SAVE THE TENDERLOINS

The tenderloins are the best cuts on a deer. These small loins are located inside the body cavity, alongside the spine. Don't ruin them, as many hunters do, by either (a) leaving them on the carcass as the deer ages, in which case the outer portion dries out, gets leathery, and has to be discarded, or (b) eating them within hours after the kill, in which case they don't age enough to be as tender as they should be. Instead, remove the tenderloins shortly after field dressing and put them in the fridge for at least a couple of days. Then cook them rare on a grill and enjoy.

301 BUILD A BETTER BURGER

Venison burgers can be dry and bitter or moist and delicious. The difference is a phone call. You're going to do a careful job of trimming fat, and that will go a long way. But you should also call your local butcher (or the meat counter at the grocery store) and ask them to set aside some beef fat. Unlike venison fat, beef fat is sweet. Unlike pork fat, it doesn't prevent you from cooking your burger medium-rare. Grind in roughly 1 pound of beef fat per 10 pounds of meat, depending on how lean you like your burger.

INDEX

ABOUT THE AUTHORS

SCOTT BESTUL Scott Bestul is a Field Editor for *Field & Stream* magazine. After graduating from Minnesota's Winona State University in 1985, Bestul had just started a teaching career when he sold his first story to *Sports Afield* magazine. He began freelancing for various outdoor publications soon after and was rescued from starvation in 1996 by the late John Merwin, who recruited him to write for F&S's regional pages. Since then, Bestul has figured heavily in the magazine's whitetail features, covering some of modern deer hunting's top trends, techniques, equipment, and hunters. He has chased deer in 16 states and logs many hundreds of hours each year scouting, planting food plots, running a chainsaw, hanging tree stands and, naturally, hunting. Bestul lives in southeast Minnesota's bluff country with his wife Shari and two kids, Brooke and Bailey. He co-authors *Field & Stream*'s popular blog, Whitetail 365, with F&S's long-time editor, Dave Hurteau.

DAVE HURTEAU is the Deputy Editor of *Field & Stream* magazine. One of eight children, he grew up hunting the boondocks north of New York's Adirondack Mountains. After graduating from the University of Rochester in 1991, he launched the *Finger Lakes Outdoorsman* magazine from an Ithaca, NY, apartment. He moved to Manhattan in 1994 and began his career with *Field & Stream* magazine, working as Assistant and then Associate Editor. Three years later he was back in the boonies, but still writing for the magazine, eventually parlaying a freelance stint into another full-time editorial position. In one capacity or another, Hurteau has been with *Field & Stream* for almost 20 years, during which time he has hunted and fished throughout much of the country. From upstate NY, where he now lives with his wife and two children, Hurteau handles most of the magazine's deer coverage and much of the hunting coverage in general. With Scott Bestul, he co-authors the Whitetail 365 blog on fieldandstream.com.

FROM THE AUTHORS

SCOTT BESTUL I'd like to thank Mariah Bear, Conor Buckley, Rob James and everyone at Weldon Owen for the amazing effort they put into this book. To the folks at F&S—Anthony Licata, Mike Toth, Slaton White, and the entire crew—I'm so deeply grateful for your friendship, guidance, patience and expertise. And there's no suitable payback for the work of Dave Hurteau, who —in addition to being among the sharpest editors on the planet—is one of my dearest friends and most cherished hunting companions.

I dedicate this book to Brooke and Bailey, who make coming home from the deer woods as exciting as heading out there, and the late John Merwin, who could bust my chops and save my bacon, all in the same phone call.

DAVE HURTEAU I've been a control freak on this project since day one; so thank you to Mariah Bear, Rob James, Ian Cannon, Conor Buckley, Will Mack, and Barbara Genetin for putting up with my nit-picking. Much of what I know about deer hunting I learned directly from Scott Bestul, and I would have no business co-authoring a book on deer without the expertise he has so generously shared. All of the Whitetail Handbook contributors have been excellent and willing teachers. Thank you to my colleagues and mentors at F&S, especially Anthony Licata, Mike Toth, Slaton White, Jean McKenna, Colin Kearns, the great David E. Petzal, and the late John Merwin and Maggie Nichols. I dedicate this book to my wife, Robin, the bravest person I know.

ABOUT THE MAGAZINE

In every issue of *Field & Stream* you'll find a lot of stuff: beautiful artwork and photography, adventure stories, wild game recipes, humor, reviews, commentary, and more. That mix is what makes the magazine so great and what's helped it remain relevant since 1895. But at the heart of every issue are the skills. The tips that explain how to pick the perfect stand location every time, the tactics that help you bag that trophy buck, the lessons that you'll pass on to your kids about the joy of the outdoors— those are the stories that readers have come to expect from *Field & Stream*.

You'll find a ton of those skills in *The Total Deer Hunter Manual*, but there's not a book big enough to hold them all in one volume. Besides, whether you're new to deer hunting or an old pro, there's always more to learn. You can continue to expect *Field & Stream* to teach you those essential skills in every issue. Plus, there's all that other stuff in the magazine, too, which is pretty great. To order a subscription, visit www.fieldandstream.com/subscription.

ABOUT THE WEBSITE

When *Field & Stream* readers aren't hunting or fishing, they kill hours (and hours) on www.fieldandstream.com. And once you visit the site, you'll understand why.

First, if you enjoy the skills and opinions in this book, there's plenty more online—within our extensive archives of stories from the writers featured here as well as our network of 50,000-plus experts who can answer all of your questions about the outdoors.

At fieldandstream.com, you'll get to explore the world's largest online destination for hunters and anglers. Our blogs, written by the leading experts in the outdoors, cover every facet of hunting and fishing and provide constant content that instructs, enlightens, and always entertains. Our adventure videos contains footage that's almost as thrilling to watch as it is to experience for real. And our photo galleries include the best wildlife and outdoor photography you'll find anywhere.

Perhaps best of all is the community you'll find at fieldandstream.com. It's where you can argue with other readers about the best trout fly or the perfect venison chili recipe. It's where you can share photos of the fish you catch and the game you shoot. It's where you can enter contests to win guns, gear, and other great prizes.

And it's a place where you can spend a lot of time. Which is okay. Just make sure to reserve some hours for the outdoors, too.

CREDITS

Text created by: *Scott Bestul:* Greatest Deer features, 2, 10, 11, 12, 13, 14, 15, 16, 17, 18, 19, 20, 21, 22, 23, 24, 28, 40, 42, 48, 50, 51, 54, 55, 56, 57, 58, 59, 60, 63, 64, 65, 67, 68, 71, 75, 76, 77, 79, 82, 83, 84, 85, 86, 87, 89, 91, 92, 93, 94, 96, 98, 103, 104, 105, 106, 116, 117, 118, 119, 120, 121, 122, 127, 128, 129, 130, 131, 137, 140, 141, 143, 144, 145, 159, 160, 161, 179, 180, 181, 182, 183, 184, 185, 186, 187, 188, 189, 190, 191, 192, 193, 194, 195, 196, 201, 202, 204, 207, 209, 210, 214, 216, 219, 220, 222, 223, 224, 226, 227, 228, 235, 236, 240, 242, 248, 256, 258, 260, 264, 268, 274, 276, 277, 278, 279, 281, 283, 285, 287

Dave Hurteau: Greatest Hunter features, chapter introductions, 1, 3, 4, 5, 6, 7, 8, 9, 25, 26, 27, 30, 31, 32, 33, 34, 35, 36, 41, 44, 45, 46, 47, 49, 52, 53, 61, 62, 66, 69, 70, 74, 78, 80, 81, 88, 90, 95, 97, 99, 107, 108, 109, 113, 115, 124, 126, 132, 133, 134, 135, 136, 138, 139, 142, 146, 147, 148, 150, 152, 155, 156, 157, 162, 163, 164, 166, 167, 168, 169, 170, 171, 172, 173, 174, 175, 176, 177, 178, 197, 199, 203, 205, 206, 208, 215, 217, 229, 230, 237, 238, 243, 252, 254, 255, 257, 259, 261, 263, 265, 267, 269, 271, 272, 290, 291, 292, 293, 295, 296, 297, 298, 299, 300, 301

Gerald Alamy: 37, 38, 39, 101, 102, 110, 112, 231, 253, 262, 273, 286 *Bernie Barringer:* 211, 212, 246 *Jace Bauserman:* 213 *Phil Bourjaily:* 153, 154, 165 *Will Brantley:* 114, 158, 225 *Travis Faulkner:* 43, 244, 282 *James Guthrie:* 151 *Mark Hicks:* 29, 232, 234, 247 *Steven Hill:* 198, 233, 239, 275, 280, 284 *Keith McCafferty:* 249, 250 *David E. Petzal:* 149 *Lawrence Pyne:* 72, 73, 100, 111, 123, 125, 251, 266, 270, 294 *Bill Vaznis:* 200, 218, 221, 241, 245

Photography courtesy of: *Charles Alsheimer:* 39, 53, 243 *Ameristep:* 140, 203 (1, 5) *Antlers by Klaus:* Greatest Deer (Jordan Buck, Del Austin, Mel Johnson, Mike Beatty) *Bear Archery:* 160 (right) *Bedlans Sporting Goods, Inc.:* 154 (Winchester M100) *Beretta:* 149 (Blaser R8) *Scott Bestul:* 115, 120, 194, 238 *Jeff Bast:* 229 *Boone and Crockett Club:* Greatest Deer (Ed Broder, Timothy Beck, Kevin Petrzilka, Doug Burris) *BPI Outdoors:* 164 (bottom) *Denver Bryan/ Images on the*

Wildside: 3, 16, 42, 45, 49, 74, 85, The Plan chapter intro, 91, 108, 183, 201, 227, 239 (deer), 240, 245, 267, 272, 292, back matter *Marius Bugge*: 266 (Benoit) *Bushnell*: 146, 147 (scope and binoculars) *Code Blue, LLC*: 119 (2) *Jim Cole/Images on the Wildside*: 71 *Cowans Auctions*: 154 (Manlicher–Schoenauer) *Peter Eades/ Images on the Wildside*: 20, 47, 60, 88, 258, 284 *EBSCO*: 203 (13) *John Eriksson/ Images on the Wildside*: 5 (deer), 13, 23, 41 (bottom), 54, 122, 204, 252, 257, 265, 275 *Evolved*: 99 *Gorilla Treestands*: 201 (3) *John Hafner*: 259 *Milo Hanson*: Greatest Deer (Milo Hanson) *Howard Communications, Inc.*: 21 *Dave Hurteau*: 129, 154 (Remington M8) *Tim Irwin/ Images on the Wildside*: 83, 131, 138, 162, 163, 196 *Ithaca Gun Company*: 153 (Deerslayer) *Istock*: 234 *Alexander Ivanov*: 46 *James D. Julia, Inc.*: 154 (Winchester M70 & M1886, Marlin M1893), 249 *Donald M. Jones*: 15, 55, 159, 211, 287, 290 *Timothy G. Kent*: 215, 273 *Kimber*: 149 (Sonora) *Bill Kinney*: front cover, table of contents (p. 7), 72, 198 *Bill Konway*: 7, 175 *Lance Krueger*: 41 (top), 50, 51 (deer), 51, 59, 132 *Lonlauber.com*: Author intro, 58, 179, The Plan chapter intro, 208, 221, 235, 248, 276, 277, 294 *Anthony Licata*: Editor's intro *Lucky's Hunting Blinds*: 279 *Marlin Firearms*: 148 (X7), 149 (M1895) *McMillian*: 149 (Long Range) *Leroy Merz Antique Firearms*: 154 (Remington M14) *Primary Weapons*: 151 *Primos Hunting*: 203 (10), 268 *PSE Archery*: 160 (left) *Remington*: 149 (M7600), 153 (M870) *Dan Saelinger*: 269 *Savage Arms*: 149 (M11/111), 153 (220 Slug Gun), 154 (M99) *Sturm, Ruger & Co., Inc.*: 148 (American), 149 (Gunsite Scout, American) *Shutterstock*: Endpapers, half title, full title, TOC (p6, p8, p10), You Might Be Deer Crazy, Spot 10 Modern Deer Hunting Trends, 5 (acorns), 6, section opener (background), The Deer chapter intro, 10, 17, Greatest Deer Hunters, 18, 25, 29–32, 35, 37, 40, 51 (target), Where to Aim, 65, 68, 75, 78, 80, 81, 89, 98, 103, 105, 110, 119 (1, 3–8), 124, 127, 152, 156–158, 169, 170, 181, 182, 203 (4–5, 7–9, 11–12), 209, 214, 228, 239 (leaf), 251, 256, 266 (deer), 282, 285, 301, Index, Credits, imprint page *Ten Point Crossbow Technologies*: 161 *Thompson Center Arms*: 147 (rifle), 148 (Venture, Dimension), 163, 164 (top) *Tre Taylor/ Images on the Wildside*: 3, 126, 136 *Weatherby Vanguard*: 149 (Mark V, Series 2) *Winchester Repeating Arms*: 149 (M 70), 154 (M94) *Bill Winke*: Greatest Deer (Tony Lovstuen) *Peter Yang/August*: 171, 219

Illustrations created by: *Conor Buckley*: 2, 22, 44, 53, 66, 109, 117, 124, 135, 158, 218, 223, 226, 258, 261, 293 *Hayden Foell*: 4, 24, 25, 40, 94, 98, 101, 114, 154, 165 *flyingchili.com*: 199 *Michael Howeler*: Author intro, Hurteau On, Bestul On *Raymond Larrett*: 1, 202, 222, 224, 260 *Jason Lee*: 166 *William Mack*: section opener icons *Dan Marsiglio*: 187–193, 225, 296, 299 *Robert L. Prince*: 173, 207 *Paula Rogers*: 11,12, 67, 105, 106, 114, 177, 180 *Pete Sucheski*: 38, 111, 231 *Mike Sudal*: 181, 262 *Bryon Thompson*: 102, 216 *Lauren Towner*: 36, 123, 136, 152, 172, 174, 210, 300

weldon**owen**

PRESIDENT, CEO Terry Newell
VP, PUBLISHER Roger Shaw
EXECUTIVE EDITOR Mariah Bear
PROJECT EDITOR Rob James
EDITORIAL ASSISTANT Ian Cannon
CREATIVE DIRECTOR Kelly Booth
ART DIRECTOR William Mack
DESIGNER Barbara Genetin
ILLUSTRATION COORDINATOR Conor Buckley
PRODUCTION DIRECTOR Chris Hemesath
PRODUCTION MANAGER Michelle Duggan

Weldon Owen would also like to thank Amy Bauman, Andrew Joron,
Katie Schlossberg, and Marisa Solis for editorial assistance and Daniel
Triassi for design assistance.

FIELD & STREAM

EXECUTIVE VICE PRESIDENT Eric Zinczenko
EDITOR-IN-CHIEF Anthony Licata
EXECUTIVE EDITOR Mike Toth
MANAGING EDITOR Jean McKenna
DEPUTY EDITORS Dave Hurteau, Colin Kearns, Slaton L. White
COPY CHIEF Donna L. Ng
SENIOR EDITOR Joe Cermele
ASSISTANT EDITOR Kristyn Brady
DESIGN DIRECTOR Sean Johnston
PHOTOGRAPHY DIRECTOR John Toolan
DEPUTY ART DIRECTOR Pete Sucheski
ASSOCIATE ART DIRECTORS Kim Gray, James A. Walsh
PRODUCTION MANAGER Judith Weber
DIGITAL DIRECTOR Nate Matthews
ONLINE CONTENT EDITOR David Maccar
ONLINE PRODUCER Kurt Shulitz
ASSISTANT ONLINE EDITOR Martin Leung

2 Park Avenue
New York, NY 10016
www.fieldandstream.com

Field & Stream and Weldon Owen are divisions of

BONNIER

Library of Congress Control Number
on file with the publisher
Flexi Edition ISBN 978-1-61628-608-8
Hardcover Edition ISBN 978-1-61628-634-7
10 9 8 7 6 5 4 3 2 1
2013 2014 2015 2016
Printed in China by 1010 Printing International

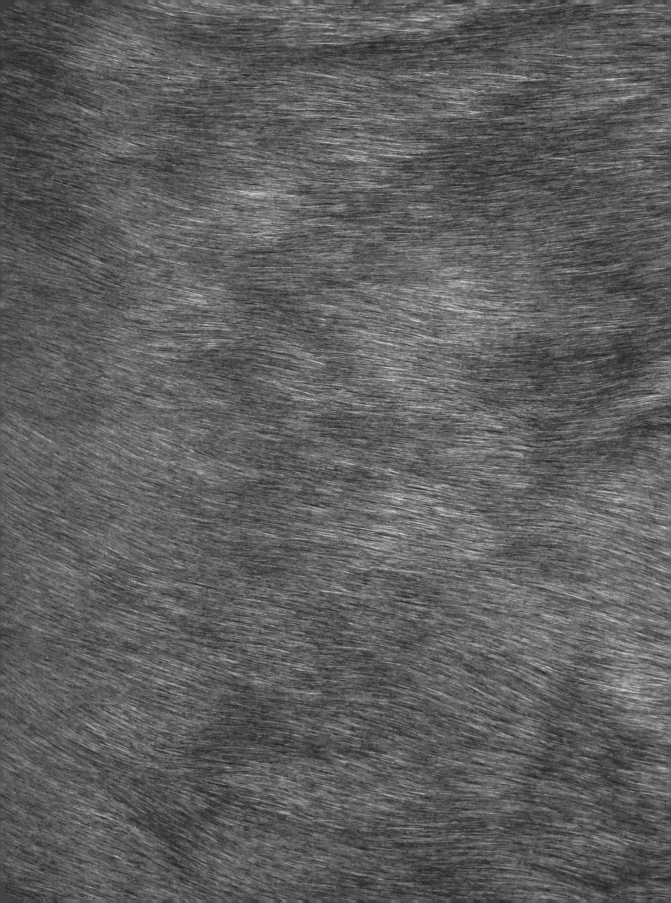